SPECTRUM®

Grade 6

Published by Spectrum®
an imprint of Carson-Dellosa Publishing
Greensboro, NC

Spectrum®
An imprint of Carson-Dellosa Publishing LLC
P.O. Box 35665
Greensboro, NC 27425 USA

ISBN 978-1-4838-1325-7

01-023157897

SPECTRUM®

Math

Chapter 1

Lesson 1.1 Number Properties

There are certain rules or properties of math that are always true.

The **Commutative Properties** of addition and multiplication state that the order in which numbers are added or multiplied does not change the result.

$$a + b = b + a \quad \text{and} \quad a \times b = b \times a$$
$$2 + 3 = 5 \qquad\qquad 5 \times 2 = 10$$
$$3 + 2 = 5 \qquad\qquad 2 \times 5 = 10$$

The **Associative Properties** of addition and multiplication state that the way in which addends or factors are grouped does not change the result.

$$(a + b) + c = a + (b + c) \quad \text{and} \quad (a \times b) \times c = a \times (b \times c)$$
$$(2 + 3) + 4 = 2 + (3 + 4) \qquad\qquad (2 \times 4) \times 5 = 2 \times (4 \times 5)$$
$$5 + 4 = 2 + 7 \qquad\qquad\qquad 8 \times 5 = 2 \times 20$$
$$9 = 9 \qquad\qquad\qquad\qquad 40 = 40$$

The **Identity Property of Addition** states that the sum of an addend and 0 is the addend.
$$5 + 0 = 5$$

The **Identity Property of Multiplication** states that the product of a factor and 1 is that factor. $4 \times 1 = 4$

The **Properties of Zero** state that the product of a factor and 0 is 0. $5 \times 0 = 0$

The properties of zero also state that the quotient of zero and any non-zero divisor is 0. $0 \div 5 = 0$

Name the property shown by each statement.

a	**b**
1. $2 \times 8 = 8 \times 2$ _As_____	$2 + (3 + 4) = (2 + 3) + 4$ _____
2. $35 \times 1 = 35$ _____	$32 + 25 = 25 + 32$ _____
3. $4 \times (6 \times 2) = (4 \times 6) \times 2$ _____	$0 \times 9 = 0$ _____
4. $45 + 0 = 45$ _____	$18 \times 0 = 0 \times 18$ _____

Rewrite each expression using the property indicated.

5. Associative; $(3 + 5) + 2 =$ _____	Commutative; $5 \times 7 =$ _____
6. Identity; $0 + 4 =$ _____	Associative; $3 \times (2 \times 5) =$ _____
7. Commutative; $7 + 9 =$ _____	Associative; $(2 + 5) + 4 =$ _____
8. Identity; $7 \times 1 =$ _____	Identity; $37 + 0 =$ _____
9. Properties of Zero; $0 \times 12 =$ _____	Properties of Zero; $0 \div 6 =$ _____

Lesson 1.2 The Distributive Property

The **Distributive Property** combines the operations of addition and multiplication.

$$a \times (b + c) \qquad = \qquad (a \times b) + (a \times c)$$
$$3 \times (2 + 5) \qquad\qquad (3 \times 2) + (3 \times 5)$$
$$3 \times 7 \qquad\qquad\qquad 6 \quad + \quad 15$$
$$21 \qquad\qquad\qquad\qquad 21$$

Indicate which operation should be done first.

$$\textbf{a} \qquad\qquad\qquad\qquad \textbf{b}$$

1. $(2 \times 5) + (2 \times 3)$ _____ $7 \times (3 + 5)$ _____

2. $(6 + 9) \times 4$ _____ $(3 \times 5) + (3 \times 7)$ _____

Rewrite each expression using the Distributive Property.

3. $4 \times (6 + 2) =$ _____ $(2 \times 5) + (2 \times 4) =$ _____

4. $(5 \times 1) + (5 \times 6) =$ _____ $4 \times (2 + 6) =$ _____

5. $8 \times (4 + 3) =$ _____ $(5 \times 0) + (5 \times 1) =$ _____

Write each missing number.

6. $(5 \times 3) + (n \times 4) = 5 \times (3 + 4)$ _____ $7 \times (n + 3) = (7 \times 2) + (7 \times 3)$ _____

7. $n \times (5 + 3) = (6 \times 5) + (6 \times 3)$ _____ $(5 \times 7) + (n \times 4) = 5 \times (7 + 4)$ _____

8. $(4 \times 5) + (4 \times 2) = 4 \times (5 + n)$ _____ $3 \times (n + 5) = (3 \times 4) + (3 \times 5)$ _____

Replace a with 2, b with 5, and c with 3. Then, find the value of each expression

9. $a \times (b + c) =$ _____ $(a \times b) + (a \times c) =$ _____

10. $(c \times a) + (c \times b) =$ _____ $b \times (a + c) =$ _____

Lesson 1.2 The Distributive Property

The **Distributive Property** states: $a \times (b + c) = (a \times b) + (a \times c)$

The same property also means that: $a \times (b - c) = (a \times b) - (a \times c)$

This can help solve complex multiplication problems:

$26 = 20 + 6$ $17 \times 26 = (17 \times 20) + (17 \times 6) = 340 + 102 = 442$

$18 = 20 - 2$ $47 \times 18 = (47 \times 20) - (47 \times 2) = 940 - 94 = 846$

Using the Distributive Property, rewrite each expression in a way that will help solve it. Then, solve.

a   **b**

1. $22 \times 102 =$ _____ $=$ _____ $39 \times 25 =$ _____ $=$ _____

2. $146 \times 33 =$ _____ $=$ _____ $28 \times 16 =$ _____ $=$ _____

3. $36 \times 35 =$ _____ $=$ _____ $51 \times 106 =$ _____ $=$ _____

4. $19 \times 256 =$ _____ $=$ _____ $45 \times 17 =$ _____ $=$ _____

5. $57 \times 38 =$ _____ $=$ _____ $48 \times 45 =$ _____ $=$ _____

6. $82 \times 80 =$ _____ $=$ _____ $51 \times 82 =$ _____ $=$ _____

7. $43 \times 142 =$ _____ $=$ _____ $264 \times 67 =$ _____ $=$ _____

8. $12 \times 39 =$ _____ $=$ _____ $58 \times 35 =$ _____ $=$ _____

Lesson 1.3 Multi-Digit Multiplication

	Multiply 3,263 by 3.	Multiply 3,263 by 40.	Add.
3263 × 43	3263 × 3 ‾‾‾‾‾‾ 9789	3263 × 40 ‾‾‾‾‾‾ 130520	3263 × 43 ‾‾‾‾‾‾ 9789 +130520 ‾‾‾‾‾‾ 140,309

Multiply.

	a	b	c	d
1.	324 × 27	816 × 16	255 × 44	2165 × 23
2.	5150 × 22	7182 × 12	6324 × 36	4522 × 63
3.	886 ×374	763 ×618	654 ×523	985 ×447
4.	2186 × 342	1898 × 475	3688 × 259	2864 × 723

Lesson 1.4 Multi-Digit Division

983 is between 840 (28 × 30) and 1120 (28 × 40), so the tens digit is 3.

143 is between 140 (28 × 5) and 168 (28 × 6), so the ones digit is 5.

```
        3
2 8 ) 9 8 3
  − 8 4 0     subtract
    1 4 3
```

```
        3 5 r3
2 8 ) 9 8 3
  − 8 4 0        subtract
    1 4 3
  − 1 4 0        subtract
        3        remainder
```

Divide.

	a	b	c	d	e
1.	18)94	27)68	22)88	19)78	25)64
2.	43)88	12)84	32)865	24)768	31)913
3.	27)815	54)725	45)880	23)615	18)324

Lesson 1.5 Reciprocal Operations

Multiplication and division are reciprocal, or opposite, operations. You can use reciprocal operations to check your answers when you work math problems.

$15 \times 4 = 60$ $60 \div 15 = 4$

$8 \times 7 = 56$ $56 \div 8 = 7$

Multiply or divide. Use the reciprocal operation to check your answers.

	a	b	c	d
1.	392 × 22	239 × 60	931 × 77	496 × 28
2.	193 × 55	529 × 31	695 × 75	972 × 93
3.	21)2898	22)7898	71)5893	32)4832
4.	11)3498	33)5214	42)4914	12)8328

Lesson 1.6 Greatest Common Factor

A **factor** is a divisor of a number. (For example, 3 and 4 are both factors of 12.) A **common factor** is a divisor that is shared by two or more numbers (1, 2, 4, and 8). The **greatest common factor** is the largest common factor shared by the numbers (8).

To find the greatest common factor of 32 and 40, list all of the factors of each.

$$32 \begin{cases} 1 \times 32 \\ 2 \times 16 \\ 4 \times 8 \end{cases} 1, 2, 4, 8, 16, \text{ and } 32 \qquad 40 \begin{cases} 1 \times 40 \\ 2 \times 20 \\ 4 \times 10 \\ 5 \times 8 \end{cases} 1, 2, 4, 5, 8, 10, 20, \text{ and } 40$$

The greatest common factor is 8.

List the factors of each number below. Then, list the common factors and the greatest common factor.

	Factors	Common Factors	Greatest Common Factor
1. 8			
12			
2. 6			
18			
3. 24			
15			
4. 4			
6			
5. 5			
12			
6. 16			
12			

Lesson 1.7 Least Common Multiple

Find the least common multiple by listing multiples of each number until finding the first one that is shared.

$$8 — 8, 16, 24$$
$$12 — 12, 24$$

The Least Common Multiple is 24.

Find the least common multiple for each set of numbers.

	a		**b**	
1.	51 and 18	_____	104 and 76	_____
2.	54 and 64	_____	20 and 26	_____
3.	78 and 110	_____	42 and 63	_____
4.	23 and 92	_____	75 and 15	_____
5.	28 and 32	_____	12 and 16	_____
6.	9, 45, and 81	_____	21, 45, and 6	_____
7.	17, 24, and 53	_____	86, 68, and 20	_____

Lesson 1.8 Multiplying Decimals

The number of digits to the right of the decimal point in the product is the sum of the number of digits to the right of the decimal point of the factors.

$$\begin{array}{r} 0.4 \\ \times\ 0.2 \\ \hline 0.08 \end{array}$$

$$\begin{array}{r} 0.28 \\ \times\ 0.6 \\ \hline 0.168 \end{array}$$

$$\begin{array}{r} 3.2432 \\ \times\ 0.13 \\ \hline 97296 \\ +32432 \\ \hline 0.421616 \end{array}$$

If needed, add zeros as place holders.

Multiply.

	a	b	c	d	e
1.	$\begin{array}{r}0.7\\\times\ 8\end{array}$	$\begin{array}{r}0.08\\\times\ 0.5\end{array}$	$\begin{array}{r}0.325\\\times\ 0.3\end{array}$	$\begin{array}{r}1.68\\\times\ 8\end{array}$	$\begin{array}{r}25\\\times0.7\end{array}$
2.	$\begin{array}{r}0.03\\\times3.06\end{array}$	$\begin{array}{r}0.162\\\times\ 0.3\end{array}$	$\begin{array}{r}8.03\\\times\ 3.5\end{array}$	$\begin{array}{r}0.297\\\times\ 7.1\end{array}$	$\begin{array}{r}76.4\\\times\ 3.6\end{array}$
3.	$\begin{array}{r}53.64\\\times\ 0.37\end{array}$	$\begin{array}{r}328.1\\\times\ 0.63\end{array}$	$\begin{array}{r}9.806\\\times\ 31\end{array}$	$\begin{array}{r}600.3\\\times0.034\end{array}$	$\begin{array}{r}895\\\times0.63\end{array}$
4.	$\begin{array}{r}27.1\\\times3.54\end{array}$	$\begin{array}{r}3.263\\\times\ 18\end{array}$	$\begin{array}{r}1.253\\\times\ 12\end{array}$	$\begin{array}{r}58.9\\\times0.038\end{array}$	$\begin{array}{r}0.82\\\times0.82\end{array}$
5.	$\begin{array}{r}0.283\\\times\ 0.6\end{array}$	$\begin{array}{r}0.178\\\times\ 53\end{array}$	$\begin{array}{r}0.83\\\times0.23\end{array}$	$\begin{array}{r}3.6\\\times0.025\end{array}$	$\begin{array}{r}48.2\\\times0.26\end{array}$

Lesson 1.9 Dividing by Two Digits

Multiply the divisor and dividend by 10, by 100, or by 1,000 so the divisor is a whole number.

$$3.5\overline{)14.0} = 3.5\overline{)140}$$
Multiply by 10.
$$\begin{array}{r} 4 \\ -140 \\ \hline 0 \end{array}$$

$$0.42\overline{)16.80} = 42\overline{)1680}$$
Multiply by 100.
$$\begin{array}{r} 40 \\ -168 \\ \hline 0 \end{array}$$

$$0.27\overline{)81.00} = 27\overline{)8100}$$
Multiply by 1,000.
$$\begin{array}{r} 300 \\ -8100 \\ \hline 0 \end{array}$$

Divide.

	a	b	c	d
1.	$2.3\overline{)5.06}$	$3.4\overline{)289}$	$5.2\overline{)2.08}$	$7.2\overline{)10.8}$
2.	$0.45\overline{)18}$	$0.22\overline{)1.166}$	$0.63\overline{)25.2}$	$0.98\overline{)63.7}$
3.	$0.032\overline{)96}$	$0.015\overline{)0.45}$	$0.068\overline{)0.017}$	$0.012\overline{)0.0144}$
4.	$2.4\overline{)0.96}$	$0.62\overline{)24.8}$	$0.016\overline{)0.08}$	$0.85\overline{)5.1}$

Chapter 2

NAME _____

Lesson 2.1 Multiplying Fractions and Mixed Numbers

Multiply fractions.

$\frac{3}{8} \times \frac{2}{3} = \frac{3 \times 2}{8 \times 3}$ Multiply numerators together.
Multiply denominators together.

$= \frac{6}{24} = \frac{1}{4}$ Simplify.

Multiply mixed numbers.

$2\frac{3}{4} \times 3\frac{1}{3} = \frac{11}{4} \times \frac{10}{3}$ Rename each mixed number as an improper fraction.

$\frac{11}{4} \times \frac{10}{3} = \frac{110}{12} = \frac{55}{6}$ Multiply.

$= 9\frac{1}{6}$ Simplify.

Multiply. Write answers in simplest form.

	a	b	c	d
1.	$\frac{2}{5} \times \frac{2}{3} =$	$\frac{3}{4} \times \frac{5}{6} =$	$\frac{7}{8} \times \frac{5}{7} = \frac{5}{8}$	$\frac{2}{5} \times \frac{3}{4} =$
2.	$\frac{7}{12} \times \frac{3}{4} =$	$\frac{2}{3} \times \frac{8}{9} =$	$\frac{4}{5} \times \frac{3}{8} =$	$\frac{3}{7} \times \frac{3}{5} =$
3.	$\frac{1}{6} \times \frac{2}{3} =$	$\frac{11}{12} \times \frac{2}{3} =$	$\frac{2}{5} \times \frac{2}{5} =$	$\frac{3}{4} \times \frac{3}{7} =$
4.	$1\frac{1}{3} \times 2\frac{1}{8} =$	$2\frac{1}{2} \times 1\frac{3}{4} =$	$2\frac{5}{8} \times 2\frac{3}{5} =$	$1\frac{1}{2} \times 2\frac{2}{3} =$
5.	$3\frac{1}{5} \times 5\frac{2}{3} =$	$4\frac{1}{2} \times 4\frac{1}{2} =$	$2\frac{1}{3} \times 3\frac{1}{4} =$	$2\frac{4}{5} \times 3\frac{1}{8} =$
6.	$2\frac{2}{3} \times 5\frac{1}{4} =$	$2\frac{1}{3} \times 2\frac{1}{3} =$	$3\frac{1}{4} \times 1\frac{1}{8} =$	$2\frac{7}{8} \times 1\frac{1}{3} =$

Lesson 2.2 Using Visual Models to Divide Fractions

Fraction bars can be used to help divide fractions.

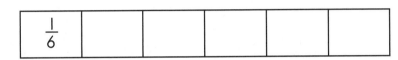

When dividing $\frac{1}{3}$ by $\frac{1}{6}$, you are finding out how many sixths are equal to $\frac{1}{3}$. When you line up the fraction bars and divide them into the appropriate pieces, you can see that $\frac{2}{6}$ is equal to $\frac{1}{3}$.

Therefore,

$$\frac{1}{3} \div \frac{1}{6} = 2$$

Use the fraction bars to solve the problems. Write answers in simplest form.

1. $\frac{1}{2} \div \frac{1}{4} =$ _____

2. $\frac{2}{3} \div \frac{1}{6} =$ _____

3. $\frac{3}{5} \div \frac{1}{15} =$ _____

Lesson 2.3 Dividing Fractions

To divide, multiply by the reciprocal of the divisor.

$\frac{4}{5} \div \frac{8}{9} = \frac{4}{5} \times \frac{9}{8} = \frac{36}{40} = \frac{9}{10}$

Divide. Write answers in simplest form.

	a	b	c	d
1.	$\frac{1}{2} \div \frac{3}{5}$	$\frac{3}{8} \div \frac{2}{3}$	$\frac{5}{8} \div \frac{3}{4}$	$\frac{2}{5} \div \frac{3}{8}$
2.	$\frac{1}{2} \div \frac{7}{8}$	$\frac{4}{5} \div \frac{3}{4}$	$\frac{5}{6} \div \frac{3}{8}$	$\frac{2}{3} \div \frac{4}{5}$
3.	$\frac{7}{8} \div \frac{1}{3}$	$\frac{7}{9} \div \frac{2}{3}$	$\frac{1}{3} \div \frac{2}{3}$	$\frac{5}{6} \div \frac{1}{3}$
4.	$\frac{3}{5} \div \frac{2}{3}$	$\frac{4}{9} \div \frac{3}{7}$	$\frac{1}{2} \div \frac{5}{8}$	$\frac{2}{3} \div \frac{7}{9}$

Lesson 2.4 Dividing Mixed Numbers

$3\frac{2}{5} \div 4$	Rename $3\frac{2}{5}$ as $\frac{17}{5}$.
$\frac{17}{5} \div \frac{4}{1}$	Rename 4 as $\frac{4}{1}$.
$\frac{9}{20} \times \frac{1}{4} = \frac{17}{20}$	Multiply by the reciprocal.

$4\frac{1}{3} \div 2\frac{3}{4}$	
$\frac{13}{3} \div \frac{11}{4}$	Rename.
$\frac{13}{3} \times \frac{4}{11} = \frac{52}{33} = 1\frac{19}{33}$	Multiply by the reciprocal.

Divide. Write answers in simplest form.

	a	b	c	d
1.	$2\frac{1}{2} \div 3\frac{1}{3}$	$1\frac{1}{8} \div 2\frac{1}{4}$	$8 \div 3\frac{1}{2}$	$2\frac{1}{3} \div 5$
2.	$4\frac{1}{2} \div 1\frac{1}{6}$	$4\frac{5}{6} \div 2\frac{2}{5}$	$4\frac{1}{3} \div 6$	$1\frac{1}{2} \div 3\frac{1}{8}$
3.	$6 \div 2\frac{1}{2}$	$1\frac{1}{2} \div 3$	$5 \div 3\frac{3}{4}$	$2\frac{1}{8} \div 3$
4.	$3\frac{3}{5} \div 4$	$3\frac{1}{3} \div 2\frac{3}{8}$	$1 \div 4\frac{1}{3}$	$9 \div 1\frac{2}{3}$

Chapter 3

Lesson 3.1 Understanding Ratios

A **ratio** compares 2 numbers. When written out, several phrases can show how the ratio should be written.

4 to 2	4:2	$\frac{4}{2}$ or $\frac{2}{1}$
6 out of 8	6:8	$\frac{6}{8}$ or $\frac{3}{4}$

Express each ratio as a fraction in simplest form.

	a	b
1.	15 feet out of 36 feet _____	5 pounds to 35 pounds _____
2.	48 rainy days out of 60 days _____	28 snow days out of 49 days _____
3.	10 pints to 20 pints _____	40 cups to 55 cups _____
4.	10 miles out of 12 miles _____	28 red bikes out of 40 bikes _____
5.	18 beetles out of 72 insects _____	63 gallons to 84 gallons _____
6.	49 dimes out of 77 coins _____	12 cakes out of 36 cakes _____
7.	15 students out of 30 students _____	3 floors out of 18 floors _____
8.	36 meters out of 100 meters _____	14 hats out of 20 accessories _____
9.	80 scores out of 90 scores _____	2 sports out of 19 sports _____
10.	42 cars out of 124 cars _____	7 messages out of 84 messages _____

Lesson 3.1 Understanding Ratios

Ratios can be written based on the number of objects in a set.

There are 2 bottles of soda and 5 bottles of water in the refrigerator.
Write the ratio of sodas to waters.

$\frac{2}{5}$

Express each ratio as a fraction in simplest form.

a

b

1. There are 2 cubes and 15 spheres in a geometry box. Write the ratio of spheres to cubes.

   _____

   There are 5 cars and 4 vans in a parking lot. Write the ratio of vans to cars.

   _____

2. There are 5 horses and 15 elephants in a circus. Write the ratio of elephants to horses.

   _____

   There are 16 horses and 14 elephants in a circus. Write the ratio of horses to elephants.

   _____

3. There are 11 blue marbles and 7 red marbles in a box. Write the ratio of red marbles to blue marbles.

   _____

   There are 12 apples and 15 oranges in a fruit basket. Write the ratio of apples to oranges.

   _____

4. There are 5 blue marbles and 16 red marbles in a box. Write the ratio of blue marbles to red marbles.

   _____

   There are 12 dogs and 7 cats in a park. Write the ratio of cats to dogs.

   _____

5. There are 14 cars and 7 vans in a parking lot. Write the ratio of cars to vans.

   _____

   There are 7 blue marbles and 8 red marbles in a bag. Write the ratio of red marbles to blue marbles.

   _____

6. There are 6 pennies and 10 dimes in a jar. Write the ratio of pennies to dimes.

   _____

   There are 24 butterflies and 16 snails on the ground. Write the ratio of butterflies to snails.

   _____

Lesson 3.2 Solving Ratios

A proportion can be used in problem solving.

The ratio of apples to oranges is 4 to 5. There are 20 oranges in the basket. How many apples are there?

$\frac{4}{5} = \frac{n}{20}$ Set up a proportion, using n for the missing number.

$4 \times 20 = 5 \times n$ Cross-multiply.

$\frac{80}{5} = n$ Solve for n.

$16 = n$ There are 16 apples.

Solve.

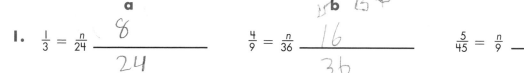

     a   **b**   **c**

1. $\frac{1}{3} = \frac{n}{24}$ $\dfrac{8}{24}$ $\frac{4}{9} = \frac{n}{36}$ $\dfrac{16}{36}$ $\frac{5}{45} = \frac{n}{9}$ 1

2. $\frac{3}{5} = \frac{n}{15}$ $\dfrac{9}{15}$ $\frac{10}{70} = \frac{n}{7}$ 1 $\frac{25}{40} = \frac{n}{16}$ _____

3. $\frac{7}{12} = \frac{n}{36}$ $\dfrac{21}{36}$ $\frac{13}{26} = \frac{n}{4}$ _____ $\frac{7}{1} = \frac{n}{3}$ 21

4. $\frac{8}{5} = \frac{n}{40}$ $\dfrac{64}{40}$ $\frac{2}{6} = \frac{n}{33}$ _____ $\frac{5}{13} = \frac{n}{39}$ _____

5. $\frac{5}{6} = \frac{n}{18}$ $\dfrac{15}{18}$ $\frac{9}{8} = \frac{n}{32}$ 36 $\frac{2}{3} = \frac{n}{15}$ 10

Lesson 3.2 Solving Ratios

The missing number can appear any place in a proportion.
Solve the same way.

$\frac{2}{3} = \frac{6}{n}$

$3 \times 6 = 2 \times n$

$\frac{18}{2} = n$

$9 = n$

$\frac{3}{5} = \frac{n}{10}$

$3 \times 10 = 5 \times n$

$\frac{30}{5} = n$

$6 = n$

$\frac{3}{n} = \frac{6}{8}$

$3 \times 8 = 6 \times n$

$\frac{24}{6} = n$

$4 = n$

$\frac{n}{4} = \frac{3}{6}$

$4 \times 3 = 6 \times n$

$\frac{12}{6} = n$

$2 = n$

Solve.

	a	b	c
1.	$\frac{n}{3} = \frac{3}{9}$ _____	$\frac{5}{3} = \frac{15}{n}$ _____	$\frac{2}{n} = \frac{1}{4}$ _____
2.	$\frac{15}{30} = \frac{2}{n}$ _____	$\frac{4}{6} = \frac{n}{24}$ _____	$\frac{n}{7} = \frac{15}{21}$ _____
3.	$\frac{6}{n} = \frac{15}{20}$ _____	$\frac{n}{12} = \frac{9}{18}$ _____	$\frac{9}{2} = \frac{27}{n}$ _____
4.	$\frac{7}{9} = \frac{n}{63}$ _____	$\frac{15}{n} = \frac{12}{4}$ _____	$\frac{40}{100} = \frac{n}{25}$ _____
5.	$\frac{35}{n} = \frac{4}{8}$ _____	$\frac{16}{4} = \frac{36}{n}$ _____	$\frac{n}{12} = \frac{25}{30}$ _____

Lesson 3.3 Solving Ratio Problems

Tables can be used to help find missing values in real-life ratio problems.

A car can drive 60 miles on two gallons of gas. Create a table to find out how many miles the car can travel on 10 gallons of gas.

Gas	2 gallons	4 gallons	6 gallons	8 gallons	10 gallons
Miles	60 miles	120 miles	180 miles	240 miles	300 miles

Complete the tables to solve the ratio problems. Circle your answer in the table.

1. You can buy 4 cans of green beans at the market for $2.25. How much will it cost to buy 12 cans of beans?

Cans	4 cans	8 cans	12 cans
Cost	$2.25		

2. An ice-cream factory makes 180 quarts of ice cream in 2 hours. How many quarts could be made in 12 hours?

Ice Cream	180 quarts					
Hours	2 hours	4 hours	6 hours	8 hours		

3. A jet travels 650 miles in 3 hours. At this rate, how far could the jet fly in 9 hours?

Distance	650 miles		
Hours	3 hours		

4. A bakery can make 640 bagels in 4 hours. How many can they bake in 16 hours?

Bagels	640 bagels			
Hours	4 hours			

Lesson 3.4 Understanding Unit Rates

A **rate** is a special ratio that compares quantities of two different types of items—for example, *340 miles per 10 gallons (340 mi./10 gal.)*. In a **unit rate**, the second quantity is always 1, such as in *34 miles per gallon (34 mi./1 gal.)*. This allows you to see how many of the first item corresponds to just one of the second item.

Suppose you want to divide students equally between buses for a field trip. To see how many students should go on each bus, find the unit rate.

If there are 160 students and 4 buses, how many students should go on each bus?

$\frac{160}{4} = \frac{s}{1}$ To find the number of students for one bus, divide by the number of buses total.

$\frac{160}{4} = \frac{40}{1}$ The unit rate is $\frac{40}{1}$, or 40 students per bus.

SHOW YOUR WORK

Solve each problem by finding the unit rate.

1. John can create 20 paintings in 4 weeks. How many paintings can he create each week?

   1.

2. Sasha can walk 6 miles in 3 hours. If she has to walk 1 mile, how long will it take her?

   2.

3. Todd keeps his 4-room house very clean. It takes him 1 hour and 36 minutes to clean his whole house. How long does it take him to clean one room?

   3.

4. Victoria can make 8 necklaces in 4 days. How long does it take her to make one necklace?

   4.

5. Byron has his own bakery. He bakes 84 cakes each week. How many cakes can he make in one day?

   5.

6. Charlie buys 3 computer tables for $390. How much did he pay for each table?

   6.

Lesson 3.5 Understanding Percents

The symbol **%** (percent) means $\frac{1}{100}$ or 0.01 (one hundredth).

$$7\% = 7 \times \frac{1}{100}$$
$$= \frac{7}{1} \times \frac{1}{100}$$
$$= \frac{7}{100}$$

$$6\% = 6 \times 0.01$$
$$= 0.06$$

$$23\% = 23 \times \frac{1}{100}$$
$$= \frac{23}{100}$$

$$47\% = 47 \times 0.01$$
$$= 0.47$$

Write the fraction and decimal for each percent. Write fractions in simplest form.

	Percent	Fraction	Decimal
1.	2%	_____	_____
2.	8%	_____	_____
3.	27%	_____	_____
4.	13%	_____	_____
5.	68%	_____	_____
6.	72%	_____	_____
7.	56%	_____	_____
8.	11%	_____	_____
9.	3%	_____	_____
10.	22%	_____	_____
11.	17%	_____	_____
12.	83%	_____	_____
13.	97%	_____	_____
14.	43%	_____	_____

Lesson 3.6 Finding Percents Using Fractions

35% of $60 = 35\% \times 60$

$\qquad = \frac{35}{100} \times 60$

$\qquad = \frac{7}{20} \times \frac{60}{1} = \frac{420}{20} = \frac{42}{2}$

$\qquad = 21$

40% of $32 =$

$40\% \times 32 = \frac{40}{100} \times 32$

$\qquad = \frac{2}{5} \times \frac{32}{1} = \frac{64}{5}$

$\qquad = 12\frac{4}{5}$

Complete the following. Write each answer in simplest form.

	a	b
1.	8% of 65 = _____	95% of 80 = _____
2.	30% of 32 = _____	25% of 28 = _____
3.	150% of 12 = _____	25% of 30 = _____
4.	28% of 7 = _____	10% of 38 = _____
5.	40% of 20 = _____	15% of 45 = _____
6.	80% of 80 = _____	20% of 75 = _____
7.	45% of 70 = _____	18% of 45 = _____
8.	4% of 92 = _____	16% of 90 = _____
9.	90% of 60 = _____	25% of 86 = _____
10.	12% of 40 = _____	9% of 60 = _____
11.	60% of 60 = _____	95% of 20 = _____
12.	21% of 50 = _____	3% of 25 = _____

Lesson 3.7 Finding Percents Using Decimals

26% of 73.2 $26\% = 26 \times 0.01 = 0.26$

$$
\begin{array}{r}
7\,3.2 \\
\times\quad 0.2\,6 \\
\hline
4\,3\,9\,2 \\
+\;1\,4\,6\,4 \\
\hline
1\,9.0\,3\,2
\end{array}
$$

26% of 73.2 = 19.032

Complete the following.

	a	**b**
1.	32% of 64 = _____	26% of 40 = _____
2.	2.5% of 89 = _____	1.2% of 385 = _____
3.	58% of 12 = _____	250% of 8 = _____
4.	73% of 8.4 = _____	49% of 86 = _____
5.	0.8% of 256 = _____	11% of 29 = _____
6.	120% of 35 = _____	7.5% of 60 = _____
7.	84% of 7 = _____	40% of 95 = _____
8.	20% of 45 = _____	22% of 142 = _____
9.	9.2% of 63 = _____	80% of 80 = _____
10.	7% of 112 = _____	62% of 45 = _____
11.	16% of 16 = _____	12% of 200 = _____
12.	1.8% of 240 = _____	18% of 15 = _____

Lesson 3.8 Finding Percents

Use these methods to find the percent one number is of another number:

50 is what percent of 80?

$50 = n\% \times 80$

$50 = \frac{n}{100} \times 80$ $50 = \frac{80n}{100}$

$5000 = 80n$

$5000 \div 80 = 80n \div 80$

$62.5 = n$

50 is 62.5% of 80.

$\frac{1}{4}$ is what percent of $\frac{5}{8}$?

$\frac{1}{4} = n\% \times \frac{5}{8}$

$\frac{1}{4} = \frac{n}{100} \times \frac{5}{8}$ $\frac{1}{4} = \frac{5n}{800}$

$800 = 20n$

$800 \div 20 = 20n \div 20$

$40 = n$

$\frac{1}{4}$ is 40% of $\frac{5}{8}$.

Complete the following.

	a	**b**
1.	12 is _____% of 20.	0.9 is _____% of 4.5.
2.	15 is _____% of 100.	16 is _____% of 25.
3.	0.9 is _____% of 6.	$\frac{1}{3}$ is _____% of $\frac{5}{6}$.
4.	1.8 is _____% of 18.	45 is _____% of 50.
5.	48 is _____% of 64.	16 is _____% of 40.
6.	19 is _____% of 95.	39 is _____% of 26.
7.	1.8 is _____% of 6.	5.6 is _____% of 2.8.
8.	12 is _____% of 32.	64 is _____% of 51.2.
9.	$\frac{3}{8}$ is _____% of $\frac{3}{4}$.	1.4 is _____% of 5.6.
10.	0.6 is _____% of 0.5.	$\frac{7}{10}$ is _____% of $\frac{7}{8}$.

Chapter 4

Lesson 4.1 Integers as Opposite Numbers

Every positive number has an opposite, negative number. A negative number is less than 0.

Draw a number line to show the opposite of each number.

	a	**b**
1.	What is the opposite of 8?	What is the opposite of 25?
2.	What is the opposite of −10?	What is the opposite of −7?
3.	What is the opposite of 12?	What is the opposite of −9?
4.	What is the opposite of −6?	What is the opposite of 2?
5.	What is the opposite of 11?	What is the opposite of −14?
6.	What is the opposite of −20?	What is the opposite of 16?

Name the opposite of each number.

7.	The opposite of 10 is _____.	The opposite of 1 is _____.
8.	The opposite of −3 is _____.	The opposite of 7 is _____.
9.	The opposite of −4 is _____.	The opposite of −8 is _____.
10.	The opposite of 13 is _____.	The opposite of −15 is _____.
11.	The opposite of −32 is _____.	The opposite of 27 is _____.
12.	The opposite of 17 is _____.	The opposite of −20 is _____.

Lesson 4.2 Integer Values in Real Life

Integers can be used to describe real-life situations.

A driver is going 15 miles per hour below the speed limit. The integer −15 can describe this situation. The negative sign shows that the speed is less than the speed limit.

Use integers to represent each real-life situation.

	a	b
1.	45 feet below sea level _____	a gain of 8 yards on a play _____
2.	$528 deposit into a checking account _____	62° above zero _____
3.	stock market increases of 345 points _____	an 8-pound weight loss _____
4.	7,500 feet above sea level _____	withdrawal of $80 from an ATM _____
5.	a 10-pound weight gain _____	stock market decrease of 250 points _____
6.	3 units to the right on a number line _____	8 units to the left on a number line _____
7.	10 units to the left on a number line _____	7 units to the right on a number line _____
8.	$60 deposit into a savings account _____	withdrawal of $95 from an ATM _____
9.	stock market decrease of 97 points _____	34° below zero _____
10.	100 feet below sea level _____	a gain of 15 yards on a play _____
11.	a 25-pound weight loss _____	stock market increase of 390 points _____
12.	95° above zero _____	6,000 feet above sea level _____

Lesson 4.3 Absolute Value

The **absolute value** of a number is its distance from zero.

Absolute value is represented by vertical lines on either side of an integer.

What is the absolute value of 8? $|8| = 8$

What is the absolute value of −8? $|-8| = 8$

Find the absolute value of each integer.

	a	b	c
1.	$|4| = \underline{4}$	$|-13| = \underline{13}$	$-|10| = \underline{}$
2.	$-|-7| = \underline{7}$	$|11| = \underline{11}$	$|-2| = \underline{}$
3.	$-|12| = \underline{12}$	$-|5| = \underline{5}$	$|1| = \underline{}$
4.	$|-14| = \underline{14}$	$-|8| = \underline{8}$	$-|-13| = \underline{}$
5.	$|3| = \underline{3}$	$|-7| = \underline{7}$	$-|4| = \underline{}$
6.	$-|-15| = \underline{15}$	$|9| = \underline{9}$	$|-12| = \underline{}$
7.	$|16| = \underline{16}$	$|-6| = \underline{6}$	$-|20| = \underline{}$
8.	$-|40| = \underline{40}$	$-|-24| = \underline{24}$	$|17| = \underline{}$
9.	$|33| = \underline{33}$	$-|-41| = \underline{}$	$|-19| = \underline{}$
10.	$|26| = \underline{26}$	$|-18| = \underline{}$	$-|35| = \underline{}$
11.	$-|53| = \underline{53}$	$|-21| = \underline{}$	$|30| = \underline{}$
12.	$|25| = \underline{25}$	$-|-21| = \underline{}$	$|-47| = \underline{}$

Lesson 4.4 Comparing and Ordering Integers

Integers are the set of whole numbers and their opposites.

Positive integers are greater than zero. **Negative integers** are less than zero. Zero is neither positive nor negative. A negative integer is less than a positive integer. On a number line, an integer and its opposite are the same distance from zero. The smaller of two integers is always the one to the left on a number line.

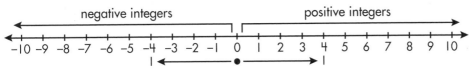

The opposite of 4 is −4. They are both 4 spaces from 0.

$$-7 < -2$$
−7 is to the left of −2.

$$-4 > -9$$
−4 is to the right of −9.

Use integers to name each point on the number line.

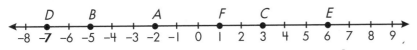

a	b	c
1. A _____	D _____	F _____
2. E _____	C _____	B _____

Use > or < to compare each pair of numbers.

3. 2 ☐ 7	−1 ☐ −4	5 ☐ 0
4. −4 ☐ 1	0 ☐ −8	−8 ☐ −10
5. 7 ☐ −7	−2 ☐ 0	4 ☐ 6
6. 1 ☐ −1	6 ☐ 3	−6 ☐ −3
7. 4 ☐ −2	−6 ☐ −4	3 ☐ −3

Order from least to greatest.

a	b
8. −3, −5, 0 _____	8, −8, 2 _____
9. 0, 5, −3, −7 _____	4, −1, 2, −2 _____
10. −6, 5, −2, −3, 2 _____	5, −8, −2, −3, 0 _____

Lesson 4.5 Using Integers in the Coordinate Plane

Positive and negative coordinates can be graphed using the coordinate plane system.

The first number in an ordered pair represents its point on the x-axis. The second number represents the point on the y-axis.

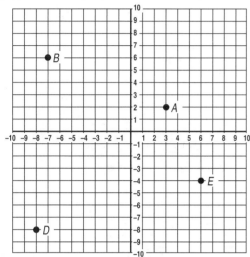

Point A: (3, 2)

Point B: (–7, 6)

Point C: (6, –4)

Point D: (–8, –8)

Use the coordinate grid to answer the questions.

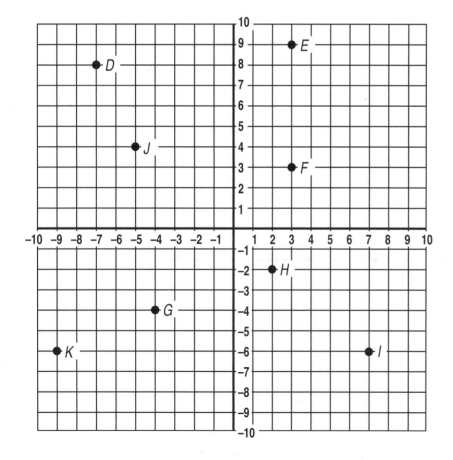

Write the ordered pair for each coordinate.

1. D _____

2. E _____

3. G _____

4. H _____

5. K _____

Name the point located at each ordered pair.

6. (–5, 4) _____

7. (7, –6) _____

8. (–9, –6) _____

9. (3, 3) _____

10. (–7, 8) _____

Lesson 4.6 Problem Solving in the Coordinate Plane

Use the coordinate grid to answer the questions.

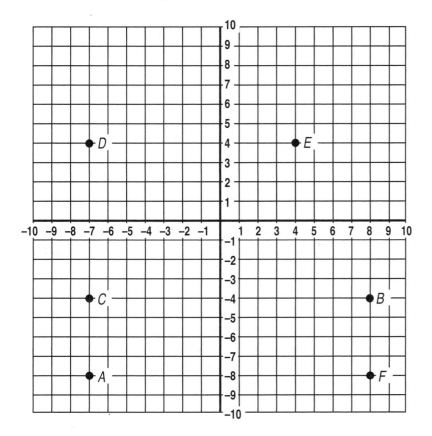

A – stream   D – school

B – home   E – park

C – bookstore   F – fire station

How far is it from the fire station to the bookstore?

Begin at the fire station.

First move __15__ units left. Then, move __4__ units up.

__15__ + __4__ = __19__ units

It takes __19__ units to get from the fire station to the bookstore.

1. How far is it from school to the park? _____ units

2. How far is it from the stream to the fire station? _____ units

3. How far is it from the bookstore to home? _____ units

4. How far is it from the stream to the school? _____ units

5. How far is from the fire station to home? _____ units

Chapter 5

Lesson 5.1 Using Exponents

A **power** of a number represents repeated multiplication of the number by itself. $10^3 = 10 \times 10 \times 10$ and is read 10 to the third power.

In **exponential** numbers, the **base** is the number that is multiplied, and the **exponent** represents the number of times the base is used as a factor. In 2^5, 2 is the base and 5 is the exponent.

2^5 means 2 is used as a factor 5 times.
$2 \times 2 \times 2 \times 2 \times 2 = 32 \quad 2^5 = 32$

Scientific notation for a number is expressed by writing the number as the product of a number between one and ten, and a power of ten.

3,000 can be written as $3 \times 1,000$ or 3×10^3.
3×10^3 is scientific notation for 3,000.

Some powers of 10 are shown in the table at right.

10^1	10	10
10^2	10×10	100
10^3	$10 \times 10 \times 10$	1,000
10^4	$10 \times 10 \times 10 \times 10$	10,000
10^5	$10 \times 10 \times 10 \times 10 \times 10$	100,000

Use the table above to write each number in scientific notation.

	a	b	c
1.	30 _____	4,000 _____	50,000 _____
2.	600,000 _____	700 _____	90 _____
3.	40,000 _____	100,000 _____	400 _____

Write each power as the product of factors.

4.	3^3 _____	5^5 _____	1^6 _____
5.	12^2 _____	8^3 _____	6^3 _____
6.	7^4 _____	4^4 _____	11^4 _____

Use exponents to rewrite each expression.

7.	$3 \times 3 \times 3$ _____	8×8 _____	$7 \times 7 \times 7 \times 7 \times 7$ _____
8.	24×24 _____	$4 \times 4 \times 4$ _____	$6 \times 6 \times 6 \times 6 \times 6 \times 6$ _____
9.	$2 \times 2 \times 2 \times 2$ _____	$38 \times 38 \times 38$ _____	$5 \times 5 \times 5 \times 5 \times 5$ _____

Evaluate each expression.

10.	a^4 if $a = 2$ _____	x^3 if $x = 4$ _____	n^7 if $n = 1$ _____
11.	n^2 if $n = 8$ _____	b^4 if $b = 3$ _____	x^3 if $x = 5$ _____
12.	a^5 if $a = 3$ _____	x^3 if $x = 6$ _____	n^2 if $n = 11$ _____

Lesson 5.2 Parts of an Expression

A **variable** is a symbol, usually a letter of the alphabet, that stands for an unknown number, or quantity. a = variable

An **algebraic expression** is a combination of numbers, variables, and at least one operation. $x + 13$

A **term** is a number, variable, product, or quotient in an algebraic expression. In $3a + 5$, $3a$ is a term and 5 also is a term.

The term $3a$ means $3 \times a$. The number 3 is the coefficient of a. A **coefficient** is a number that multiplies a variable. In the expression $x + 5$, the coefficient of x is understood to be 1.

An **equation** is a sentence that contains an equal sign. $x + 13 = 25$

Identify each of the following as an *expression* or an *equation*.

a	b	c
1. $3 + x$ _____	$7 + 4 = 11$ _____	$55 \times n$ _____
2. $x - 7 = 15$ _____	$b - 45$ _____	$24 = 6 \times 4$ _____

For each term below, identify the coefficient and the variable.

a	b
3. $3x$ coefficient _____ variable _____	$4y$ coefficient _____ variable _____
4. z coefficient _____ variable _____	$5n$ coefficient _____ variable _____
5. $7b$ coefficient _____ variable _____	m coefficient _____ variable _____
6. r coefficient _____ variable _____	$6d$ coefficient _____ variable _____

Translate each phrase into an algebraic expression.

7. five more than n _____   eight decreased by x _____

8. x added to seven _____   the product of n and 11 _____

Translate each sentence into an equation.

9. Six times a number is 18. _____   Seventy less than a number is 29. _____

10. Eight divided by a number is 2. _____   The product of 7 and 12 is 84. _____

Write the following expressions in words.

11. $6 - n = 3$ _____

12. $5 \times 13 = 65$ _____

Lesson 5.3 Writing Expressions

An **equation** is a number sentence that contains an equal sign.
An **expression** is a number phrase without an equal sign.
Equations and expressions may contain only numerals, or they also may contain variables. A
variable is a symbol, usually a letter, that stands for an unknown number.

	Equation	Expression
Numerical	$3 \times 5 = 15$	$9 + 2$
Variable	$2n + 2 = 18$	$a - 5$

All equations and expressions express an idea.

3×4 means "three 4s." $6 \div 3 = 2$ means "6 divided by 3 is 2."

$n - 7$ means "n decreased by 7" or "a number decreased by 7."

$4n + 2 = 6$ means "four times a number, plus 2, is 6" or "4ns, plus 2, is 6."

Translate each phrase into an expression or an equation.

a   **b**

1. x increased by 5 _____   12 divided by a number _____

2. seven ns _____ c less than 7 _____

3. a number added to 15 is 23 _____   one-fourth of x _____

4. p added to 6 _____   the product of 15 and m _____

Translate each sentence into an equation. Use n for an unknown number.

5. 11 decreased by a number is 7. _____

6. 8 times a number, plus 4, is 84. _____

7. A number divided by 5 is 6. _____

Write each expression in words.

8. $n - 5$ _____

9. $3n \div 6$ _____

Lesson 5.4 Equivalent Expressions

Equivalent expressions are created by simplifying values and combining terms.

$4(6x - 5) = 24x - 20$ Multiply each value by 4 to create an equivalent expression.

$3(4^3 + 7x) = 3(64 + 7x)$ First, calculate the value of the exponents.
$3(64 + 7x) = 192 + 21x$ Then, use the distributive property to create the equivalent expression.

$t + t + t = 3t$ Use multiplication in place of repeated addition.

Create expressions equivalent to the ones below.

1. $7(4z + 8b)$ _____

2. $8(2x + 3^2)$ _____

3. $4(r + r + r + r)$ _____

4. $9(3 + 8x)$ _____

5. $4^2(3 + 6t)$ _____

6. $\dfrac{t + t + t}{4}$ _____

7. $2(4s^3 + 2)$ _____

8. $30(3x + 4)$ _____

9. $6(5a + 9b)$ _____

10. $9(3x + 5^4)$ _____

11. $7(c + c + c)$ _____

12. $9(2 + 7f)$ _____

13. $7^5(4g - 8d)$ _____

14. $\dfrac{e + e + e}{5}$ _____

15. $5(3z^6 + 3)$ _____

16. $10(y + 2)$ _____

Lesson 5.5 Solving 1-Step Equations: Addition & Subtraction

Subtraction Property of Equality

If you subtract the same number from each side of an equation, the two sides remain equal.

$$x + 12 = 20$$

To undo the addition of 12, subtract 12.

$$x + 12 - 12 = 20 - 12$$
$$x + 0 = 8$$
$$x = 8$$

Addition Property of Equality

If you add the same number to each side of an equation, the two sides remain equal.

$$n - 3 = 15$$

To undo the subtraction of 3, add 3.

$$n - 3 + 3 = 15 + 3$$
$$n - 0 = 18$$
$$n = 18$$

Write the operation that would undo the operation in the equation.

	a		b
1.	$x - 4 = 3$ _____		$8 = b + 4$ _____
2.	$y + 7 = 25$ _____		$3 = a - 7$ _____

Solve each equation.

	a	b	c
3.	$a - 4 = 2$ _____	$y + 5 = 9$ _____	$x - 3 = 14$ _____
4.	$7 = x - 4$ _____	$b + 7 = 19$ _____	$y + 5 = 5$ _____
5.	$z - 7 = 5$ _____	$m - 5 = 5$ _____	$n + 1 = 1$ _____
6.	$x + 7 = 10$ _____	$x - 3 = 18$ _____	$x + 0 = 9$ _____
7.	$b + 4 = 4$ _____	$b - 8 = 12$ _____	$n + 8 = 12$ _____
8.	$z - 10 = 20$ _____	$z + 5 = 20$ _____	$x - 2 = 8$ _____

Write and solve the equation for each problem below.

9. Kelley went to the movies. She took 20 dollars with her. When she came home, she had 6 dollars. How much money did she spend? _____

9.

10. There are 27 students in Mrs. Yuen's homeroom. Twelve of them have home computers. How many students do not have home computers?

_____

10.

Lesson 5.5 Solving 1-Step Equations: Addition & Subtraction

Solve each equation.

a	b	c

1. $9 + d = 16$ _____ $y + 3 = 9$ _____ $12 + a = 27$ _____

2. $18 - b = 4$ _____ $23 - c = 21$ _____ $w - 11 = 11$ _____

3. $n + 8 = 41$ _____ $7 + m = 20$ _____ $9 + s = 9$ _____

4. $t - 18 = 5$ _____ $36 - a = 36$ _____ $15 - b = 0$ _____

5. $17 = c + 3$ _____ $29 = 5 + b$ _____ $36 = 35 + n$ _____

6. $2 = d - 4$ _____ $19 = 25 - a$ _____ $12 = t - 12$ _____

Write an equation for each problem. Then, solve the equation.

7. Ruben read 37 pages in his history book over the weekend. He read 21 pages on Saturday. How many pages did he read on Sunday?

_____ He read _____ pages on Sunday.

8. The Garcias ate 9 pieces of toast for breakfast. If there are 33 slices of bread left, how many slices were in the loaf of bread?

_____ There were _____ slices in the loaf of bread.

9. In a 25-kilometer triathlon, competitors swim 2 kilometers, run 5 kilometers, and bike the rest. How far do they bike?

_____ They bike _____ kilometers.

Lesson 5.6 Solving 1-Step Equations: Multiplication & Division

Division Property of Equality

If you divide each side of an equation by the same nonzero number, the two sides remain equal.

$$3y = 21$$

To undo multiplication by 3, divide by 3.

$$\frac{3y}{3} = \frac{21}{3}$$

$$y = 7$$

Multiplication Property of Equality

If you multiply each side of an equation by the same number, the two sides remain equal.

$$\frac{a}{4} = 4$$

To undo division by 4, multiply by 4.

$$\frac{a}{4} \times \frac{4}{1} = 5 \times 4$$

$$a = 20$$

Write the operation that would undo the operation in each equation.

	a		b
1.	$5 \times n = 40$ _____		$\frac{y}{5} = 80$ _____
2.	$\frac{x}{2} = 8$ _____		$a \times 7 = 42$ _____

Solve each equation.

	a	b	c
3.	$3 \times a = 9$ _____	$\frac{x}{5} = 5$ _____	$\frac{n}{4} = 3$ _____
4.	$\frac{x}{3} = 3$ _____	$n \times 4 = 4$ _____	$3 \times y = 24$ _____
5.	$5 \times b = 10$ _____	$\frac{b}{8} = 2$ _____	$4 \times a = 20$ _____
6.	$\frac{m}{3} = 1$ _____	$8 \times n = 20$ _____	$\frac{x}{5} = 2$ _____
7.	$4 \times n = 1$ _____	$\frac{n}{4} = 5$ _____	$\frac{b}{3} = 27$ _____
8.	$n \times 15 = 30$ _____	$\frac{n}{4} = 10$ _____	$n \times 12 = 36$ _____
9.	$\frac{n}{18} = 2$ _____	$n \times 3 = 18$ _____	$n \times 2 = 20$ _____
10.	$\frac{n}{2} = 20$ _____	$\frac{n}{16} = 1$ _____	$n \times 3 = 3$ _____
11.	$5 \times b = 30$ _____	$\frac{b}{5} = 30$ _____	$n \times 8 = 24$ _____
12.	$\frac{n}{4} = 1$ _____	$\frac{b}{2} = 2$ _____	$n \times 6 = 48$ _____

Lesson 5.6 Solving 1-Step Equations: Multiplication & Division

Solve each equation.

	a	b	c
1.	$2 \times d = 18$ _____	$a \times 4 = 20$ _____	$5 \times n = 30$ _____
2.	$y \div 3 = 4$ _____	$t \div 9 = 3$ _____	$\frac{a}{5} = 3$ _____
3.	$8 \times s = 64$ _____	$p \times 16 = 16$ _____	$7 \times r = 42$ _____
4.	$\frac{n}{5} = 10$ _____	$n \div 3 = 12$ _____	$a \div 8 = 6$ _____
5.	$25 = 5 \times d$ _____	$0 = a \times 57$ _____	$32 = b \times 2$ _____
6.	$19 = \frac{x}{1}$ _____	$7 = b \div 4$ _____	$9 = \frac{c}{7}$ _____

Write an equation for each problem. Then, solve the equation.

7. Taryn practiced piano the same amount of time every day for 6 days. If she practiced a total of 12 hours, how many hours did she practice each day?

_____ She practiced _____ hours each day.

8. A group of friends decided to equally share a package of trading cards. If there were 48 cards in the package and each person received 12, how many friends were in the group?

_____ There were _____ friends in the group.

9. Twenty-five cars can take the ferry across the river at one time. If 150 cars took the ferry, and it was full each time, how many times did the ferry cross the river?

_____ The ferry crossed the river _____ times.

Lesson 5.7 Solving Inequalities

Inequalities can be solved the same way that equations are solved.

$6 + q > 14$

$6 + q - 6 > 14 - 6$

$q > 8$

1. Subtract 6 from both sides of the inequality to isolate the variable on one side of the inequality.

2. The variable q represents a value that is greater than 8.

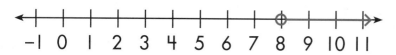

A number line can be used to represent the possible values of the variable. An open circle shows that the values do not include 8. For inequalities that use $\leq$ or $\geq$, a closed circle indicates that the values do include that point.

Solve the inequalities and represent the possible values of the variable on a number line.

1. $6 > z - 2$

2. $g + 7 < -12$

3. $d - 5 < 7$

4. $15 > k + 2$

5. $1 + x > -16$

6. $y + 8 < -9$

7. $8 \leq 8 + r$

8. $w + 8 \geq 11$

Lesson 5.7 Solving Inequalities

Solve the inequalities and represent the possible values of the variable on a number line.

1. $x - 2 < 12$

2. $-1 + y > 17$

3. $p + 2 < -13$

4. $-7 + v < -17$

5. $6 + s \geq -6$

6. $f + 2 \geq 8$

7. $-10 > w - 1$

8. $-3 + g \leq 9$

Lesson 5.8 Dependent and Independent Variables

Sometimes word problems contain dependent and independent variables. The **dependent variable** in a problem is the value that is affected by the other values in the problem. The **independent variable** is the value that affects the outcome of the dependent variable.

If a car has to travel 200 miles, the speed (s) the car is driving is the independent variable and the time (t) it takes to make the trip is the dependent variable. This can be represented by the formula, $200 = s \times t$, and can be solved by creating a table.

Dependent Variable	Time	5 hours	4 hours	$3\frac{1}{3}$ hours
Independent Variable	Speed	40 miles/hr.	50 miles/hr.	60 miles/hr.

Use tables to identify the variables and find possible solutions to the problems.

1. Maria has to buy apples at the grocery store. Apples cost $1.25 per pound. How much will Maria spend on apples?

   What equation will you use? _____

Dependent Variable				
Independent Variable				

2. When a tree is planted, it is 6 feet tall. Each month, it grows by 2 feet. How tall will it get over time?

   What equation will you use? _____

_____ **Variable**	Height			
_____ **Variable**	Time	3 months	6 months	2 years

Lesson 5.8 Dependent and Independent Variables

Use tables to identify the variables and find possible solutions to the problems.

1. Students have been assigned to read a book that is 150 pages. Every student reads at a different speed. Depending on reading speed, how many days will it take different students to read the assigned book?

Write the equation: _____

_____ **Variable**	Time (Days)			
_____ **Variable**	Reading Speed	15 pages/ day	20 pages/ day	30 pages/ day

2. As a candle burns, it decreases in height by 2 inches every hour. If the candle is 12 inches tall when it is lit, how will the height change over time?

Write the equation: _____

Dependent Variable	Height (inches)			
Independent Variable	Time (hours)			

3. As a daffodil grows, it increases in height by 3 inches every 2 days. If the daffodil plant starts at 1 inch on day one, how will the height change over time?

Write the equation: _____

Dependent Variable				
Independent Variable				

4. The temperature in an oven increases by 8° every minute. If the starting temperature of the oven is 250, how will the temperature change over time?

Write the equation: _____

_____ **Variable**				
_____ **Variable**				

Lesson 6.1 Calculating Area: Triangles

The area (A) of a triangle is one-half the of the base (b) times the height (h).

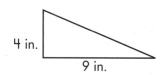

4 in.
9 in.

$$A = \frac{1}{2} \times b \times h$$

or

$$A = \frac{1}{2}bh$$

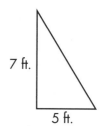

7 ft.
5 ft.

$A = \frac{1}{2} \times 9 \times 4$

$= \frac{1}{2} \times 36$

$= 18$

$A = 18$ square inches

$A = \frac{1}{2} \times 5 \times 7$

$= \frac{1}{2} \times 35$

$= 17\frac{1}{2}$

$A = 17\frac{1}{2}$ square feet

Find the area of each right triangle.

     a   **b**

1.

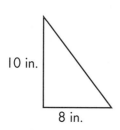

10 in.
8 in.

$A = $ _____ sq. in.

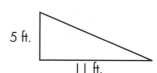

5 ft.
11 ft.

$A = $ _____ sq. ft.

2.

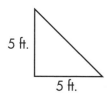

5 ft.
5 ft.

$A = $ _____ sq. ft.

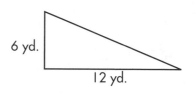

6 yd.
12 yd.

$A = $ _____ sq. yd.

Lesson 6.1 Calculating Area: Triangles

The area of a triangle is related to the area of a rectangle.

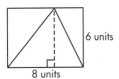

6 units

The dashed line indicates the height of the triangle.

rectangle: $A = 8 \times 6 = 48$ sq. units

triangle: $A = \frac{1}{2}(8)(6) = 24$ sq. units

8 units

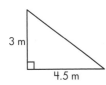

3 m

$A = \frac{1}{2}(4.5)(3) = 6\frac{3}{4}$ sq. m

Notice that in a right triangle the height is the length of one of the legs. This is not the case with acute and obtuse triangles.

4.5 m

Find the area of each triangle below.

a	**b**	**c**

1.

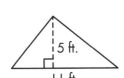

5 ft.

11 ft.

$A =$ _____ sq. ft.

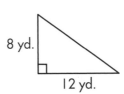

8 yd.

12 yd.

$A =$ _____ sq. yd.

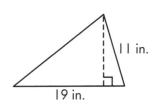

11 in.

19 in.

$A =$ _____ sq. in.

2.

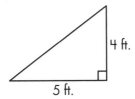

4 ft.

5 ft.

$A =$ _____ sq. ft.

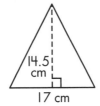

14.5 cm

17 cm

$A =$ _____ sq. cm

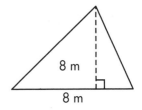

8 m

8 m

$A =$ _____ sq. m

Lesson 6.2 Calculating Area: Quadrilaterals

Area is the number of square units it takes to cover a figure. To find the **area of a rectangle**, multiply the length by the width. $A = lw$

7 units

2 units

$A = 7 \times 2$
$A = 14$ square units

8 units

$A = s \times s = 8 \times 8$
$A = 64$ square units

Find the area of each rectangle below.

| | **a** | **b** | **c** |

1.

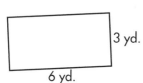 3 yd.
6 yd.

 18 m

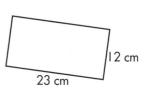 12 cm
23 cm

$A =$ _____ sq. yd.

$A =$ _____ sq. m

$A =$ _____ sq. cm

2.

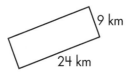 9 km
24 km

 23 in.

8 ft.
6 ft.

$A =$ _____ sq. km

$A =$ _____ sq. in.

$A =$ _____ sq. ft.

Find the length of each rectangle below.

3.

 6 in.

4.5 ft.

9 m

$A = 54$ sq. in.
$\ell =$ _____ in.

$A = 58.5$ sq. ft.
$\ell =$ _____ ft.

$A = 81$ sq. m
$\ell =$ _____ m

Lesson 6.2 Calculating Area: Quadrilaterals

A parallelogram is a polygon with 2 sets of parallel sides. To find the **area of a parallelogram**, multiply the measure of its base by the measure of its height: $A = b \times h$ or $A = bh$.

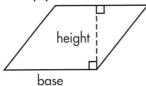

$b = 8$ in. and $h = 7$ in. What is A?

$A = b \times h$ $A = 8 \times 7 = 56$ in.^{2} or 56 square inches.

Find the area of each parallelogram.

a	b	c

1.

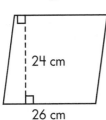

24 cm

26 cm

$A =$ _____ sq. cm

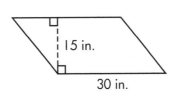

15 in.

30 in.

$A =$ _____ sq. in.

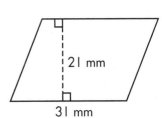

21 mm

31 mm

$A =$ _____ sq. mm

2.

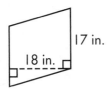

17 in.

18 in.

$A =$ _____ sq. in.

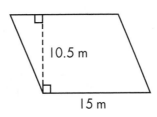

10.5 m

15 m

$A =$ _____ sq. m

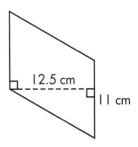

12.5 cm

11 cm

$A =$ _____ sq. cm

Lesson 6.3 Calculating Area: Other Polygons

To find the area of an irregular shape, separate the shape into its component figures and find the area of each one.

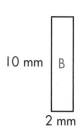

7 mm
3 mm
B 10 mm
A
5 mm

This figure can be divided into two rectangles, as shown by the dotted line.

To find the missing side measurement of shape A, look at the vertical measurements you already know: 10 mm and 7 mm. Because the missing side must be the difference between 10 and 7, subtract to get the answer: $10 - 7 = 3$ mm.

A 3 mm
3 mm

To find the area of shape A, multiply $l \times w$.
$$3 \times 3 = 9 \text{ mm}$$

10 mm B
2 mm

Follow the same steps to find the area of shape B.
$$5 - 3 = 2 \text{ mm}$$
$$A = 10 \times 2 = 20 \text{ mm}$$

Then, add the two areas together to get the area of the entire irregular shape.
$$9 + 20 = 29 \text{ square mm}$$

Find the area of each figure.

	a	**b**	**c**

1.

5 mm
2 mm
10 mm
9 mm

$A =$ _____ sq. mm

10 yd.
8 yd.   8 yd.
3 yd.

$A =$ _____ sq. yd.

8 cm
4 cm   3 cm
2 cm

$A =$ _____ sq. cm

2.

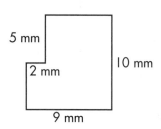

3 in.
9 in.   5 in.
8 in.

$A =$ _____ sq. in.

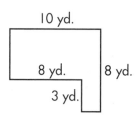

2 mm
2 mm   6 mm
4 mm

$A =$ _____ sq. mm

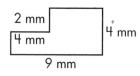

2 mm
4 mm   4 mm
9 mm

$A =$ _____ sq. mm

NAME _____

Lesson 6.3 Calculating Area: Other Polygons

Some irregular shapes are made up of more than one type of figure.

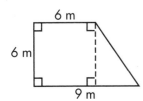

This figure can be divided into a square and a triangle.

area of square
$A = 6 \times 6 = 36$

area of triangle
$A = \frac{1}{2} \times 3 \times 6 = 9$

The area of the figure is $36 + 9 = 45$ square meters.

Find the area of each figure.

| | a | b | c |

1.

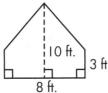

$A =$ _____ sq. ft.

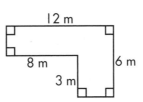

$A =$ _____ sq. m

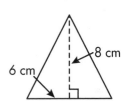

$A =$ _____ sq. cm

2.

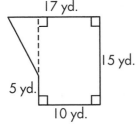

$A =$ _____ sq. yd.

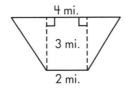

$A =$ _____ sq. mi.

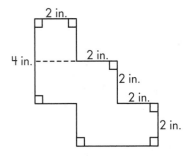

$A =$ _____ sq. in.

Lesson 6.4 Volume of Rectangular Solids

The **volume** (V) of a rectangular solid is the product of the measure of its length (ℓ), the measure of its width (w), and the measure of its height (h). $V = \ell \times w \times h$

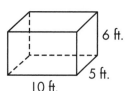

$V = 10 \times 5 \times 6$

$= 50 \times 6$

$= 300$

The volume is 300 cubic feet.

Find the volume of each rectangular solid.

	a	**b**	**c**

1.

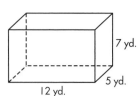

7 yd.

5 yd.

12 yd.

$V =$ _____ cu. yd.

8 in.

8 in.

8 in.

$V =$ _____ cu. in.

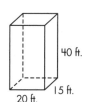

40 ft.

15 ft.

20 ft.

$V =$ _____ cu. ft.

2.

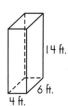

14 ft.

6 ft.

4 ft.

$V =$ _____ cu. ft.

5 in.

5 in.

4 in.

$V =$ _____ cu. in.

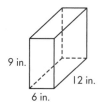

9 in.

12 in.

6 in.

$V =$ _____ cu. in.

Lesson 6.4 Volume of Rectangular Solids

Find the volume of each rectangular solid.

a	b	c

1.

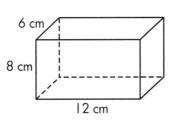

$V =$ _____ cu. cm

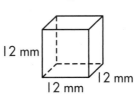

$V =$ _____ cu. mm

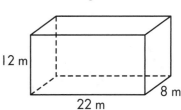

$V =$ _____ cu. m

2.

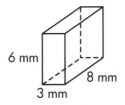

$V =$ _____ cu. mm

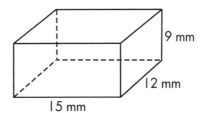

$V =$ _____ cu. mm

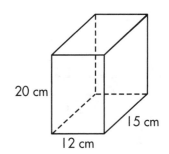

$V =$ _____ cu. cm

3.

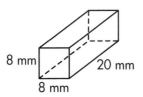

$V =$ _____ cu. mm

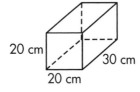

$V =$ _____ cu. cm

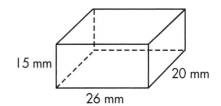

$V =$ _____ cu. mm

Lesson 6.4 Volume of Rectangular Solids

The volume of a rectangular solid with fractional edge lengths can also be measured by packing the solid with cubes that share a common denominator with the edge lengths. In this rectangular solid, each side length has a denominator of 5, so the solid can be packed with $\frac{1}{5}$ inch cubes to determine its volume.

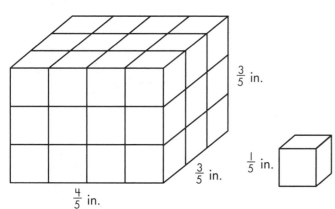

First, calculate the volume of the cube itself.

$\frac{1}{5} \times \frac{1}{5} \times \frac{1}{5} = \frac{1}{125}$ cubic inches

Next, add up the cubes in the solid. You can see from the top layer that there are 12 cubes per layer, and $12 \times 3 = 36$.

Last, multiply the number of cubes times the volume of one cube.

$36 \times \frac{1}{125} = \frac{36}{125}$ cubic inches

This is the same answer you get when you use the formula $l \times w \times h$. $\qquad \frac{4}{5} \times \frac{3}{5} \times \frac{3}{5} = \frac{36}{125}$

Find the volume of each rectangular solid.

a   **b**

1.

$\frac{3}{7}$ in.

$\frac{2}{7}$ in.

$\frac{5}{7}$ in.

$V =$ _____ cu. in.

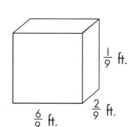

$\frac{1}{9}$ ft.

$\frac{2}{9}$ ft.

$\frac{6}{9}$ ft.

$V =$ _____ cu. ft.

2.

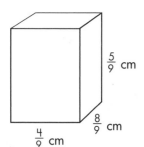

$\frac{5}{9}$ cm

$\frac{8}{9}$ cm

$\frac{4}{9}$ cm

$V =$ _____ cu. cm

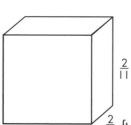

$\frac{2}{11}$ ft.

$\frac{2}{11}$ ft.

$\frac{10}{11}$ ft.

$V =$ _____ cu. ft.

Lesson 6.5 Surface Area: Rectangular Solids

The **surface area** of a solid is the sum of the areas of all surfaces of the solid. A rectangular solid has 6 surfaces.

The area of each surface is determined by finding:

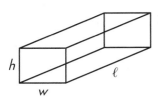

length × width, length × height, width × height

The total surface area is found using this formula:

$SA = 2\ell w + 2\ell h + 2wh$

If $\ell = 10$ m, $w = 6$ m, and $h = 4$ m, the surface area is found as follows:

$SA = 2(10 \times 6) + 2(10 \times 4) + 2(6 \times 4)$

$SA = 2(60) + 2(40) + 2(24) = 120 + 80 + 48 = 248$ m^2

Find the surface area of each rectangular solid.

a	b	c

1.

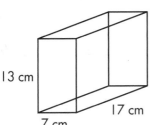

13 cm, 17 cm, 7 cm

SA = _____ cm^2

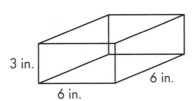

3 in., 6 in., 6 in.

SA = _____ in.^{2}

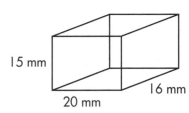

15 mm, 20 mm, 16 mm

SA = _____ mm^2

2.

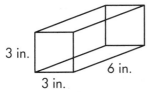

3 in., 3 in., 6 in.

SA = _____ in.^{2}

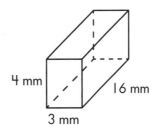

4 mm, 3 mm, 16 mm

SA = _____ mm^2

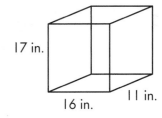

17 in., 16 in., 11 in.

SA = _____ in.^{2}

Lesson 6.5 Surface Area: Rectangular Solids

Find the surface area of each rectangular solid.

a	b	c

1.
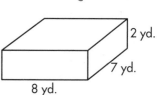
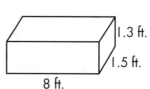

2 in.
5 in.
3 in.

SA = _____ sq. in.

1.3 ft.
1.5 ft.
8 ft.

SA = _____ sq. ft.

2 yd.
7 yd.
8 yd.

SA = _____ sq. yd.

2.
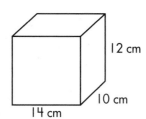
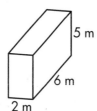
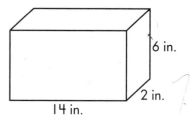

12 cm
10 cm
14 cm

SA = _____ sq. cm

5 m
6 m
2 m

SA = _____ sq. m

6 in.
2 in.
14 in.

SA = _____ sq. in.

3.
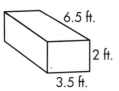
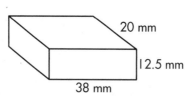
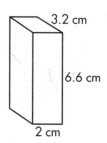

6.5 ft.
2 ft.
3.5 ft.

SA = _____ sq. ft.

20 mm
12.5 mm
38 mm

SA = _____ sq. mm

3.2 cm
6.6 cm
2 cm

SA = _____ sq. cm

Lesson 6.6 Surface Area: Pyramids

The **surface area** of a solid is the sum of the areas of all surfaces of the solid. The surface area of a square pyramid is the sum of the area of the square base and each of the 4 triangular sides.

side

Each triangle's area is $\frac{1}{2}$ base × height. In a pyramid, **base** refers to the side length and **height** refers to the slant height, or length. So surface area or $SA = (\text{side} \times \text{side}) + 4(\frac{1}{2} \text{side} \times \text{length})$.

$SA = s^2 + 2s\ell$ SA is given in **square units**, or **units^2**.

slant height, or *length* (ℓ) of the side

If $s = 6$ cm and $\ell = 10$ cm, what is the surface area?

$SA = s^2 + 2s\ell$

$SA = 6^2 + 2 \times 6 \times 10 = 36 + 120 = 156$ cm^2

Find the surface area of each square pyramid.

1.

a

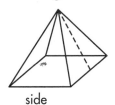

44
176
4'   88
176
264

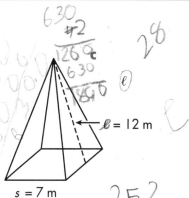

$\ell = 11$ in.

$s = 8$ in.

$SA = \underline{264}$ in.^{2}

b

$\ell = 10.5$ cm

$s = 15$ cm

$SA = \underline{1890}$ cm^2

c

630
+2
1260
630
860

$\ell = 12$ m

$s = 7$ m

$SA = \underline{252}$ m^2

2.

$\ell = 21$ ft.

$s = 9$ ft.

$SA = \underline{567}$ ft.^{2}

378
189
189
2
378
189

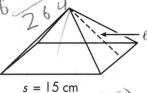

$\ell = 8$ cm

$s = 10$ cm

$SA = \underline{240}$ cm^2

160
80
240

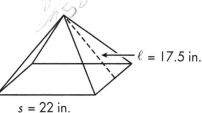

$\ell = 17.5$ in.

$s = 22$ in.

$SA = \underline{1155}$ in.^{2}

385
2
770
385
1155

22
17.5
385.0

Lesson 6.7 Graphing Polygons: Rectangles

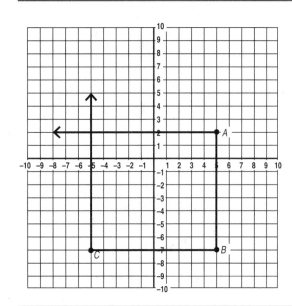

Coordinate planes can help you solve problems with polygons, such as rectangles.

If points A (5, 2), B (5, −7), and C (−5, −7) are vertices of a rectangle, where does vertex D fall?

Connect the vertices and then draw lines straight from points A and C to find where vertex D will fall.

Point D occurs at point (−5, 2).

Use the coordinate grids to find the missing vertex of each polygon.

1. a rectangle with points at (0, 2), (−6, 2), and (−6, 4)

The missing point is at _____.

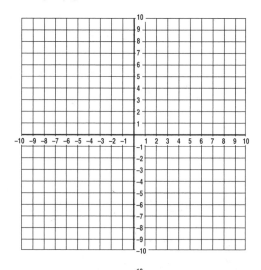

2. a rectangle with points at (3, −4), (3, 5), and (−2, 5)

The missing point is at _____.

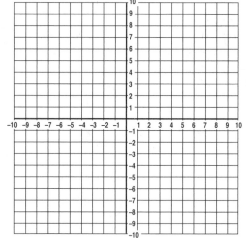

Lesson 6.8 Graphing Polygons: Right Triangles

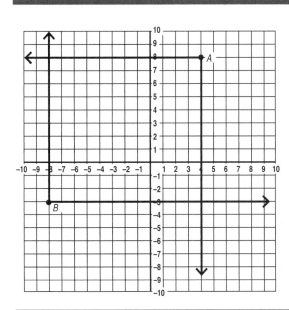

Triangle problems can also be solved through graphing on the coordinate plane.

If points A (4, 8) and B (−8, −3) are vertices of the hypotenuse (longest side) of a right triangle, where does vertex C fall?

Connect the vertices and then draw lines straight from points A and B to find where vertex C will fall.

Point C can occur at point (−8, 8) or point (4, −3).

Use the coordinate grids to find the missing vertex of each polygon.

1. a right triangle with points at (3, 2) and (−5, 6)

   The missing point is at _____ or _____.

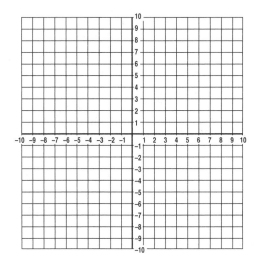

2. a right triangle with points at (−4, −6) and (5, 2)

   The missing point is at _____ or _____.

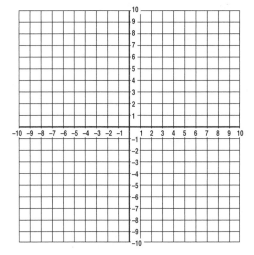

Chapter 7

Lesson 7.1 Asking Statistical Questions

A **statistical question** has answers that will vary.

"How old are students in my school?" is a statistical question because not every answer will be the same.

"How old am I?" is not a statistical question because there is only one answer.

Read each question and write *statistical* or *not*.

a	b
1. How tall are the students in my class?	What does this apple cost?
2. What grades did students score on the test?	How fast can dogs run 100 yards?
3. How many marbles are in the jar?	Does a chocolate bar weigh more than a pack of jelly beans?
4. What was the difference in rainfall between March and April?	How many miles can cars travel on a gallon of gas?
5. Will I score a basket in the game tonight?	How often do adults eat breakfast?

Lesson 7.2 Describing Data

Data can be described by how the values relate to each other and how they are spread out.

10, 7, 8, 8, 23, 45, 77, 90, 90

The data is spread over 83 points.

The center value of the data is 23.

The lowest value in the data is 7.

All of the values are greater than 0.

The highest value in the data is 90.

8 and 90 appear twice each in the data.

Write three descriptions of each data set.

1. 62, 68, 63, 67, 69, 63, 67

A. _____

B. _____

C. _____

2. 0, 0, 2, 8, 6, 10, 100

A. _____

B. _____

C. _____

3. 0, 8, 20, 45, 84, 92, 45

A. _____

B. _____

C. _____

Lesson 7.3 Measures of Center: Mean

The **mean** of a data set is computed by adding all of the numbers in the data together and dividing by the number of values contained in the data set.

84, 66, 102, 114, 78, 90

84 + 66 + 102 + 114 + 78 + 90 = 534   1. Add all of the values in the data set together.

$$\begin{array}{r} 89 \\ 6\overline{)534} \end{array}$$

2. Divide the sum by the number of values in the data set.

89

3. The mean of the data set is 89.

Find the mean of each data set.

a	b
1. 48, 64, 80, 48	85, 75, 90, 60, 80
2. 84, 140, 105, 119, 105, 84, 105	102, 78, 114, 96, 96, 102
3. 119, 140, 119, 91, 91, 126, 91	96, 108, 78, 96, 72, 102
4. 52, 52, 64, 80	55, 90, 70, 90, 85
5. 112, 140, 77, 126, 91, 77, 133	90, 84, 72, 102, 84, 66
6. 99, 89, 46, 97, 17, 75	60, 31, 24, 50, 44, 88

Lesson 7.4 Measures of Center: Median

The **median** of a data set is the middle number when the values are placed in order from least to greatest. If there are an even number of values in the data set, the median is the average of the two middle terms.

35, 29, 26, 37, 21, 38, 38

21, 26, 29, 35, 37, 38, 38   1. Put the data in order from least to greatest.

———————→ 35 ←———————   2. Count in from the outside to find the middle value.

35   3. The median of this data set is 35.

Find the median of each data set.

a   **b**

1. 23, 31, 32, 34, 39, 38, 38, 34, 38   24, 20, 28, 19, 18, 11, 19, 18, 19

   _____   _____

2. 19, 11, 28, 13, 23, 14, 28   3, 9, 6, 2, 1, 10, 1, 2, 1

   _____   _____

3. 26, 34, 24, 37, 36, 22, 34, 26, 34   10, 2, 3, 4, 6, 7, 6

   _____   _____

4. 23, 32, 38, 40, 30, 34, 23   15, 21, 23, 16, 19, 14, 23, 14, 23

   _____   _____

5. 10, 3, 5, 1, 7, 8, 5, 1, 5   51, 87, 77, 93, 67, 81, 77, 93, 77

   _____   _____

6. 78, 35, 85, 93, 62, 95, 88, 51, 45   97, 64, 25, 26, 8, 24, 36, 72, 56

   _____   _____

Lesson 7.5 Measures of Center: Mode

The **mode** of a data set is the value that occurs the most often. Sometimes a data set has more than one mode.

2, 6, 1, 8, 10, 3, 10, 1, 10

1, 1, 2, 3, 6, 8, 10, 10, 10   1. Put the data in order from least to greatest.

(1, 1) 2, 3, 6, 8, 10, (10, 10)   2. Look for values that occur more than once.

10   3. The value that occurs the most times is the mode.

Find the mode for each data set.

a	b
1. 3, 2, 8, 5, 1, 4, 4, 3, 4	39, 25, 40, 38, 22, 37, 40
_____	_____
2. 24, 16, 26, 12, 28, 23, 28, 26, 28	118, 115, 108, 124, 106, 120, 108
_____	_____
3. 16, 18, 12, 15, 21, 26, 26	32, 28, 22, 36, 24, 35, 24, 32, 24
_____	_____
4. 253, 295, 204, 151, 118, 277, 277	22, 16, 14, 15, 25, 21, 21
_____	_____
5. 95, 73, 55, 69, 72, 65, 73, 72, 73	3, 8, 4, 2, 7, 10, 4
_____	_____
6. 14, 93, 14, 96, 13, 5, 84, 69, 93	92, 44, 32, 82, 86, 59, 22, 32
_____	_____

Lesson 7.6 Finding Measures of Center

The **mean** is the average of a set of numbers. To find the mean, add all the numbers and divide by the number of values in the set.

The **median** is the middle number of a data set. If there are two middle numbers, the median is the average of the two.

The **mode** is the number that appears most often in a data set.

Example: 12, 15, 18, 23, 8, 10, and 12
Mean: $12 + 15 + 18 + 23 + 8 + 10 + 12 = 98$ $\frac{98}{7} = 14$

To find the median, arrange the numbers in order.   8, 10, 12, <u>12</u>, 15, 18, 23
Median: 12   Mode: 12

Find the mean, median, and mode of each data set. Show your work.

a	b
1. 32, 35, 25, 43, 43	8, 12, 23, 12, 15

a	b
mean _____	mean _____
median _____	median _____
mode _____	mode _____

2. 10, 18, 12, 14, 12, 12   17, 15, 15, 28, 20, 26

mean _____   mean _____

median _____   median _____

mode _____   mode _____

3. 52, 61, 79, 78, 56, 79, 71   37, 50, 67, 83, 34, 49, 37

mean _____   mean _____

median _____   median _____

mode _____   mode _____

Lesson 7.7 Using Measures of Center

Measures of center can be used to describe a data set. Each measure of center allows for different observations about the set.

The **mean** is the most popular measure of center. It is the average, so it provides the clearest picture of the center of the data, but only if there are no outliers (values that are far away from the majority of the numbers in the set).

The **median** is the most useful measure when the data set contains outliers.

The **mode** is the most useful measure when the values in the data set are non-numerical.

Tell which measure of center would be best for describing each data set.

                a   b

1. 3, 4, 5, 5, 7, 6, 21   62, 65, 72, 68, 66

   _____   _____

2. 54, 72, 85, 67, 93, 85, 61, 89   red, blue, green, red, blue, yellow, blue

   _____   _____

3. $14.60, $7.25, $15.70, $15.25, $14.90   8, 25, 19, 19, 25, 9, 9, 18, 25, 9, 8, 7, 10

   _____   _____

4. 0, 1, 3, 5, 5, 5, 7, 9, 9, 11, 15, 99   A, B, C, A, B, C, D, A, B, B

   _____   _____

Lesson 7.8 Measures of Variability: Range

The **range** of a data set is the difference between the largest value and smallest value contained in the data set.

11, 12, 15, 15, 13, 12

11, 12, 12, 13, 15, 15   1. Put the data set in order from least to greatest.

<u>11</u>, 12, 12, 13, 15, <u>15</u>   2. Find the largest value and smallest value.

15 − 11 =   3. Subtract.

4   4. The range of this data set is 4.

Find the range of each data set.

a	b
1. 11, 10, 12, 9	79, 79, 79, 84
2. 25, 30, 32, 23, 27, 22	96, 94, 101, 96, 91, 92
3. 36, 33, 37, 37, 41, 33	506, 508, 510, 509
4. 277, 280, 287, 276	10, 8, 9, 12, 6, 8
5. 12, 9, 16, 9	95, 92, 89, 97, 94, 88

Lesson 7.9 Measures of Variability: Interquartile Range

The **interquartile range** (IQR) of a data set is the difference between the median of the lower half of a data set and the median of the upper half of the same data set.

13, 15, 9, 35, 25, 17, 19

9, 13, 15, 17, 19, 25, 35	1. Put the data set in order from least to greatest.
9, 13, 15　17　19, 25, 35	2. Find the lower half, median, and upper half of the data set.
Q1=13　　　Q3=25	3. Find the medians of the lower half and upper half.
25 − 13 =	4. Subtract.
12	5. The interquartile range of the data set is 12.

Find the interquartile range for each set of data.

a	**b**
1. 6, 1, 3, 8, 5, 11, 1, 5	80, 90, 95, 85, 70
median: _____	median: _____
Q1: _____	Q1: _____
Q3: _____	Q3: _____
IQR: _____	IQR: _____
2. 70, 75, 90, 100, 95	45, 43, 13, 11, 5, 2
median: _____	median: _____
Q1: _____	Q1: _____
Q3: _____	Q3: _____
IQR: _____	IQR: _____
3. 45, 39, 17, 16, 4, 1	29, 58, 15, 75, 22, 16, 64
median: _____	median: _____
Q1: _____	Q1: _____
Q3: _____	Q3: _____
IQR: _____	IQR: _____

Lesson 7.10 Measures of Variability: Mean Absolute Deviation

The **mean absolute deviation** (MAD) of a data set is a value that shows if the data set is consistent. The closer the mean absolute deviation of a data set to zero, the more consistent it is.

17, 19, 8, 32, 21, 24, 19

8, 17, 19, 19, 21, 24, 32	1. Put the data set in order from least to greatest.
Mean = 20	2. Find the mean of the data set.
12, 3, 1, 1, 1, 4, 12	3. Find the absolute value of the difference between the mean and each value in the set. (For example, 20 − 8 = 12; $\lvert 12 \rvert$ = 12)
Mean = 8.71	4. Find the mean of those absolute values.
MAD = 8.71	5. The mean absolute deviation of this data set is 8.71. This tells us that the values in the set are on average about 8.71 away from the middle.

Find the mean absolute deviation of each data set. Round each answer to two decimal places.

a	**b**

1. 10, 16, 18, 15, 15, 10, 23   41, 56, 38, 45, 55, 51, 52

   mean: _____   mean: _____

   value differences: value differences:

   _____   _____

   MAD: _____   MAD: _____

2. 10, 12, 18, 25, 25, 11, 22   22, 33, 44, 55, 66, 88, 55, 55, 11, 22

   mean: _____   mean: _____

   value differences: value differences:

   _____   _____

   MAD: _____   MAD: _____

Lesson 7.11 Using Measures of Variability

The **range** of a data set is the difference between the largest value and smallest value contained in the data set.

The **interquartile range** (IQR) of a data set is the difference between the median of the lower half of a data set and the median of the upper half of the same data set.

The **mean absolute deviation** (MAD) of a data set is a value that helps understand if the data set is consistent. If the mean absolute deviation of a data set is close to zero, the data set is more consistent.

Complete the table by listing the measures of variability for each data set. Round answers to two decimal places.

Data	Range	IQR	MAD
1. 43, 48, 80, 53, 59, 65, 58, 66, 70, 50, 76, 62	_____	_____	_____
2. 12, 47, 26, 25, 38, 45, 35, 35, 41, 39, 32, 25, 18, 30	_____	_____	_____
3. 99, 45, 23, 67, 45, 91, 82, 78, 62, 51	_____	_____	_____
4. 10, 2, 5, 6, 7, 3, 4	_____	_____	_____
5. 23, 56, 45, 65, 59, 55, 61, 54, 85, 25	_____	_____	_____
6. 55, 63, 88, 97, 58, 90, 88, 71, 65, 77, 75, 88, 95, 86	_____	_____	_____

Lesson 7.12 Plotting Data: Stem-and-Leaf Plots

A set of data can be organized into a **stem-and-leaf plot** by using place values.

87, 38, 35, 76, 48, 57, 68, 44, 63, 49, 63, 64, 71

The tens digits are the stems and the ones digits are the leaves.

Stem	Leaves
3	5 8
4	4 8 9
5	7
6	3 3 4 8
7	1 6
8	7

Key: 3 | 5 = 35

This allows you to see the least (35), the largest (87), the range (52), the median (63), and the mode (63).

Create a stem-and-leaf plot for each set of data. Include a key for each plot.

	a	**b**
1.	14, 31, 34, 21, 13, 28, 33	63, 38, 72, 54, 50, 79, 64, 39, 57, 49
2.	48, 38, 34, 25, 27, 37, 49	88, 96, 99, 75, 87, 93, 81, 84, 91, 73
3.	19, 25, 38, 17, 24, 33, 13	26, 37, 25, 33, 35, 46, 27, 45, 23, 41

Lesson 7.13 Plotting Data: Box-and-Whisker Plots

Box-and-whisker plots are helpful in interpreting the distribution of data. For example, the results of a test might include these 15 scores:

66, 56, 75, 77, 98, 72, 48, 83, 73, 89, 65, 74, 87, 85, 81

The numbers should be arranged in order:

48, 56, 65, 66, 72, 73, 74, 75, 77, 81, 83, 85, 87, 89, 98

The median is 75. The **lower quartile** is the median of the lower half (66). The **upper quartile** is the median of the upper half (85). Draw a box around the median with its ends going through the quartiles. Each quartile contains one-fourth of the scores.

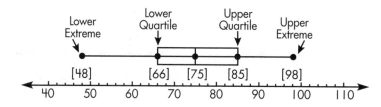

Answer the questions using the box-and-whisker plot above.

1. Half of the students scored higher than _____ on the test.

2. _____ scores are represented in the box part of the plot.

3. The range of the scores on the test is _____.

The scores on a recent daily quiz were 10, 15, 20, 20, 30, 30, and 40.

4. What is the median of these scores? _____

5. What is the lower quartile? _____

6. What is the upper quartile? _____

7. Using the number line below, draw a box-and-whisker plot for these scores.

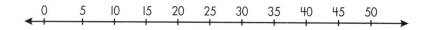

Lesson 7.14 Plotting Data: Line Graphs

Mrs. Martin's homeroom and Mr. Lopez's homeroom had a canned food drive. The **line graph** shows how many cans were collected after each day.

On Monday, how many more cans did Mr. Lopez's class collect than Mrs. Martin's class?

Mr. Lopez's class collected ___5___ more cans than Mrs. Martin's class on Monday.

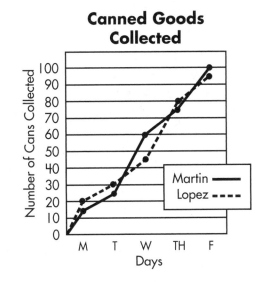

Canned Goods Collected

Use the line graph above to answer the following questions

1. On Monday, whose homeroom collected the most cans?   _____

2. By Tuesday, how many cans had Mr. Lopez's homeroom collected?   _____

3. On which day was the difference between the number of cans collected by each homeroom the greatest?   _____

4. Which homeroom collected the most cans on that day?   _____

5. How many cans total had been collected by both homerooms by Tuesday?   _____

6. On what day did Mrs. Martin's homeroom bring in the most cans?   _____

7. On what day did Mr. Lopez's homeroom bring in the most cans?   _____

8. On what day did Mrs. Martin's homeroom bring in the least number of cans?   _____

9. By Wednesday, how many cans had been collected by both homerooms?   _____

10. How many cans were collected by both homerooms during the week?   _____

Lesson 7.15 Plotting Data: Histograms

A **histogram** displays data using bars of different heights. It is different from a bar graph because it shows data grouped into ranges. Both axes of a histogram should be numerical.

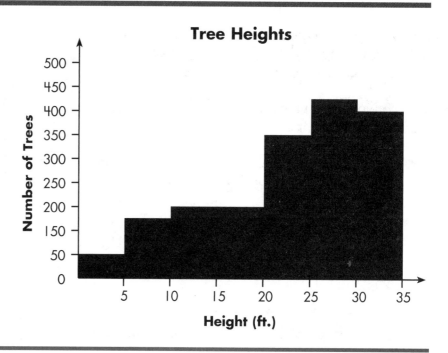

Tree Heights

Use the histogram above to answer the following questions.

1. How many trees were measured in all? _____

2. In what range did the most trees fall? _____

3. In what range did the least trees fall? _____

4. What percentage of trees were less than 20 feet tall? _____

5. What percentage of trees were greater than 20 feet tall? _____

6. How many more trees were 30–35 feet tall than 20–25 feet tall? _____

7. What is the range of heights shown? _____

8. Predict how many trees would be in the 35–40 foot range if it were included on the graph. _____

9. Explain the basis for your prediction.

_____

10. Draw a star above the bar where a tree that measures 21 feet would be included.

Lesson 7.16 Summarizing Data Sets

Use measures of center and variability to help summarize these data sets. Round answers to two decimal places. Plot the data using a stem-and-leaf plot to show how the data is spread.

1. Your class just took a science test. These are the scores: 97, 99, 81, 78, 34, 96, 63, 100, 85, 83, 85, 88, 79, 82, 94, 85, 83, and 72.

   mode: _____   range: _____

   median: _____   IQR: _____

   mean: _____   MAD: _____

   Write 2 to 3 sentences that describe this data set.

   _____

   _____

   _____

   _____

Stem	Leaves

2. The soccer team at Wilson Middle School played ten games this year. They scored 4, 3, 1, 5, 3, 2, 5, 3, 2, and 4 goals in their games.

   mode: _____   range: _____

   median: _____   IQR: _____

   mean: _____   MAD: _____

   Write 2 to 3 sentences that describe this data set.

   _____

   _____

   _____

   _____

Stem	Leaves

Lesson 7.16 Summarizing Data Sets

Use measures of center and variability to help summarize these data sets. Round answers to two decimal places. Then, plot the data using a box-and-whisker plot to show how the data is spread.

1. The height of twelve 6th graders is collected in inches. Their heights are 60, 54, 48, 64, 52, 50, 68, 64, 58, 56, 56, and 64.

   mode: _____   Box-and-Whisker Plot

   median: _____

   mean: _____

   range: _____

   IQR: _____

   MAD: _____

   Write 2 to 3 sentences that describe this data set.

   _____

   _____

2. A teacher decides to collect information on how long students spend doing homework each evening. She talks to 15 students and receives this data (in minutes): 30, 15, 60, 45, 15, 45, 45, 60, 75, 30, 45, 30, 45, 15, and 45.

   mode: _____   Box-and-Whisker Plot

   median: _____

   mean: _____

   range: _____

   IQR: _____

   MAD: _____

   Write 2 to 3 sentences that describe this data set.

   _____

   _____

Lesson 7.16 Summarizing Data Sets

Use measures of center and variability to help summarize this data set. Round answers to two decimal places. Then, plot the data using a line graph to show how the data is spread.

A school keeps track of how many students are buying notebooks each month from the school store. It collected this information.

Month	Notebooks Sold
Jan.	25
Feb.	30
Mar.	15
Apr.	20
May	15
June	5
July	0
Aug.	35
Sept.	20
Oct.	15
Nov.	20
Dec.	30

mode: _____

median: _____

mean: _____

range: _____

IQR: _____

MAD: _____

Write 2 to 3 sentences that describe this data set.

_____

_____

SPECTRUM®

Language Arts

Chapter 1

Lesson 1.1 Common and Proper Nouns

Common nouns name people, places, and things. They are general nouns (not specific). In a sentence, the noun is the person, place, or thing that can act or be acted upon.

>*teacher* – a person
>I like my *teacher*.
>
>*country* – a place
>I will visit another *country*.
>
>*book* – a thing
>What is your favorite *book*?

Proper nouns name specific people, places, and things.
>*Mrs. Crane* – a specific person
>*Mrs. Crane* is my favorite teacher.
>
>*United States of America* – a specific place
>I was born in the *United States of America*.
>
>*Animal Farm* – a specific thing
>*Animal Farm* is one of my favorite books.

Complete It

Use the word box below to complete the following sentences. Remember, common nouns are general and proper nouns are more specific. Proper nouns are also capitalized.

doctor	poem	song
Saturn	Dr. Green	planet
"Twinkle, Twinkle Little Star"		Where the Sidewalk Ends

1. I am writing a _____ for music class.

2. I took my cat to see _____ when he had a cold.

3. The planet with the rings is called _____.

4. My mom takes me to the _____ when I'm sick.

5. My _____ came in third place in the poetry contest.

6. Mars is the closest _____ to the earth.

7. _____ is one of my favorite books.

8. My little sister likes to sing _____ before she goes to bed.

Lesson 1.1 Common and Proper Nouns

Proof It
Correct the mistakes in the use of common and proper nouns using proofreading marks.

/	– lowercase letter
≡	– capitalize letter
^	– insert words or letters

John Muir

John muir was born in 1838 in dunbar, scotland. From a very young age, he had a love of Nature. He traveled all over the world. He came to the united states to observe nature and take notes on what he saw. He wrote many nature Books. John Muir was concerned for the welfare of the land. He wanted to protect it. He asked president theodore roosevelt for help. The National parks System was founded by John Muir. This System sets aside land for Parks. The first national park was yellowstone national park. John Muir is also the founder of the sierra club. The people in this Club teach others about nature and how to protect it. John Muir is known as one of the world's greatest conservation leaders.

Try It
Write a biography about someone you think is a hero. Use at least six common and six proper nouns correctly in your biography.

_____

_____

_____

_____

_____

_____

_____

Lesson 1.2 Regular and Irregular Plural Nouns

A **plural noun** names more than one person, place, or thing. Most nouns are made plural by adding an **s** to the end of the word.

cars   cups   football**s**

Nouns ending in the letters **s**, **x**, or **z** or in a **ch** or **sh** sound need **es**.

boss**es**   tax**es**   waltz**es**

If a word ends in the letter **y**, then the **y** is changed to an **i** before adding the **es**.

countr**ies**   cit**ies**   fl**ies**

However, words that end in **y** with a vowel before the **y** only add the **s**.

boy**s**   key**s**   donkey**s**

If a noun ends in **f** or **fe**, and the **f** sound can still be heard in the plural form, just add **s**. If the final sound of the plural form is **v**, then change the **f** to **v** and add **es**.

roof**s** (**f** sound)   cal**ves** (**v** sound)

Lesson 1.2 Regular and Irregular Plural Nouns

Try It
Use the lines to explain how the nouns were made into their plural forms. The first one is done for you.

Column A	**Column B**	
match	matches	<u>If the noun ends in ch, add an es.</u>
eyebrow	eyebrows	_____
volcano	volcanoes	_____
wolf	wolves	_____
trophy	trophies	_____
toothbrush	toothbrushes	_____
sheriff	sheriffs	_____

Find It
Write the irregular plural noun form of the following singular nouns on the lines provided. Use a dictionary if you need help.

1. ox _____
2. trout _____
3. man _____
4. series _____
5. axis _____
6. mouse _____

7. sheep _____
8. salmon _____
9. woman _____
10. crisis _____
11. oasis _____
12. radius _____

Lesson 1.3 Personal and Intensive Pronouns

A **pronoun** is a word used in place of a noun.

A **subject pronoun** can be the subject of a sentence. *I, you, he, she,* and *it* are subject pronouns.

    I found the ball.   *It* is my favorite sport.

An **object pronoun** can be the object of a sentence. *Me, you, him, her,* and *it* are object pronouns.

    Matt gave the ball to *me*.   Matt threw *it*.

Possessive pronouns show possession. *My, mine, your, yours, his, her, hers,* and *its* are possessive pronouns.

    Anna gave *my* ball to Matt.

The plural forms of personal pronouns include:

    Subject: *we, you, they*   Object: *us, you, them*
    Possessive: *our, ours, your, yours, their, theirs*

Intensive pronouns end in *–self* or *–selves* and usually appear right after the subject of a sentence. They emphasize the subject.

    I *myself* am too tired to go to the movies.
    You *yourselves* are responsible for the outcome of the game.

Complete It

Complete each of the following sentences with an intensive pronoun. Remember, intensive pronouns end with *–self* or *–selves*.

  1. Jessa _____ baked all these muffins.

  2. The Boy Scouts _____ set up all these tents.

  3. The smoke _____ did all this damage to the house.

  4. We _____ created the website in just a couple of days.

  5. Oliver _____ wrote that poem.

  6. You _____ must clean up all these dominoes.

  7. The doctor _____ checked on each of the patients.

  8. The kids in Pilar's class _____ raised over $100 for the charity.

Lesson 1.3 Personal and Intensive Pronouns

Identify It

The following skit contains subject, object, and possessive plural pronouns. Identify what each boldfaced plural pronoun is replacing on the line. Then, write whether the pronoun is a subject, object, or possessive on the line. The first one has been done for you.

Matt and Anna are on **their** _____Matt and Anna, possessive_____ way to the

park to play. On the way, **they** _____ meet Andrew and Stephanie.

"**We** _____ are on **our**

_____ way to the park," said Matt. "Can **you**

_____ join **us** _____?"

"Can **we** _____ play with **your**

_____ ball?" asked Stephanie. "**Ours**

_____ is missing."

"**Yours** _____ is missing? That's too bad," said

Anna. "Sure, **you** _____ can play with **our**

_____ ball."

Matt, Anna, Andrew, and Stephanie all walked to the park. They would all play together.

"I'll throw the ball to you," said Matt to Andrew. "Then you can throw the ball

to **them** _____," Matt said pointing to Anna and Stephanie.

"Hey," yelled Anna. "I see a ball ahead. Could it be Andrew and Stephanie's ball?"

"Yes, it could be **their**

_____ ball," answered Matt. Matt showed Andrew and Stephanie the ball. Sure enough, it was **theirs**

_____.

Lesson 1.4 Demonstrative Pronouns

A pronoun is a word used in place of a noun. Pronouns can be a subject, object, or possessive of the sentence. Pronouns can also be demonstrative.

Demonstrative pronouns replace nouns without naming the noun.

this   that   these   those

This is fun. (refers to an event or experience, for example, a roller coaster)
That was wonderful. (refers to an event or experience, for example, a movie)
These are good. (refers to a basket of apples)
Those are better. (refers to a barrel of pears)

This and these are usually used when the person or object is closer to the writer and speaker. That and those are usually used when the person or object is farther away from the writer or speaker.

This is fast (the roller coaster here), but that is faster (the roller coaster over there).
These look good (the apples in the basket that is close), but those look better (the pears in the barrel across the room).

Demonstrative pronouns, like other pronouns, add variety to your writing and speaking.

Match It
Draw a line to match the demonstrative pronoun in Column A with the objects of the sentence in Column B.

Column A	Column B
this	many newspapers across the room
that	one magazine at the library
these	one wallet in a pocket
those	many pencils on the desk

this	many ants on the ground
that	one book on the shelf
these	many bananas at the store
those	one experience at a baseball game

Lesson 1.4 Demonstrative Pronouns

Proof It

Proof the following dialogue. Use the proofreading marks in the key to delete the demonstrative pronouns that are incorrect and insert the correct words.

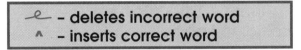

ℓ	– deletes incorrect word
^	– inserts correct word

Lauren and Devin like shopping at the mall. But sometimes they can be hard to please.

"Lauren, look at those!" (holding up earrings next to her ears)

Devin sighed, "I like this better." (pointing to earrings on a counter farther away)

"Maybe I don't want earrings at all," said Lauren. "What about these?" (waving her arm in the air to display a bracelet)

"No," said Devin. "Now, these is perfect!" (pointing to a belt hanging on the far wall)

"Devin, look at those. (pointing to a clock on the wall) I think the store is closing," cried Lauren.

"Yes, and these (pointing to the price tag on the belt) won't make my mom very happy," said Devin.

"Come on," replied Lauren. "Let's come back again tomorrow!"

Try It

Write more dialogue about Lauren and Devin's trip to the mall the next day. Be sure to use all four demonstrative pronouns: *this, that, these,* and *those.*

_____

_____

_____

_____

_____

_____

Lesson 1.5 Relative Pronouns

A pronoun is a word used in place of a noun. Pronouns can be the subject, the object, or the possessive of a sentence.

Relative pronouns are pronouns that are related to nouns that have already been stated. They combine two sentences that share a common noun.

who   whose   that   which

The woman, *who* is a doctor, wasn't at the party.
Who refers to the noun *woman*.

The parents, *whose* children were at the party, were ready to go.
Whose refers to the noun *parents*.
(This relative pronoun shows possession.)

The note *that* you read is incorrect.
That refers to the noun *note*.

The newspaper articles, *which* are long, must be cut.
Which refers to the noun *newspaper articles*.

Complete It
Complete the following sentences by choosing the correct relative pronoun in parentheses. Circle the correct answer.

1. Someone (who, that) likes kiwi usually likes strawberries.

2. Bicyclers (which, whose) bikes are ready can go to the starting line.

3. He likes movies (which, that) have a lot of action.

4. The man, (who, whose) lives across the street, is an actor.

5. The car (who, that) you drove is blocking the driveway.

6. The bananas, (which, that) are the ripest, are used in the recipe.

Lesson 1.5 Relative Pronouns

Solve It

Solve the following riddle. Use a relative pronoun to fill in the blanks.

that	who
which	whose

Who bakes apple pies?

The man _____ grows apples bakes pies.

Who makes the best apple pies?

The man _____ apples are the sweetest bakes the best pies.

What didn't get baked into the pie?

The apple _____ had a bruise did not go in the pie.

What won the prize?

The pies, _____ were the sweetest, won the prize.

Try It

Try writing a riddle of your own. Follow the example above. Ask questions that require an answer with a relative pronoun. Use each relative pronoun at least once.

_____

_____

_____

_____

_____

_____

_____

_____

_____

_____

_____

Lesson 1.6 Indefinite Pronouns

Indefinite pronouns are pronouns that do not specifically name the noun that comes before them (as do the relative pronouns).

> *all   another   any   anybody   anyone   anything   each   everybody*
> *everyone   everything   few   many   nobody   none   one   several*
> *some   somebody   someone*

> *Many* were invited to the party, but only a few came.
> We donated *everything* from the attic to the charity foundation.
> They looked everywhere for copies of the report, but found *none*.

Identify It
Underline the indefinite pronouns in the following paragraph.

The fair was approaching. Each of the cooks in town made ice cream cones for the fair. The cooks were put in pairs. One made the ice cream while another made the cones. You wouldn't think there would be any problems. However, there were some. One wanted the same flavor. Another wanted cherry. Someone wanted chocolate. Several even ate two scoops. That means someone had none. Everyone would think that is unfair. But the cooks were ready for anything. They made snow cones and everybody ate those instead. What else could happen? The sun melted the ice cream and the snow cones. Cooks quickly handed napkins to everyone with ice cream or snow cones. Then, they made milkshakes. Everything turned out fine.

Lesson 1.7 Pronoun Shifts

A **pronoun shift** happens when a writer changes pronouns in the middle of a sentence or paragraph. This can confuse the reader.

> After *we* got our chickens, *we* discovered that *you* really need to be ready to take care of them in all kinds of weather.

In the example, the writer changes from *we* (first-person plural) to *you* (second-person singular).

Identify It

A pronoun shift occurs in each item below. Find and circle it.

1. As a photographer, he has an interesting career, because they get to meet so many people.

2. As new players on the team, we were nervous, but you just need to remember that everyone is new at some point.

3. If you want to ride this roller coaster, they need to be 48 inches tall.

4. Aunt Samantha said that when she was a baby, you didn't have to ride in car seats.

5. Mr. Green said he gave their students all the instructions before the test.

6. They gave us her outgrown clothes.

7. After the choir concert, we singers gathered backstage to celebrate their success.

8. As a magician, she must work hard to safeguard their secrets.

Lesson 1.7 Pronoun Shifts

Complete It

Complete each sentence below by writing the correct pronoun on the line. In some cases, either *he* or *she* is an acceptable answer.

1. As a professional athlete, he must work out nearly every day if _____ wants to stay in shape.

2. They did not go to the Girl Scouts meeting, so _____ didn't hear the news.

3. Since they are under the age of 12, the children need to be accompanied by _____ parents.

4. Since he is leaving for college this fall, _____ is getting a car.

5. As the soccer coach requested, I met with her, and _____ said I'm welcome to join the team.

6. When they got home, _____ wanted to have a snack.

7. I need to get my permission slip signed if _____ want to go to the art museum next week.

8. Is Jorge going to join you and me at the pool, or will he call _____ first?

9. Mr. Crawley said he would host a class picnic, and _____ promised to make his taco salad.

10. As a chef, she must be willing to experiment if _____ wants to develop new dishes.

Try It

On the lines below, write a short paragraph about an experience you've had with your classmates. Circle each pronoun you use, and proofread your paragraph to be sure there are no pronoun shifts.

_____

_____

_____

_____

_____

_____

Lesson 1.8 Verbs: Regular Present and Past Tense

A **verb** is a word that tells the action or the state of being of a sentence. In this sentence, *walk* is the verb. It tells the action of the sentence.

> The students *walk* home.

In this sentence, *shared* is the verb. It tells the action of the sentence.

> Kevin *shared* his cake with Carol at the party last night.

In the first sentence the action is taking place now. In the second sentence the action took place in the past. Add **ed** to the present tense of a **regular verb** to make it past tense. If the word already ends in the letter **e**, just add the letter **d**.

Complete It

Write each word in present tense in the first sentence and then in past tense in the second sentence.

1. act   Today, I _____.   Yesterday, I _____.
2. mend   Today, I _____.   Yesterday, I _____.
3. cook   Today, I _____.   Yesterday, I _____.
4. bake   Today, I _____.   Yesterday, I _____.
5. answer   Today, I _____.   Yesterday, I _____.
6. cycle   Today, I _____.   Yesterday, I _____.
7. wave   Today, I _____.   Yesterday, I _____.
8. scream   Today, I _____.   Yesterday, I _____.
9. bike   Today, I _____.   Yesterday, I _____.
10. jump   Today, I _____.   Yesterday, I _____.
11. mow   Today, I _____.   Yesterday, I _____.
12. yell   Today, I _____.   Yesterday, I _____.
13. rake   Today, I _____.   Yesterday, I _____.
14. whisper   Today, I _____.   Yesterday, I _____.
15. divide   Today, I _____.   Yesterday, I _____.

Lesson 1.8 Verbs: Regular Present and Past Tense

Proof It

Proofread the following announcement. Use the proofreading marks to correct mistakes with the present and past tense forms of verbs and insert the correctly spelled words. Not all of the verbs are from this lesson.

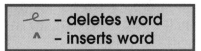

e - deletes word

^ - inserts word

Hello from Northland Auditorium, home of the Riverdale Cook-Off and Bake-Off. The chefs are ready for the bake-off. The chefs cook meals last night. The judges award prizes for the best meals last night. The chefs baked today. Early this morning, the judges call the chefs over. They talk with them about their recipes. The judges will now observed the baking. Judge Wilson and Judge Boggs looked over many of the cooks' shoulders. They laughed. It must be good news. I don't think they would joked if it weren't. Two cooks answered a question for the judges. They act nervous. The judges tasted all of the baked goods. What will win the blue ribbon? Will cookies, cakes, brownies, or candy captured the top prize? The judges now handed a note to the announcer. The winner is....

Try It

Write a first-hand account of a school event. Include both present and past tense regular verbs.

_____

_____

_____

_____

_____

_____

_____

_____

Lesson 1.9 Verbs: Irregular Present and Past Tense

Irregular verbs are verbs that do not follow the same rules as regular verbs when forming their past tense. They must be learned. Below is a list of many common irregular verbs in their present and past tense forms.

Present:	Past:	Present:	Past:
am	was	lay	laid
are (plural)	were (plural)	leave	left
begin	began	let	let
bite	bit	lie	lay
break	broke	make	made
bring	brought	put	put
build	built	read	read
catch	caught	ride	rode
choose	chose	ring	rang
come	came	rise	rose
cut	cut	run	ran
dig	dug	say	said
do	did	see	saw
draw	drew	set	set
drink	drank	sing	sang
drive	drove	sink	sank
eat	ate	sit	sat
fall	fell	sleep	slept
feed	fed	speak	spoke
feel	felt	stand	stood
fight	fought	sting	stung
fly	flew	take	took
get	got	teach	taught
give	gave	tear	tore
go	went	tell	told
grow	grew	think	thought
has	had	throw	threw
hold	held	wear	wore
is	was	win	won
keep	kept	write	wrote
know	knew		

Lesson 1.9 Verbs: Irregular Present and Past Tense

Identify It
Underline the irregular present and past tense verbs in this paragraph.

Aikido

They jump. They fall. They fly through the air. Who are they? They are students of Aikido. Aikido is a Japanese form of self-defense. Partners work together. They use wrists, joints, and elbows to block, pin, and throw each other. They learn the moves together and work in harmony with each other. Aikido is an art that tests both mind and body. It is a spiritual art. The founder of Aikido was born in 1883. He wrote hundreds of techniques. Aikido grew throughout Japan and throughout the world. Thousands of students take Aikido today. Aikido means *the way of harmony.*

Challenge:
Identify the regular present and past tense verbs and give their other form.

Try It
Write a paragraph about one of your hobbies or activities. Use at least six present tense irregular verbs and six past tense irregular verbs. Use a dictionary if you need help.

_____

_____

_____

_____

_____

_____

_____

_____

_____

_____

_____

_____

_____

_____

Lesson 1.10 Subject-Verb Agreement

Subject-verb agreement means verbs must agree in number with the subject of the sentence. If the subject is singular, then use a singular verb. If the subject is plural, use a plural verb.

The apple *tastes* good.   The apples *taste* good.

The flower *is* beautiful.   The flowers *are* beautiful.

If the subject is a compound subject, two subjects connected by the word *and*, then a plural verb is needed.

Tyler and Inez *bake* pies.   Tyler *bakes* pies.

If the subject is a compound subject connected by the words *or* or *nor*, then the verb will agree with the subject that is closer to the verb.

Neither Tyler **nor** Inez *likes* blueberry pie. (Inez likes)

Does Tyler **or** his brothers *like* banana cream pie? (brothers like)

If the subject and the verb are separated by a word or words, be sure that the verb still agrees with the subject.

Inez as well as her sisters *works* at the bakery.

Complete It

Circle the correct verb for each sentence.

1. Jill (jump, jumps) rope after school.

2. Jill and Katie (jump, jumps) rope after school.

3. Jill and her friends (jump, jumps) rope after school.

4. Jill as well as her friends (jump, jumps) rope after school.

5. Ross (like, likes) veggie lasagna.

6. Ross and Regina (like, likes) veggie lasagna.

7. Ross and his brothers (like, likes) veggie lasagna.

8. Ross as well as his parents (like, likes) veggie lasagna.

9. Does Jill or her friends (want, wants) to ride with me?

10. Neither Jill nor Katie (want, wants) to go to the movies.

Lesson 1.10 Subject-Verb Agreement

Rewrite It

Rewrite the following paragraph, correcting the subject-verb agreement mistakes as you go. Remember to be on the lookout for subjects and verbs that are separated.

Sea turtles grows in many sizes and colors. They ranges between 100 and 1300 pounds. Instead of teeth, sea turtles has beaks in their jaws. Which of their senses is most keen? That would be their sense of smell. A female sea turtle lay her eggs on land. Unfortunately, sea turtles are in danger. But in the last 100 years, the population have become almost extinct. What can we do to ensure the survival of sea turtles? We can all helps by keeping our oceans clean. We can educate ourselves about the causes of habitat destruction. We can spread the word to others. Knowledge are a powerful tool in the world of our environment. The sea turtles is counting on us.

_____

_____

_____

_____

_____

_____

_____

_____

_____

_____

_____

_____

Try It

Write a nonfiction paragraph about a reptile or insect that interests you. Underline the subjects of each sentence and circle the verbs.

_____

_____

_____

_____

_____

_____

Lesson 1.11 Action Verbs

Action verbs tell the action of the sentence. Action verbs come in both regular and irregular forms. They have present, past, and future tense forms, too.

Sandy and Karen *visit* every spring.
Sandy and Karen *visited* last year.
Sandy and Karen *will visit* next winter.

I bet Stan and Mike *eat* the whole apple pie.
I *ate* the whole apple.
I *will eat* the apple after I wash it.

Solve It

Look at the following pictures. On the line below each picture, write the action verb that the subject in the picture is doing.

1._____

2. _____

3._____

4. _____

5._____

6. _____

Lesson 1.11 Action Verbs

Match It

One verb that is used often in dialogue is *said*. Try to bring more variety to your writing by using other action verbs as a substitute for the verb *said*. Match the sentences in Column A with an action verb in Column B that could be substituted for the verb *said* in the sentence.

Column A	**Column B**
1. "Hey! We're over here!" said Marty _____	**a.** concluded
2. "I like taking walks at the park, too," said Kim. _____	**b.** began
3. "I promise it won't happen again," said Alex. _____	**c.** yelled
4. "Oh, I don't want to do more homework," said Justin. _____	**d.** reported
5. "We received 8 inches of snow over night," said the weather person. _____	**e.** added
	f. complained
6. "Those are the results of my survey," said the professor. _____	**g.** cautioned
7. "Be careful riding on the wet pavement," said Mom. _____	**h.** groaned
8. "Would you like some more lemonade?" said the server. _____	**i.** vowed
9. "I don't like what's on my sandwich," said the customer. _____	**j.** asked
10. "Let's start today's lesson," said the teacher. _____	

Try It

Write a letter to a friend or relative. Tell him or her about a recent event in school or another activity in which you participated. Use at least 10 action verbs. Underline the verbs in your letter.

_____

_____

_____

_____

_____

_____

_____

_____

_____

Lesson 1.12 Helping Verbs

Helping verbs are not main verbs. They help to form some of the tenses of the main verbs. Helping verbs express time and mood.

shall	may	would	has	can
will	have	should	do	did
could	had	must		

The forms of the verb *to be* are also helping verbs:

is	are	was	were	am	been

Verbs ending in **ing** can be a clue that there is a helping verb in the sentence. Sometimes, there is more than one helping verb in a sentence. This is called a **verb phrase**.

The Olympic star *would practice* for hours.
The Olympic star *was practicing* for hours and hours.
The Olympic star *had been practicing* for hours and hours.

Complete It

Choose a helping verb or verb phrase from the box to complete each sentence. Underline the main verb of the sentence that it helps. The main verb does not always directly follow the helping verb. Sometimes there is another word in between. Some sentences can have more than one answer.

have	has	should	must	shall
had	could	would	can	had been

1. _____ we dance to this song?

2. That _____ be the right direction, but I'm not sure.

3. Rick and Dana _____ waiting for hours when they finally got in.

4. _____ you go with me to the movies?

5. The children _____ go with their older brothers.

6. I _____ been a fan of hers for years.

7. It _____ been days since we've seen each other.

8. We _____ take this train; it will get us home faster.

9. It _____ be this way, I see a familiar house.

10. This assignment _____ taken a long time to finish.

Lesson 1.13 Linking Verbs

Linking verbs connect a subject to a noun or adjective. They do not express an action.

The most common linking verbs are the forms of the verb *to be:*

| is | are | was | were | been | am |

Other linking verbs are those of the five senses:

| smell | look | taste | feel | sound |

Other linking verbs reflect a state of being:

| appear | seem | become | grow | remain |

A noun or adjective will follow these linking verbs in the sentence.

Identify It
Circle the linking verb and underline the noun or adjective that is linked in each sentence.

1. The crowd appears excited.

2. The crowd thought the play was good.

3. The lettuce tastes bitter.

4. The line seems long.

5. Syd, Mitzi, and Deb were runners.

6. Mr. Thomas became successful after much hard work.

7. The runners feel great running in the fresh air.

8. The lights grew dim as the play began.

9. The singer's voice sounds weak compared to the others.

10. Her future remains uncertain.

11. It was a long day.

12. Dinner sounds great.

13. They are late.

14. I am hungry.

15. The snack is tasty.

Lesson 1.14 Transitive Verbs

Transitive verbs transfer their action to a direct or indirect object. If the object doesn't receive the action of the verb, the meaning of the verb is not complete.

> The hail storm *broke* the *car windows*.
> Transitive verb = broke
> Object = car windows (what was broken)

The meaning of the verb *broke* would not be complete without the object *car windows*.

The object and receiver of a transitive verb can be either a direct object or an indirect object.

A **direct object** receives the action directly from the subject.

> They *sent* a *claim*.
> Transitive verb = sent
> Direct object = claim (what was sent)

An **indirect object** is the person to whom or for whom the action is directed.

> They *sent the insurance agency* a *claim*.
> Transitive verb = sent
> Direct object = claim (what was sent)
> Indirect object = the insurance agency (to whom the claim was sent)

Match It

The partial sentence in Column B completes the sentence started in Column A. Column A contains the subjects of the sentences and the transitive verbs. Column B contains the direct and indirect objects. Draw a line from Column A to the sentence ending that makes the most sense in Column B.

Column A	**Column B**
1. Karen's father bought	his fans a story.
2. The outfielder caught	the ice cubes for later.
3. The artist drew	a picture.
4. The boys drank	the ball.
5. The teacher gave	soy beans and pumpkins.
6. The team ate	several pizzas.
7. The swimmers swam	many laps.
8. The farmer grew	them gold stars.
9. The author wrote	her a present.
10. Marie froze	the lemonade.

Lesson 1.15 Gerunds, Participles, and Infinitives

Gerunds, **participles**, and **infinitives** are other kinds of verbs. These verbs take the role of another part of speech in some circumstances.

A **gerund** is when a verb is used as a noun. A verb can take the form of the noun when the ending **–ing** is added.

> *Cooking* is one of my favorite activities.
> (The subject *cooking* is a noun in the sentence.)

A **participle** is when a verb is used as an adjective. A verb can take the form of an adjective when the endings **–ing** or **–ed** are added.

> Those *falling* snowflakes from the sky are pretty.
> (*falling* modifies *snowflakes*)

> The *ordered* parts should be here on Monday.
> (*ordered* modifies *parts*)

An **infinitive** is when a verb is used as a noun, adjective, or adverb. A verb can take the form of a noun, adjective, or adverb when preceded by the word *to*.

> *To agree* with the professor can be important.
> (The verb *to agree* acts as the subject, noun, of the sentence.)
> The last student *to report* on the subject led the research team.
> (The verb *to report* acts as an adjective modifying *student*.)
> Roger observed the long movie *to report* on it for the paper.
> (The verb *to report* acts as an adverb modifying *observed*.)

Complete It

Choose a verb from the box to fill in the blanks in the sentences.

to catch	joking	sleeping
to drink	reported	to warn

1. _____ is Jed's favorite activity on the weekends.

2. She jumped high _____ the ball.

3. The _____ comedians performed at school.

4. Jim takes plenty of water _____ on long runs.

5. The _____ details of the event were surprising.

6. _____ the public of the oncoming storm was her job.

Lesson 1.15 Gerunds, Participles, and Infinitives

Identify It

The following sentences contain verbs that are acting as gerunds, participles, or infinitives. Identify which by placing a **G** for gerund, a **P** for participle, or an **I** for infinitive after each sentence. Then, underline the gerund, participle, or infinitive.

1. Acting is all Sally wants to do. _____

2. The students singing on stage are from our school. _____

3. Logs burned in this fireplace are small. _____

4. To jump for the shot would be the best thing to do. _____

5. Matthew brought a sandwich to eat in case the meeting ran long. _____

6. Ann watched the special on television to learn about habitats. _____

7. Amy studied the styles of ancient Rome to sew the appropriate costume. _____

8. Running is an excellent exercise. _____

9. Karen brings sweaters to wear in case it gets cold at night. _____

10. The sound of children laughing is a wonderful sound. _____

11. To finish your homework early is a good idea. _____

12. The polished car sparkled in the sunlight. _____

Try It

Make a list of six verbs. Write them on the lines below. Then, change them to gerunds, participles, and infinitives and use them in sentences. Write your new sentences on the lines provided.

_____ _____ _____

_____ _____ _____

_____

_____

_____

_____

_____

_____

Lesson 1.16 Adjectives

Adjectives are words used to describe a noun or pronoun. Most adjectives are common adjectives. Common adjectives are not proper, so they are not capitalized.

The *cold* water felt good on the *hot* day.
Water and *day* are the nouns. The adjectives *cold* and *hot* describe the nouns.

Proper adjectives are formed from proper nouns and are always capitalized.
The children wanted snow cones and *French* fries at the amusement park.
The proper adjective *French* describes the noun, *fries*.

Solve It
The words in the box are adjectives of the senses. Find and circle these words in the puzzle. They can be horizontal, vertical, diagonal, forward, and backward.

bright	loud	fresh	sour	cool
dim	sharp	sweet	spicy	rough
pretty	soothing	woodsy	tart	soft

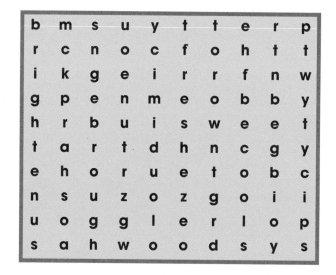

Lesson 1.16 Adjectives

Identify It
Circle the common adjectives and underline the proper adjectives in the paragraph.

Marblehead Lighthouse

Lighthouses are tall towers with bright lights that guide ships at night or in the fog. One famous lighthouse is located in Marblehead, Ohio, on Lake Erie. It is one of Lake Erie's most-photographed landmarks. Marblehead Lighthouse is the oldest lighthouse in continuous operation on the Great Lakes. It has been in operation since 1822. The 65-foot high tower is made of limestone. Throughout the years, the lighthouse has been operated by 15 lighthouse keepers. Two of the 15 keepers were women. Lighthouse keepers had many duties. They lighted the projection lamps, kept logs of passing ships, recorded the weather, and organized rescue efforts. As technology changed with time, the type of light used also changed. Electric light replaced lanterns in 1923. Today a 300mm lens flashes green signals every six seconds. It can be seen for up to 11 nautical miles. The lighthouse no longer has a resident keeper. The United States Coast Guard now operates the Marblehead Lighthouse. The lighthouse beacon continues to warn sailors and keep those on the lake waters safe.

Try It
Choose 10 of the 15 sensory adjectives from the puzzle on page 108. Use each of the 10 adjectives in a sentence.

_____

_____

_____

_____

_____

_____

_____

_____

_____

_____

_____

_____

Lesson 1.17 Adverbs

Adverbs are words used to modify a verb, an adjective, or another adverb.

An adverb tells *how*, *why*, *when*, *where*, *how often*, or *how much*.

Adverbs often end in **ly** (but not always).
> *how* or *why*: softly, courageously, forcefully
> *when* or *how often*: sometimes, yesterday, always
> *where*: here, inside, below
> *how much*: generously, barely, liberally

Match It
The categories in Column A are missing their adverbs. Select adverbs from Column B and write them in the appropriate category in Column A.

Column A	**Column B**
Category 1: *how* or *why*	scarcely
_____	today
_____	cleverly
_____	outside
	joyfully
Category 2: *when* or *how often*	entirely
_____	there
_____	tomorrow
_____	never
	luckily
Category 3: *where*	wholly
_____	up
_____	
_____	
Category 4: *how much*	
_____	
_____	
_____	

Lesson 1.17 Adverbs

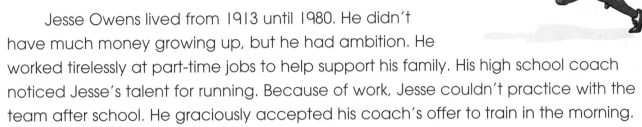

Identify It
Circle the adverbs in the following paragraphs. Underline the verbs, adjectives, or adverbs they modify.

An All-American Hero

Jesse Owens lived from 1913 until 1980. He didn't have much money growing up, but he had ambition. He worked tirelessly at part-time jobs to help support his family. His high school coach noticed Jesse's talent for running. Because of work, Jesse couldn't practice with the team after school. He graciously accepted his coach's offer to train in the morning.

Jesse was anxiously recruited by many colleges and accepted an offer to the Ohio State University. However, since he was African American, he received no scholarships, despite the fact that he broke several world records while attending OSU. He continued to energetically work, study, and train. In the Berlin Olympic Games in 1936, he became the first American to win four gold medals in a single game. He also broke many track records. Remarkably, his records lasted more than 20 years.

What is even more remarkably significant is his dedication to the well-being of others that he actively exhibited later in life. He became a spokesman for living a life guided by hard work and loyalty. He eagerly sponsored and participated in youth sports programs in underprivileged neighborhoods. After his death in 1980, his wife continued to operate the Jesse Owens Foundation. Jesse Owens truly deserved the Medal of Freedom he was awarded in 1976. It is the highest honor a United States civilian can receive.

Try It
Write a sentence for each adverb in the verb box. Be sure your adverbs modify verbs, adjectives, or other adverbs.

actively	energetically
after	several
anxiously	tirelessly

_____

_____

_____

_____

_____

_____

Lesson 1.18 Conjunctions

Conjunctions connect individual words or groups of words in sentences. There are three types of conjunctions.

Coordinate conjunctions connect words, phrases, or independent clauses that are equal or of the same type. Coordinate conjunctions are *and*, *but*, *or*, *nor*, *for*, *yet*, and *so*.

> The horse's mane is soft *and* shiny.

Correlative conjunctions are used with pairs and are used together. *Both/and*, *either/or*, and *neither/nor* are examples of correlative conjunctions.

> *Neither* pizza *nor* pasta was listed on the menu.

Subordinate conjunctions connect two clauses that are not equal. They connect dependent clauses to independent clauses in order to complete the meaning. *After*, *as long as*, *since*, and *while* are examples of subordinate conjunctions.

> We can't save for our spring vacation *until* we get part-time jobs.

Match It

Match the words in Column A with their relationship in Column B.

Column A	Column B
1. provided that the light is green	equal (coordinate)
2. cold and fluffy snow	pairs (correlative)
3. either smooth or crunchy	dependent (subordinate)

4. both mushrooms and olives	equal (coordinate)
5. before it gets dark	pairs (correlative)
6. purple or blue shirt	dependent (subordinate)

7. after the race	equal (coordinate)
8. neither pennies nor nickels	pairs (correlative)
9. music and dance	dependent (subordinate)

Lesson 1.18 Conjunctions

Identify It

Identify whether the following sentences use coordinate, correlative, or subordinate conjunctions by writing a **CD** for coordinate, **CR** for correlative, or **S** for subordinate before each sentence. Then, underline the conjunctions.

1. _____ Bobcats, members of the lynx family, are found in North America and Northern Eurasia.

2. _____ Although they are members of the lynx family, they differ in a number of ways.

3. _____ Bobcats have smaller ear tufts and feet than lynxes.

4. _____ Because of the terrain, bobcats can have different body types.

5. _____ Bobcats living in northern territories are smaller and have pale coats.

6. _____ Bobcats living in southern territories are larger and have dark coats.

7. _____ Bobcats can be found in swampy areas but also desert areas.

8. _____ Bobcats hunt both during the night and during the day.

9. _____ Though smaller in size, bobcats are more aggressive than lynxes.

10. _____ Bobcats can climb and swim well.

11. _____ Not only bobcats but all big cats are exploited for their fur.

12. _____ Because of this and other threats to the cat family, conservation groups are working to halt species extinction.

Try It

Write six sentences that use conjunctions. Write two sentences using coordinate conjunctions, two sentences using correlative conjunctions, and two sentences using subordinate conjunctions.

_____

_____

_____

_____

_____

_____

_____

Lesson 1.19 Interjections

An **interjection** is a word or phrase used to express surprise or strong emotion.

Common interjections include: *ah; alas; aw; cheers; eeek; eh; hey; hi; huh; hurray; oh; oh, no; ouch; uh; uh-huh; uh-uh; voila; wow; yeah*

Exclamation marks are usually used after interjections to separate them from the rest of the sentence.

> *Hurray!* We are the champions!

If the feeling isn't quite as strong, a comma is used in place of the exclamation point.

> *Yeah,* the Oakdale Grizzlies had a great basketball season!

Sometimes question marks are used as an interjection's punctuation.

> *Well?* How does the team look for next year?

Solve It

What interjection from the above list would you choose to add to the following sentences? Use the pictures to help you decide. Write them on the blank in the sentences.

1. _____ It's so good to see you.

2. _____ We've made it to the top.

3. _____ I really scraped up my knee!

4. _____ Tonight we celebrate!

5. _____ Dessert is served.

6. _____ I hope I do better on the next test.

Lesson 1.19 Interjections

Rewrite It

Rewrite the following dialogue. Add interjections where you think they are appropriate to make the dialogue more exciting and interesting. Choose interjections from the previous page, or add some of your own.

"We're about ready to land. Look at that landscape," exclaimed Dana as the plane made its descent at the Kona International Airport on the big island, Hawaii. The guide book says this airport sits on miles of lava rock."

"How can that be?" asked Gabriella.

"There are five volcanoes on Hawaii. One is extinct, one is dormant, and three are still active," answered Dana.

"There are active volcanoes here?" asked Gabriella.

"The one that caused the lava flow beneath this airport is Hualalai," reported Dana. "It is still considered active. In the 1700s, it spewed lava all the way to the ocean. The airport is on top of one of the flows. The world's largest volcano, Mauna Loa, and the world's most active volcano, Kilauea, are also here on Hawaii."

"Dana, are you sure you want to vacation on this island?" asked Gabriella.

"I plan to visit all of the volcanoes," answered Dana.

"I'm hitting the beach. I've got some serious surfing to do!" exclaimed Gabriella.

_____
_____
_____
_____
_____
_____
_____
_____
_____
_____
_____
_____
_____
_____
_____
_____
_____

Lesson 1.20 Prepositions

Prepositions are words or groups of words that show the relationship between a noun or pronoun (the object of the sentence) and another word in the sentence.

> They sat *upon the dock*.

In this sentence, *upon* is the preposition, and *dock* is the object of the preposition.

<u>Common prepositions:</u>

above	below	in	under
across	beneath	inside	until
after	beside	into	up
along	between	near	with
around	by	off	within
at	down	on	without
away	during	outside	
because	except	over	
before	for	to	
behind	from	toward	

Complete It

Complete the following sentences by circling the preposition that works best in the sentence.

1. Look (behind, down from) your car before you back out.

2. I really like the little café right (across, away from) the street.

3. The kitty likes watching the birds (outside, toward) the window.

4. Our cats only live (around, inside) the house.

5. Edna stored the photographs (through, underneath) her bed.

6. Cedric can't go on the field trip (within, without) his permission slip.

7. The commentators predicted the outcome of the game (before, until) it was over.

8. The snow piled (on top of, over to) the ice.

Lesson 1.20 Prepositions

Identify It

Circle the prepositions and underline the objects of the prepositions in the paragraph.

What Is the West Wing?

The West Wing is located in the White House. The President of the United States has his office in the West Wing. It is called the Oval Office. The West Wing houses the executive staff's offices, in addition to the president's office. The chief of staff's office is across from the Oval Office. The vice president works beside the chief of staff. The press secretary and the communication director's offices are along the main corridor. The Roosevelt Room (a conference room), the Cabinet Room (the cabinet is a group of advisers who are heads of government departments), and the President's secretary's office are a little farther down the corridor. Outside of the press secretary's window is the Rose Garden. The West Colonnade runs alongside the Rose Garden. The Press Room is inside the West Colonnade. The Press Room sits on top of an old swimming pool. The swimming pool is a remnant of Franklin D. Roosevelt's administration. That completes the tour of the West Wing.

Try It

Write a paragraph describing the rooms in your home. Tell where the rooms are located and what sits outside of some of the windows. Circle the prepositions you used.

_____

_____

_____

_____

_____

_____

_____

_____

_____

_____

_____

_____

Lesson 1.21 Prepositional Phrases

Prepositional phrases include the prepositions and the objects (nouns or pronouns) that follow the prepositions. A prepositional phrase includes the preposition, the object of the preposition, and the modifiers (describes other words) of the object. Prepositional phrases often tell about *when* or *where* something is happening.

> They sat *upon the dock*.

If the noun in the prepositional phrase above had modifiers, they would also be included in the prepositional phrase.

> They sat *upon the wooden dock*.

Match It

Match the beginnings of sentences in Column A with the prepositional phrases that match them best in Column B.

Column A

1. The clouds are

2. We can leave

3. Let's have dinner

4. The lake lies far

5. When alphabetizing the files, put the As

6. Annie can't baby sit, so Laurie is coming

7. It was raining so hard it was difficult to see

8. Swimming is permitted if you stay

Column B

within the limits.

in the sky.

after the movie.

in her place.

outside the window.

in front of the Bs.

in the morning.

beyond the forest.

Lesson 1.21 Prepositional Phrases

Solve It

The following sentences describe the above scene. However, the prepositions are missing. Look at the picture and complete the sentences.

1. The kids played _____ the fence.

2. A cat looked _____ a window.

3. A squirrel sat _____ the roof.

4. Chimney smoke rose _____ the house.

5. The basement was _____ the house.

6. The clouds floated _____ the sky.

7. The tree sat _____ the fence.

8. A jogger ran _____ the street.

Try It

Write four sentences that include prepositional phrases. Underline the prepositional phrases in your sentences.

_____

_____

_____

_____

Lesson 1.22 Articles

Articles are specific words that serve as adjectives before a noun. *A*, *an*, and *the* are articles.

The is a **definite article**. That means it names a specific noun.
>   I go to *the* school on *the* corner.
The article *the* tells that the person goes to a specific school on a specific corner.

A and *an* are **indefinite articles**. They do not name a specific noun.
>   I would like to go to *a* school on *a* corner.
The article *a* tells that the person wants to go to a school on a corner, but not a specific school or corner.

Use *a* when the noun it precedes begins with a consonant or a vowel that sounds like a consonant.
>   a dog   a cat   a skunk   a one-way street

Use *an* when the noun it precedes begins with a vowel or sounds like it starts with a vowel.
>   an envelope   an olive   an island   an honest person

Complete It
Complete the following sentences by circling the correct answer in parentheses.

1. Mike and Jen rented the apartment above (a, an, the) bookstore.

2. Henry wants to get (a, an, the) car with four doors.

3. An amoeba is (a, an, the) one-celled animal.

4. Coordinating the play turned out to be quite (a, an, the) ordeal.

5. Todd wants to rent (a, an, the) canoe for the weekend.

6. Kay brought (a, an, the) orange to go with her lunch.

7. (A, An, The) orange sweater looked best on Karley.

8. Not (a, an, the) hour went by that they didn't think about each other.

9. (A, An, The) Kensington Trail is beautiful.

10. Lynn wants to buy (a, an, the) blue or red bracelet.

Lesson 1.22 Articles

Proof It
Proofread the following paragraph. Change any incorrect articles to the correct ones.

> _e_ – deletes incorrect letters, words, punctuation
> ^ – inserts correct letters, words, punctuation

The Tonys

Almost everyone has heard of the Oscars, an Emmys, and a Golden Globe Awards. The Tony Awards is also a awards presentation. A Tony Awards are given for outstanding accomplishment in theater. The Tony Awards were named after Antoinette Perry, a actress, director, producer, and manager. She was known for helping young people who were interested in the acting profession. An first Tony Awards were presented in 1947 with seven categories. Today, there are 25 categories including Best Play and Best Musical. The Tony award is the medallion that shows a image of Antoinette Perry on one side. On an other side are a masks of comedy and tragedy.

Try It
What is your favorite play, movie, or television show? Write a paragraph describing your favorite. Underline the articles you used.

_____

_____

_____

_____

_____

_____

_____

_____

_____

Lesson 1.23 Declarative Sentences

Declarative sentences are sentences that make statements. They say something about a place, person, thing, or idea. When punctuating a declarative sentence, use a period at the end.

> I have several hours of homework to do.

Identify It
Identify the following declarative sentences by placing a checkmark ✓ on the line provided. Leave the other sentences blank.

1. _____ Have you ever heard of a red-eyed tree frog?

2. _____ Red-eyed tree frogs are small, colorful, musical frogs with big red eyes.

3. _____ Where do red-eyed tree frogs live?

4. _____ They primarily live in South America, Central America, and parts of Mexico.

5. _____ They like lowland rainforests close to rivers and hills.

6. _____ How small are red-eyed tree frogs?

7. _____ Female red-eyed tree frogs grow to be 3 inches long.

8. _____ Males grow to be only 2 inches long.

9. _____ Do they have any color other than red eyes?

10. _____ Their bodies are neon green with dashes of yellow and blue.

11. _____ Their upper legs are bright blue and their feet are orange or red.

12. _____ How are these tree frogs musical?

13. _____ Red-eyed tree frogs are nocturnal and can be heard in their trees at night.

14. _____ Why are these frogs called *tree frogs*?

15. _____ They live mostly in trees.

Lesson 1.24 Interrogative Sentences

Interrogative sentences are sentences that ask questions. When punctuating an interrogative sentence, use a question mark.

Do you live in the country or in the city**?**

Complete It
Complete the following sentences by circling the correct punctuation at the end of the sentences.

1. Who is your hero (? .)

2. Do you have Mr. Bell for history this year (? .)

3. What is your favorite food (? .)

4. Can we leave first thing in the morning (? .)

5. When does the bus leave (? .)

6. Green is my favorite color (? .)

7. Where are we going on the field trip next week (? .)

8. I'm going to have Mr. Stubbert for history next year (? .)

9. Why don't we go out for dinner (? .)

10. Can Charlie come over for dinner (? .)

11. How many stars are in the sky (? .)

12. I'm going to take the bus downtown (? .)

13. What's your favorite color (? .)

14. How many sisters and brothers do you have (? .)

15. Look at that unusual building (? .)

16. Have you ever seen the Grand Canyon (? .)

17. Are you going to take swimming lessons this summer (? .)

18. I am so clumsy, I dropped my tray at lunch (? .)

19. How do you want to decorate the gym for the dance (? .)

20. I like broccoli on my salad (? .)

Lesson 1.25 Exclamatory Sentences

Exclamatory sentences are sentences that reveal urgency, strong surprise, or emotion. When punctuating an exclamatory sentence, use an exclamation mark.

Watch out for the icy steps**!**

Sometimes you will find interjections in exclamatory sentences.

Yea! One more test until summer break!

Exclamation marks can also be used in dialogue, when the character or speaker is making an urgent or emotional statement.

"*Watch out!*" shouted Kelly.

Exclamation marks should be used sparingly in writing. Do not overuse them.

Match It

Match the sentences (which are missing their punctuation) in Column A with their type of sentence in Column B. Draw an arrow to make your match.

Column A	Column B
1. I will be thirteen on my next birthday	declarative
2. Hurry and open up your presents	interrogative
3. How old are you	exclamatory

4. Oh no I dropped all of my papers in a puddle	declarative
5. Is it supposed to snow all weekend	interrogative
6. Autumn is my favorite season	exclamatory

7. Where are my shoes	declarative
8. I scored 12 points in the basketball game	interrogative
9. Look out	exclamatory

Lesson 1.26 Imperative Sentences

Imperative sentences demand that an action be performed. The subjects of imperative sentences are usually not expressed. They usually contain the understood subject *you*. Imperative sentences can be punctuated with a period or an exclamation mark.

> Get on bus #610.
> (*You* get on bus #610.)
>
> Answer the phone before it stops ringing!
> (*You* answer the phone before it stops ringing!)

Identify It

Identify the following sentences by writing a **D** for declarative, an **IN** for interrogative, an **E** for exclamatory, or an **IM** for imperative after each sentence.

1. Hop over that puddle! _____

2. How many more days until spring break? _____

3. I won the contest! _____

4. I don't want anchovies on my pizza. _____

5. Let's set up a lemonade stand this summer. _____

6. What is the distance of a century bicycle ride? _____

7. Announce the winners as they come across the finish line. _____

8. The firefighter saved everyone in the house! _____

9. Think about what you want to serve at the party. _____

10. My favorite appetizer is vegetable stuffed mushrooms. _____

11. Whom do you admire most? _____

12. The fundraiser was a huge success! _____

Lesson 1.27 Simple Sentences

Simple sentences are sentences with one independent clause. **Independent clauses** present a complete thought and can stand alone as a sentence. Simple sentences do not have any dependent clauses. **Dependent clauses** do not present a complete thought and cannot stand alone as sentences.

Simple sentences can have one or more simple subjects.
> *Goats* lived at the sanctuary.
> *Goats* and *turkeys* lived at the sanctuary.

Simple sentences can have one or more simple predicates (verbs).
> The goats *played* with the other animals.
> The turkeys *played* and *talked* with the other animals.

Simple sentences can have more than one simple subject and more than one simple predicate.
> The *goats* and the *turkeys played* and *talked* with the other animals.

Match It
Each of the simple sentences in Column A has select words underlined. The sentence parts that match the underlined words are found in Column B. Match the sentences in Column A with the sentence parts in Column B.

Column A

1. Farm Sanctuary <u>rescues</u> and <u>protects</u> farm animals.

2. Farm Sanctuary <u>members</u> have helped to pass farm animal protection laws.

3. The New York <u>sanctuary</u> and the California <u>sanctuary</u> are home to hundreds of rescued farm animals.

4. Farm Sanctuary <u>offers</u> a humane education program to schools.

5. At Farm Sanctuary, <u>people</u> and <u>animals</u> <u>work</u> and <u>play</u> together.

Column B

one subject

two subjects

one predicate

two predicates

two subjects/two predicates

Lesson 1.28 Compound Sentences

Compound sentences are sentences with two or more simple sentences (independent clauses) joined by a coordinate conjunction, punctuation, or both. As in simple sentences, there are no dependent clauses in compound sentences.

A compound sentence can be two sentences joined with a comma and a coordinate conjunction.

> He didn't think he was a fan of Shakespeare, *yet* he enjoyed the play.

A compound sentence can also be two simple sentences joined by a semicolon.

> He didn't think he was a fan of Shakespeare; he enjoyed the play.

Match It

Match simple sentences in Column A with simple sentences in Column B to create compound sentences. Write the compound sentences and remember to add either a coordinate conjunction or punctuation.

Column A

1. The football game was exciting.

2. My favorite team is playing.

3. My school's colors are blue and white.

4. I'm going to get a pretzel at halftime.

5. My team won the game.

Column B

1. They have a good record this year.

2. I'm going to get pizza after the game.

3. The score was close.

4. The season isn't over yet.

5. The opposing team's colors are green and gold.

1. _____

_____

2. _____

_____

3. _____

_____

4. _____

_____

5. _____

_____

Lesson 1.29 Complex Sentences

Complex sentences have one independent clause and one or more dependent clauses. The independent and dependent clauses are connected with a subordinate conjunction or a relative pronoun. Dependent clauses do not present a complete thought and cannot stand alone as sentences. The dependent clause can be anywhere in the sentence.

Complex sentence (connected with subordinate conjunction):
> You can go to the movies *if* you finish your homework.

Complex sentence (connected with a relative pronoun):
> My mother asked me to drop off these flowers for Mrs. Hastings, *whose* house is on our way to school.

Dependent clauses follow the connecting subordinate conjunction or the relative pronoun. The dependent clause can either be the first or second part of the sentence.
> *Before* the movie, I'll finish my homework.
> I'll finish my homework *before* the movie.

Identify It
Put a checkmark on the line in front of following the complex sentences.

1. _____ I like biking because it is good exercise.

2. _____ Tony is going to order pasta with mushrooms, which is his favorite dish.

3. _____ History is my favorite subject.

4. _____ Mr. Baum, who is also the baseball coach, is my favorite teacher.

5. _____ While Kim is a good speller, Jerry is better.

6. _____ I would like a salad for lunch, yet soup sounds good, too.

7. _____ Erin made the basketball team after two weeks of tryouts.

8. _____ Although it's going to snow, I think we should still hike the trails.

9. _____ Unless it rains, we'll walk, not ride.

10. _____ We can continue hiking until it gets icy.

Lesson 1.30 Sentence Fragments

A **sentence fragment** is a group of words that is missing a subject, predicate, or both. A sentence fragment is also a group of words that doesn't express a complete thought, as in a dependent clause.

> Doesn't have good insulation. (no subject)
> Complete sentence: The window doesn't have good insulation.

> The window good insulation. (no predicate)
> Complete sentence: The window doesn't have good insulation.

> Good insulation. (no subject or predicate)
> Complete sentence: The window doesn't have good insulation.

> Since the lemonade was too sour. (not a complete thought)
> Complete sentence: We drank water since the lemonade was too sour.

Complete It

Complete the following sentence fragments by choosing a sentence fragment from the box that completes the sentences.

It was presented   **Construction began**
The statue's height   **is "Liberty Enlightening the World."**
stands on Liberty Island in the New York Harbor.

1. The Statue of Liberty _____

_____. (look for a verb phrase)

2. _____ in France in 1875.
(look for a subject and a verb)

3. _____ to the United
States on July 4, 1884. (look for a subject and verb)

4. The official name of the Statue of Liberty _____

_____. (look for a verb phrase)

5. _____
from base to torch is 152 feet, 2 inches. (look for a subject)

Lesson 1.31 Combining Sentences

Combining short, choppy sentences into longer, more detailed sentences makes writing much more interesting and easier to read. Sentences can be combined in a variety of ways.

Compound Subjects and Compound Verbs:
> The lightning is coming. The thunder is coming.
> The *thunder and lightning* are coming.

> The president of our class is honest. The president of our class is loyal.
> The president of our class is *honest and loyal*.

Adjectives and Adverbs:
> I went to a party. The party was a costume party.
> I went to a *costume party*.

> Timothy ran quickly. Timothy ran in the race.
> Timothy *ran quickly* in the race.

Making Complex Sentences (using subordinate conjunctions):
> Donna wanted to go to the reunion. Donna wanted to go if her best friend Diane went.
> Donna wanted to go to the reunion *if* her best friend Diane went.

Match It

Under Column A are five combined sentences. Under Column B are the parts of speech that were combined. Match the sentences in Column A with the parts of speech in Column B.

Column A	**Column B**
1. The salesman reluctantly attended the seminar.	combined subjects
2. Dan and Rose are taking swimming lessons.	combined verbs
3. Cam's parents lived in a beautiful neighborhood.	combined adjective
4. David climbed and descended the mountain.	combined adverb
5. The phone rang while we were eating.	subordinate conjunction

Lesson 1.32 Writing a Paragraph

A **paragraph** is made up of a group of sentences. A paragraph should have, and stick to, a single topic. Each sentence of the paragraph should focus on the topic with plenty of information and supporting details related to the topic.

Elements of a Paragraph: There are three parts to a paragraph.

1. Beginning: The topic sentence is the beginning of the paragraph. It tells the reader what the paragraph is going to be about. It expresses the feeling of the paragraph.

2. Middle: The middle is the main element of the paragraph. The sentences here give more information and supporting details about the topic sentence.

3. End: After all of the information and details are written, the end sentence sums it all up.

Writing the Paragraph: There are five steps to take when writing a paragraph.

1. Prewriting: Choose your topic and think about what information you want to include.

2. Drafting: Write your topic sentence and the other parts of your paragraph.

3. Revising: Reread your paragraph. Make sure the three parts of your paragraph are used correctly. Rewrite your paragraph and include details with adjectives and adverbs to make it more interesting.

4. Proofreading: Proofread your paragraph looking for errors in spelling and punctuation.

5. Publishing: Now's your chance to show off your work. You will publish your paragraph.

Types of Paragraphs: A few of the most common paragraphs include the following types:

Descriptive – Descriptive paragraphs give vivid details of people, places, things, or ideas.

Narrative – Narrative paragraphs give the details of an event or events in the form of a story.

Expository – Expository paragraphs give facts or explain ideas in a nonfiction format.

Persuasive – Persuasive paragraphs express an opinion and try to convince readers that this opinion is correct.

Lesson 1.32 Writing a Paragraph

Rewrite It

The sentences in the following paragraph are out of order. Rewrite the paragraph placing the topic sentence first, the summary sentence last, and the body sentences in between.

This substance has a red pigment. Horseshoe crabs' blood has copper in it. Not all living creatures have red blood; horseshoe crabs' blood is blue! Human blood has hemoglobin that has iron in it. The color of one's blood, whether a creature big or small, depends on the makeup and chemicals in the blood. This material causes the blood to appear blue.

topic sentence: _____

_____

first body sentence: _____

_____

second body sentence: _____

_____

third body sentence: _____

_____

fourth body sentence: _____

_____

end sentence: _____

_____

Try It

Write a paragraph about a topic of your choosing. Select one of the types of paragraphs. Think about your topic ideas and the five steps of writing.

_____

_____

_____

_____

_____

_____

Lesson 1.32 Writing a Paragraph

Match It

Circle the letter of the best answer to each of the following questions.

1. Which sentence would most likely be found in a persuasive paragraph?

   a. Alexandra kicked off her sandals and raced towards the waves.

   b. According to Chinese tradition, each year is assigned an animal in the Chinese zodiac.

   c. More than half of the middle school students have said they would attend an afterschool program at the community center.

2. Which of the following sentences is mostly likely from a narrative paragraph?

   a. The man peeked through the window and saw the mass of reporters waiting on his front lawn.

   b. Throughout history, pigeons have been used to carry messages.

   c. You'll notice a difference in your energy level after cutting sugar out for only one week.

3. Which sentence would make the best topic sentence?

   a. Babe Ruth's given name was George Herman Ruth.

   b. Babe Ruth is one of the greatest athletes in the history of baseball.

   c. Babe Ruth joined the Baltimore Orioles in 1914.

4. Which sentence is most likely to be a supporting detail from the middle of a paragraph?

   a. The next time you see a bat, remember how much we rely on this small, odd creature.

   b. Bats often feed on fruit, pollen, and insects.

   c. Have you ever seen a bat on clear, starry night?

Lesson 1.32 Writing a Paragraph

Try It

On the lines below, write the rough draft of a descriptive, narrative, expository, or persuasive paragraph.

_____

_____

_____

_____

_____

_____

_____

_____

_____

_____

_____

_____

_____

_____

_____

_____

_____

_____

_____

_____

_____

_____

_____

_____

_____

Proper nouns are specific people, places, and things. They are capitalized.

Capitalize days of the week.

Sunday   Monday   Tuesday   Wednesday   Thursday   Friday   Saturday

Capitalize months of the year.

January   February   March   April   May   June   July   August   September   October   November   December

Months of the year are also capitalized when they serve as adjectives.

They ran the marathon on a sunny *June* morning.

Solve It

Complete the following sentences by cracking the code and filling in the blanks. Remember to capitalize the days of the weeks when you write them.

1=A	4=D	7=G	10=J	13=M	16=P	19=S	22=V	25=Y
2=B	5=E	8=H	11=K	14=N	17=Q	20=T	23=W	26=Z
3=C	6=F	9=I	12=L	15=O	18=R	21=U	24=X	

1. I'm always groggy on a __ __ __ __ __ __, the first day of the school week.
   13 15 14 4 1 25

2. I was born on a __ __ __ __ __ __, one of the two weekend days.
   19 21 14 4 1 25

3. The day of the week with the most letters in it is __ __ __ __ __ __ __ __ __.
   23 5 4 14 5 19 4 1 25

4. __ __ __ __ __ __ is high school football night.
   6 18 9 4 1 25

5. __ __ __ __ __ __ __ is one of the two days of the week that starts with the
   20 21 5 19 4 1 25   same letter.

6. __ __ __ __ __ __ __ __ is the other.
   20 8 21 18 19 4 1 25

7. I play baseball every __ __ __ __ __ __ __ __.
   19 1 20 21 18 4 1 25

Lesson 2.1 Proper Nouns: Days of the Week, Months of the Year

Rewrite It

Rewrite the following sentences after unscrambling the names of the months. Do not forget to capitalize them.

1. The month of <u>jeun</u> is Adopt a Shelter Cat Month.

_____

2. Earth Day, a day for environmental awareness, is celebrated in <u>lpari</u>.

_____

3. Adopt a Shelter Dog Month is held in <u>cbotore</u>.

_____

4. St. Valentine is credited for bringing couples together on the 14th of <u>barufrey</u>.

_____

5. The state of Colorado has its own day, and it's celebrated in <u>stuagu</u>.

_____

6. Shogatsu is the name for New Year in Japan; it is celebrated in <u>najruay</u>.

_____

Try It

Write a paragraph about your favorite day of the week or month of the year.

_____

_____

_____

_____

_____

_____

_____

_____

_____

_____

_____

_____

Lesson 2.2 Proper Nouns: Historical Events, Names of Languages and Nationalities, Team Names

Historical events, nationalities, and team names are **proper nouns**.

Events, periods of time, and important documents from history are capitalized.
Cold War   Renaissance Period   Constitution of the United States

Names of languages and nationalities are capitalized. They are also capitalized when they are used as adjectives.
French   Hispanic   Dutch apple pie

The names of sports teams are capitalized.
Detroit Tigers

Complete It
Complete the following sentences by circling the correct answer in parentheses. Hint: Not all choices are proper and need to be capitalized.

1. The war lasting from 1939 to 1945 was (world war II, World War II).

2. The (italian, Italian) language is one of the romance languages.

3. An (era, Era) is considered to be any important period of time.

4. The season begins for (baseball teams, Baseball Teams) in April.

5. Mikhail Baryshnikov is of (russian, Russian) descent.

6. The (boston red sox, Boston Red Sox) won the World Series in 2004.

7. The (*magna carta, Magna Carta*) was written in 1215.

8. The (english, English) cocker spaniel was the number one dog in popularity in Britain from the 1930s through the 1950s.

9. The (victorian era, Victorian Era) lasted from 1839 to 1901, during the reign of Queen Victoria in England.

10. The (french, French) soufflé is a dessert served warm.

11. The first ten amendments to the *Constitution of the United States* is the (bill of rights, Bill of Rights).

12. The (battle of waterloo, Battle of Waterloo) took place in Belgium in 1815.

Lesson 2.2 Proper Nouns: Historical Events, Names of Languages and Nationalities, Team Names

Solve It

Unscramble the following letters in parentheses to complete each sentence with a word from the box. Capitalize each word when necessary.

period	patriots	world	war
address	angels	german	greek

1. The Jurassic _____ (rdieop) was a period in time that saw the rise of the dinosaurs.

2. _____ (rowdl) War II ended in Japan on V-J Day on September 2, 1945.

3. A famous speech was the Gettysburg _____ (dresads) given by Abraham Lincoln.

4. The _____ (mgnare) chocolate cake did not really originate in Germany.

5. The New England _____ (strapiot) football team has a patriotic mascot.

6. World _____ (rwa) I was also known as the *Great War*.

7. An angelic baseball team might be known as the Los Angeles _____ (saenlg).

8. The Greeks were the first Europeans to use an alphabet, what became known as the _____ (ekreg) alphabet.

Try It

Write a paragraph about your favorite sports team. Don't forget to use capitals when needed.

_____

_____

_____

_____

_____

_____

_____

_____

Lesson 2.3 Proper Nouns: Organizations, Departments of Government, Sections of the Country

Organizations, departments of government, and sections of the country are all **proper nouns** and are capitalized.

The names of organizations and associations are capitalized.
Capital Area Humane Society   *Microsoft Corporation*

Capitalize the names of departments of government.
Department of Treasury   *Department of Health and Human Services*

Directional words that point out particular sections of the country are capitalized. However, words that give directions are not capitalized.
Heather grew up on the *East Coast* of the United States.
Madilyn grew up on the *east side* of town.

Identify It
Circle the name of the organization, department of government, or section of the country in each sentence.

1. My mom and dad work for the Department of Transportation.

2. Tina and her family are moving to the Midwest this summer.

3. The National Aeronautics and Space Administration is in charge of space exploration.

4. I volunteer for the American Red Cross.

5. San Francisco is on the West Coast of the United States.

6. While walking to school, we pass the Smithson Art Association.

7. We are traveling to the Southwest next year.

8. Tasha's aunt works for the State Department.

9. Have you ever been to New England?

10. We must send in our tax forms by April 15 to the Internal Revenue Service.

11. TransUnion Carrier Services provides cardboard boxes for moving.

12. Portland, Oregon, is in the Northwest.

Lesson 2.4 Proper Nouns: Titles, Geographic Names

The titles of books, poems, songs, movies, plays, newspapers, and magazines are **proper nouns** and are capitalized. Most titles are also underlined in text. Song titles and essays, however, are in quotes.

book: _The Cat in the Hat_   song: "Atomic Dog"   magazine: _Time_

Titles associated with names are also capitalized.

Mayor Franklin   _Senator_ Santos   _Professor_ Johnson

Do not capitalize these titles if they are not directly used with the name.

The _mayor_ of our town is _Mayor_ Franklin.

Geographic names, such as the names of countries, states, cities, counties, bodies of water, public areas, roads and highways, and buildings are capitalized.

Columbia, Hawaii, Athens, Chesapeake Bay, Sierra Nevada Range, Rocky Mountain National Park, Paint Creek Trail, Globe Theatre

If the geographic name is not a specific name, do not capitalize it.

I'm going to _the lake_ for the weekend.

Complete It

Complete the following sentences by circling the best answer in parentheses.

1. My favorite song is ("Vertigo", "vertigo") by U2.

2. The (President, president) of the organization is visiting on Tuesday.

3. At 2:00 pm, (Governor, governor) Spencer is making a speech.

4. Valerie and Gerald watched the sunset from the (Eiffel Tower, eiffel tower).

5. Are you going to the (Mountains, mountains) or the beach for vacation?

6. One of my favorite books is (The Elephant Hospital, the elephant hospital).

7. Lynda walks in a park along the (Scioto River, scioto river).

8. The (Martin Luther King, Jr. Highway, Martin Luther King, Jr. highway) is located in Washington, D.C.

9. My cousin was born in (Birmingham, birmingham), England.

10. The tiny (Village, village) sits next to a canal.

Lesson 2.4 Proper Nouns: Titles, Geographic Names

Find It

Answer the following questions. If you need help, use an encyclopedia or other resource. Be sure to capitalize the answers when necessary.

1. Who is the principal of your school? _____

2. What city, state, and country do you live in? _____

3. Where were you born? _____

4. Who is the governor of your state? _____

5. What is your favorite book? _____

6. What is your favorite movie? _____

7. What is your favorite poem? _____

8. What states border the state in which you live? _____

9. What is the closest national park to where you live? _____

10. What is the name of your local newspaper? _____

11. What magazine do you like to read the most? _____

12. What is the name of one of your state's senators? _____

Try It

Use the information gathered above to write a brief biography about yourself. As in your previous answers, remember to capitalize titles and geographic names when necessary. You can also include other information about yourself in addition to the facts above.

_____

_____

_____

_____

_____

_____

_____

_____

_____

_____

Lesson 2.5 Sentences, Direct Quotations

The first word of every **sentence** is capitalized.
> *The* wind blew strongly through the trees.

The first word in **direct quotations** is also capitalized.
> My father said, "*Finish* your homework and then we'll go for a ride."
> "*I'm* almost finished now," I happily answered.

Indirect quotations are not capitalized.
> My father said he had been working on his car for weeks.

If a continuous sentence in a direct quotation is split and the second half is not a new sentence, do not capitalize it. If a new sentence begins after the split, then capitalize it as you would with any sentence.
> "Keep your hands and arms inside the car," said the attendant, "*and* stay seated."
> "Roller coasters are my favorite rides," I said. "*I* can ride them all day."

Complete It
Complete the following sentences by circling the best answer in parentheses.

1. (The, the) girls' team beat the boys' team by three seconds.

2. T.C. said, "(Baseball, baseball) is my favorite sport."

3. "(Put, put) your donated clothing in plastic bags," said the event organizer.

4. The technician said (The, the) car would be ready in a few hours.

5. "Don't rush through your homework," said the teacher, "(And, and) stay focused."

6. "Be careful as you shovel the snow," mother said. "(You, you) can hurt your back."

7. (The, the) airplane was going to be delayed.

8. Renee said, "(Would, would) you like a baseball hat when we go to the park?"

9. "(Our, our) race will begin in 10 minutes," said the announcer.

10. The sales clerk said (She, she) would hold the item for one day.

11. "Lemon cream is my favorite pie," said Lisa, "(But, but) nothing beats brownies."

12. "I can't wait until my birthday," said Jack. "(My, my) parents are giving me a party."

Lesson 2.5 Sentences, Direct Quotations

Proof It
Proofread the following dialogue correcting capitalization errors.

| ^ | – inserts correct words or punctuation |
| ≡ | – capitalize letter |

"Hi, Dad," said Jack. "we learned about tsunamis today."

"what did you learn about tsunamis?" Jack's dad asked.

Jack answered, "well, we learned that tsunamis can move up to 500 miles per hour. we also learned about how they are formed."

"the earth's crust is made up of interlocking plates," said Jack. "the plates are floating on a hot, flexible interior that drifts. The plates sometimes collide. In a subduction, an ocean plate slides under continental plates. Over the years, the plates lock, the seafloor compresses, and the coastline warps up. eventually, the pressure pops and the seafloor lunges landward. The coast lunges seaward. the plates push seawater all over, creating the tsunami. Geologists can study sedimentary layers near the seaside to tell when shifts have occurred in the past, maybe helping to understand when it might happen again."

Try It
Write a dialogue between you and a friend, teacher, or parent. Explain to the other person something you learned about in school. Remember the capitalization rules.

_____

_____

_____

_____

_____

_____

_____

_____

_____

_____

Lesson 2.6 Personal and Business Letters

A **personal letter** has five parts: heading, salutation, body, closing, and signature.

The **heading** of a personal letter is the address of the person writing the letter and the date it is written. The name of the street, the city, the state, and the month are all capitalized.

> 1245 Hollow Dr.
> Suncrest, AZ
> March 31, 2008

The **salutation** is the greeting and begins with the word *dear*. Both *dear* and the name of the person who is receiving the letter are capitalized. The salutation ends with a comma.

> *Dear Stanley,*

The **body** is the main part of the letter and contains sentences that are capitalized as normal.

The **closing** can be written in many ways; only the first word is capitalized.

> *Your friend,   Sincerely,   All the best,*

The **signature** is usually only your first name in a personal letter. It is also always capitalized.

> *Milton*

Identify It

Identify the parts of the personal letter by writing the names on the lines provided. Then, circle the capital letters.

7511 Hibernia Rd.

_____ Seattle, WA 40000

February 31, 2014

Dear Uncle Josh, _____

    How are you? My ski trip has been great. I even learned how to snowboard. I think I'll be really sore tomorrow. All of the fundraising was worth it. Thanks for helping us out. I'm glad our class got to take this trip. I hope I'll get to come back someday. _____

Thank you, _____

Mike _____

Lesson 2.6 Personal and Business Letters

A **business letter** has six parts: heading, inside address, salutation, body, closing and signature.

The **heading** of a business letter is the address of the person writing the letter and the date it is written. The name of the street, the city, the state, and the month are all capitalized.

> 4003 Fourteenth St.
> Amlin, NH 20000
> September 6, 2014

The **inside address** includes the name and complete address of the person to whom the letter is going.

> Mark Dillon, Director
> S.A.S Productions
> 100 Otterbein Ave.
> Rochester, NY 20000

The **salutation** is the greeting and begins with the word *dear*. Both *dear* and the name of the person who is receiving the letter are capitalized. The salutation ends with a colon.

> Dear Director:

The **body** is the main part of the letter and contains sentences that are capitalized as normal.

The **closing** can be written many ways. Only the first word is capitalized.

> Yours truly,   Sincerely,   Very truly,

The **signature** is your full name and is capitalized.

> Leigh D. McGregor

Try It

Write the heading, inside address, salutation, closing, and signature of a business letter. Make up the names and other information, and be sure you capitalize correctly.

heading: _____   inside address: _____

_____   _____

_____   _____

salutation: _____   closing: _____

signature: _____

Lesson 2.7 Periods: After Imperative Sentences, In Dialogue, In Abbreviations, In Initials

Sometimes, imperative sentences call for a **period**, as when the sentence is not urgent.
Pay the toll at the booth.

Periods are used in dialogue. The period goes inside the quotation mark.
Jean said, "Give Mimi a drink of water."

If the quote comes at the beginning of the sentence, use a comma at the end of the direct quotation and before the quotation mark. Place a period at the end of the sentence.
"If it gets cold, put on your jacket," said Robyn.

Use a period after each part of an abbreviation. Use a period after each letter of an initial.

M.A. (Master of Arts)   *Samuel L. Jackson*

Complete It
Complete the following sentences by adding periods where necessary.

1. Check out at the far counter

_____

2. Janet said, "Let's take a long walk"

_____

3. "Hiking is my favorite hobby," said Charlie

_____

4. Kathryn received her MA from the University of Arizona.

_____

5. My favorite actress is Vivica A Fox.

_____

6. "Jump over the puddle, so you will stay dry," yelled Eddie

_____

7. Reach a little farther, and you will have touched the top

_____

8. JRR Tolkein is my favorite author.

_____

Lesson 2.8 Question Marks

Question marks are used in sentences that ask questions, called interrogative sentences.

> *How was your trip?*

When used in quotations, question marks can be placed either inside or outside of the end quotation mark depending on the meaning of the sentence.

When the question mark is punctuating the quotation itself, it is placed inside the quote.

> *The coach asked, "How many push-ups can you do?"*

When the question mark is punctuating the entire sentence, it is placed outside the quote.

> *Did the coach say, "Try to do twice as many as you did last week"?*

A question mark is not used in sentences with indirect quotations.

> *Suhad asked the librarian for help finding the book.*

Match It

Draw a line to match the sentences in Column A with their descriptions in Column B.

Column A	Column B
1. Bill asked the guide how long the museum would be open.	interrogative sentence
2. Could you tell that funny joke again?	question mark punctuating quotation
3. Sylvia's mother asked, "What time is your track meet on Saturday?"	question mark punctuating entire sentence
4. Did the weather reporter say, "Expect six inches of snow tonight"?	indirect quotation

5. Where did you park the car?	interrogative sentence
6. Did you say, "Read page four"?	question mark punctuating quotation
7. Sam asked for a quarter to make a wish in the well.	question mark punctuating entire sentence
8. The teacher asked, "What is the square root of 64?"	indirect quotation

NAME _____

Lesson 2.8 Question Marks

Proof It
Proofread the following dialogue, correcting the misplaced and misused question marks.

> " ˇ – inserts quotations
> ↰ – moves letters, words, punctuation, text from one location to another

"Dr. Edwards," asked Eric, "what should I study in school if I want to be a vet"?

Dr. Edwards answered, Eric, anyone who wants to be a vet should study math and science. Veterinarians have to go to medical school, just like people doctors. They have to know how much and which medicines to prescribe." Dr. Edwards continued, "You must also have good social skills."

"I like working with people. Is that important"? asked Eric.

Oh, yes," exclaimed Dr. Edwards. "Doctors have to listen to their patients. In this case, the patients' guardians have to speak for them. I listen very carefully to help with my diagnosis. Sometimes, vets have to discuss serious matters with the guardians."

Eric asked the doctor what was the most important quality for a vet to possess.

"Veterinarians must love animals," answered Dr. Edwards. "We care for them and their guardians in the very best way we can. Do you still want to be a vet, Eric"?

"Absolutely! answered Eric.

Try It
Write three sentences using question marks: one interrogative sentence, one sentence where the question mark punctuates the quotation, and one sentence where the question mark punctuates the entire sentence.

_____

_____

_____

_____

Spectrum Grade 6
148

Lesson 2.9 Exclamation Points

Exclamation points are used at the end of sentences that express surprise and strong emotion, called exclamatory sentences.

We have to read all three chapters for homework!

Interjections sometimes require exclamation points.

Aha! I've come up with the answer!

If you use an exclamation point, make sure the sentence expresses surprise, urgency, or strong emotion. Don't overuse exclamation points.

Complete It

Complete the following sentences by circling the best end punctuation in parentheses.

1. Can bees talk (. ?)

2. Scientists have discovered that bees do communicate with each other (. !)

3. How do they talk (? !)

4. Bees don't talk with their voices (. !)

5. Bees talk through dance (? !)

6. What do bees talk about (. ?)

7. Bees talk about gathering food (. !)

8. One dance move tells where the food is located (. ?)

9. Another dance move tells how far the food is away (. !)

10. Are there more dance moves (? !)

11. Yes, another move tells about how much food is in a particular location (. ?)

12. Do dancing bees have a special name (? !)

13. The bees who communicate about the food are called scout bees (. !)

14. Scout bees dance for forager bees (. ?)

15. Forager bees interpret the dance and go out to get the food (. ?)

16. How do the forager bees understand what the moves mean (? !)

17. How fast the scouts dance tells how far the food is away (. ?)

18. The angle the scouts dance tells where the food is and the number of times the scouts dance tells how much food there is (. ?)

19. What an amazing story (? !)

20. Bees are amazing creatures (. !)

Lesson 2.9 Exclamation Points

Solve It

Choose a word from the box to complete the following sentences so they express strong emotion or surprise. Not all words will be used.

brave	fast	loud	show	tall
cautious	freezing	low	short	tied
close	high	luke warm	soft	warm
far	hot	mild	spicy	won

1. Don't touch the stove; it is _____!

2. Look how _____ that racecar driver took the curve!

3. Please turn down that _____ music!

4. The trapeze performer is so _____ from the ground!

5. This tour through the caves is scary; the walls are too _____!

6. It's cold outside and the water is _____!

7. The astronauts on this mission are so _____!

8. Be careful when you take a bite; the dip is very _____!

9. Yea! Our team _____ the championship!

10. The sequoia tree is so _____!

Try It

Write a paragraph describing an exciting sporting event in which you participated or watched. Use exclamation points where appropriate.

_____

_____

_____

_____

_____

_____

_____

_____

Lesson 2.10 Commas: Series, Direct Address, Multiple Adjectives

Commas have a variety of uses, such as in a series, in direct address, and with multiple adjectives.

Series commas are used when there are at least three items listed in a sentence in a row. The items can be words or phrases. Commas are used to separate them.

> My favorite foods are *pizza, pasta salad, and vegetable burritos.*
> To make a pizza you have to *roll the crust, spread the sauce, and add the toppings.*

Commas are used to separate the name of a person spoken to from the rest of the sentence. This is called a **direct address**.

> *Ken,* please answer the door.   Your delivery has arrived, *Adam.*

When more than one adjective is used to describe a noun, they are separated by commas.

> It was a *warm, breezy* day.

Make sure the adjectives equally modify the noun, and that one item is not actually an adverb modifying the adjective. There is no comma in the following sentence because *hilariously* is an adverb modifying *funny,* not *book.*

> Calvin read a *hilariously funny book.*

Identify It

Write an **S** for series, a **DA** for direct address, or an **MA** for multiple adjectives.

1. _____ Before you leave for school, eat your breakfast, put your homework in your backpack, and brush your teeth.

2. _____ I had a sweet, juicy apple for lunch.

3. _____ Finish your homework before playing video games, Craig.

4. _____ Shawn had a long, hard homework assignment.

5. _____ Chloe, your song in the concert was beautiful.

6. _____ Don't forget your maps, food, and water for your hiking trip.

7. _____ Trevor, wash your hands before dinner.

8. _____ I grabbed a book, paper, and a pencil from my desk when packing for our trip.

9. _____ It was a cold, blustery day.

Lesson 2.10 Commas: Series, Direct Address, Multiple Adjectives

Proof It
Rewrite the following dialogue, adding commas where they are needed.

| ↑ - inserts a comma |

"Reese guess what I'm doing this weekend," said Dani.

"Are you going to play basketball at the school clean your room at home or finish your science report?" answered Reese.

"None of the above, Reese" Dani said grinning. "I'm going to the best brightest show on the planet. My grandparents are taking me to see Cirque du Soleil."

Reese replied, "Isn't that the circus with only human performers?"

"Yep, that's the one," answered Dani. "The brave talented acrobats do all kinds of maneuvers high in the air on ropes. They dance swing and fly through the air."

"I think I even heard that they do some acts underwater!" said Reese.

"They also have hysterically funny clowns," added Dani. "I've heard that sometimes they even spray water on the audience!"

"I've got a nice big surprise for you Reese," beamed Dani. "My grandparents got tickets for you your brother and your sister."

"I hope we're sitting in the front row," shouted Reese, "even if we do get wet!"

Try It
Write six sentences of our own. Write two sentences with series, two with direct addresses, and two with multiple adjectives.

1. _____

2. _____

3. _____

4. _____

5. _____

6. _____

Lesson 2.11 Commas: Combining Sentences (between clauses), Set-Off Dialogue

Simple sentences may become more interesting when they are combined into compound or complex sentences. Sometimes, this means using **commas**.

Use a comma to combine two independent clauses with a coordinate conjunction. The students read three chapters, *and* they answered the questions at the end of each chapter.

When combining an independent clause with a dependent clause (a complex sentence), use a comma. The clauses are connected with a comma and subordinate conjunction.

Although the skies were sunny now, clouds were rolling in.

Commas are used when setting off dialogue from the rest of the sentence.

The salesperson said, *"Our gym has classes in aerobics, kickboxing, and cycling."*

Match It

Draw an arrow to connect the sentences in Column A with the types of sentences in Column B.

Column A	**Column B**
1. Lisa asked, "What instrument do you play in the band?"	compound sentence
	complex sentence
2. The distance is long, but the runner is strong.	
3. Unless the movie is a comedy, I don't think I want to see it.	dialogue

4. The customer asked the contractor, "How much will it cost to remodel the kitchen?"	compound sentence
	complex sentence
5. As long as the designs are good, the clothes will sell well.	dialogue
6. The portrait is modern, yet it has an antique look.	

Lesson 2.11 Commas: Combining Sentences (between clauses), Set-Off Dialogue

Proof It

Proofread the following biography. Add or delete commas as necessary.

 – deletes incorrect letters, words, punctuation
⌄ – inserts a comma

Arthur Ashe

Arthur Ashe was born in Richmond, Virginia in 1943. He started playing tennis, when he was seven years old. Although the field was dominated by white athletes Ashe won many amateur titles in his teenage years. He won a scholarship to UCLA and competed in Wimbledon for the first time during college.

Ashe continued to win many major titles. In 1968 he won the U.S. Open becoming the top male ranked player in the United States Lawn Tennis Association. Until 1973 no African American had been permitted to compete in the South African tournament. Ashe became the first. He went on to win Wimbledon and the World Championship of Tennis. He was the top-ranked tennis player in the world in 1975.

A heart attack in 1979 forced him to retire in 1980. In 1988, Ashe suffered a devastating blow when he discovered he had contracted AIDS from a previous heart operation. Ashe was terminally ill, but he remained an active spokesperson for race relations and AIDS. Arthur Ashe died in February 1993.

Try It

Write three sentences with commas of your own: one in a compound sentence, one in a complex sentence, and one with a quotation.

_____

_____

_____

_____

_____

Lesson 2.12 Commas: Personal Letters and Business Letters

Commas are used in both personal and business letters.

Personal Letters
Commas appear in four of the five parts of the personal letter.

Heading: 2633 Lane Road
                    Meridian, OH 30000
                    June 3, 2014

Salutation: Dear Kelly,

Body: comma usage in sentences

Closing: Your friend,

Business Letters
Commas appear in four of the six parts of the business letter.

Heading: 2200 Meridian Drive
                    Riverside, CA 10000
                    October 10, 2015

Inside address: Ms. Corrine Fifelski, Director
                    Lakeview Sound Design
                    907 Effington Boulevard
                    Boulder, CO 20000

Body: comma usage in sentences

Closing: Sincerely,

Identify It
Read each line from a letter. If it is missing a comma, write an **X** on the line. If not, leave the line blank.

1. _____ 1473 Oliver Drive

2. _____ Dear Tiffany

3. _____ I went to the grocery store book store and shoe store.

4. _____ Your sister,

5. _____ April 17 2004

6. _____ Portland, ME

7. _____ I have experience in customer service and I enjoy meeting new people.

8. _____ All my best

Lesson 2.12 Commas: Personal Letters and Business Letters

Rewrite It

Rewrite the following personal letter. Add all of the required commas in your rewrite.

927 Cobblestone Road
Buffalo NY 50000
September 3 2014

Dear Mimi

    How are you? I hope you had a great summer vacation. I saw something fantastic on my trip to visit my grandparents in Japan. Do you remember studying about World War II in history class? Well I got to see an actual living relic from World War II. In the middle of Tokyo there is a tree that was hit with a bomb. Remarkably, the tree survived! We saw lots of fascinating things on our trip through Japan, but the tree was my favorite. I can't wait to see you on your next trip to Buffalo and show you the pictures. I even brought you back a special souvenir a *maneki neko* cat. This means *beckoning cat,* and it's a lucky charm in Japan.

Your friend

Akira

Lesson 2.13 Quotation Marks

Quotation marks are used to show the exact words of a speaker. The quotation marks are placed before and after the exact words.

> *"Let's go to the movies tonight,"* said Janice. *"The new action adventure was released."*

Quotation marks are also used when a direct quotation is made within a direct quotation. In this case, single quotation marks are used to set off the inside quotation.

> John said, "Miss Robinson clearly said, *'The project is due tomorrow.'*"

Single quotes express what Miss Robinson said. Double quotes express what John said.

Quotation marks are used with some titles. Quotation marks are used with the titles of short stories, poems, songs, and articles in magazines and newspapers.

> *"North Carolina Takes the Championship"* – newspaper article

If a title is quoted within a direct quotation, then single quotation marks are used.

> Melissa said, "Did you read the article *'Saving Our Oceans'* in the magazine?"

Identify It

On the lines, write a **DQ** for direct quote, a **QQ** for quote within quote, a **T** for title, and a **TQ** for title in quote.

1. _____ Sandra shouted, "Our team won the game!"

2. _____ Suzie responded, "I heard the coach say, 'This was my best team ever!'"

3. _____ The magazine <u>Sports Today</u> had an article called "A Winning Season."

4. _____ "What did the article 'A Winning Season' say about our team?" Sandra asked.

5. _____ "The writer of the article thinks we could win the championship," Suzie said.

6. _____ "He said, 'The team is strong offensively and defensively and could go all the way,'" continued Suzie.

7. _____ "This is so exciting!" yelled Sandra.

8. _____ Suzie said, "Let's go check out our newspaper 'Community Times' and see what they had to say!

Lesson 2.13 Quotation Marks

Rewrite It

Rewrite the following list of famous quotations, adding quotation marks where they are needed.

1. Arthur Ashe said, From what we get, we can make a living; what we give, however, makes a life.

   _____

   _____

   _____

2. The most important thing is not to stop questioning, said Albert Einstein.

   _____

   _____

3. Mahatma Ghandi said, The weak can never forgive. Forgiveness is the attribute of the strong.

   _____

   _____

4. Although the world is full of suffering, it is full also of the overcoming of it, said Helen Keller.

   _____

   _____

Try It

Write two sentences of dialogue that include direct quotations by characters. Write two sentences that include a title. Write two direct quotations of your own.

_____

_____

_____

_____

_____

_____

Lesson 2.14 Apostrophes

Apostrophes are used in contractions and to form possessives.

Contractions are shortened forms of words. The words are shortened by leaving out letters. Apostrophes take the place of the omitted letters.

he is = he's   can not = can't

Possessives show possession, or ownership. To form the possessive of a singular noun, add an apostrophe and an **s**.

I'll carry *Harry's* notebook.

To form the possessive of plural nouns ending in **s**, simply add the apostrophe. If the plural noun does not end in an **s**, add both the apostrophe and an **s**.

The *puppies'* guardians are very happy.
The *women's* team has won every game.

Match It

The sentences in Column A contain words with apostrophes. Match these sentences to the types of apostrophes used in Column B. Draw an arrow to make your match.

Column A	Column B
1. Felicia's jacket is in my car.	contraction
2. She's my best friend.	singular possessive
3. The men's shirts are on the second floor.	plural possessive ending in **s**
4. The girls' tickets are at the box office.	plural possessive not ending in **s**

Column A	Column B
5. The parents' cars lined the street.	contraction
6. Patty's blanket is nearly done.	singular possessive
7. The children's toys are in the toy box.	plural possessive ending in **s**
8. Teddy's got the presentation.	plural possessive not ending in **s**

Lesson 2.14 Apostrophes

Complete It
Complete the following sentences by circling the best answer in parentheses.

1. (I'll, Ill) make an appointment first thing in the morning.

2. (Sams', Sam's) bicycle is outside the library.

3. The (books', book's) covers are worn.

4. Do you see the (mooses's, moose's) beautiful antlers?

5. (Don't, Do'nt) turn onto Shipman St.; it's closed.

6. You can buy your (rabbits, rabbit's) food and toys at the shelter's retail shop.

7. We'll pick up our (children's, childrens's) toys.

8. We (shouldn't, should'nt) leave without our umbrellas.

9. Did you see the (movie's, movies) review?

10. The (boys', boy's) helmets are ready to be picked up.

Try It
Write a skit with three or more characters. Use at least three contractions and at least three singular possessives and three plural possessives.

_____

_____

_____

_____

_____

_____

_____

_____

_____

_____

_____

_____

Lesson 2.15 Colons

Colons are used to introduce a series, to set off a clause, for emphasis, in time, and in business letter salutations.

Colons are used to introduce a series in a sentence.
> My favorite vegetables include the following**:** *broccoli, red peppers, and spinach.*

Colons are sometimes used instead of a comma (in more formal cases) to set off a clause.
> The radio announcer said**:** *"The game is postponed due to torrential rains."*

Colons are used to set off a word or phrase for emphasis.
> The skiers got off of the mountain as they expected the worst**:** *an avalanche.*

Colons are used when writing the time.
> Is your appointment at 9**:**00 or 10**:**00?

Business letters use colons in the salutation.
> Dear Miss Massey**:**

Identify It

Identify why the colon is used in each sentence. Write an **S** for series, **C** for clause, **E** for emphasis, **T** for time, or **L** for letter.

1. _____ The teacher said to do the following: read two chapters, answer the questions following each chapter, and write a paragraph about what was read.

2. _____ My alarm goes off at 6:15 A.M.

3. _____ The coach gave us some tips: eat right and train hard.

4. _____ All of my hard training paid off when I saw the sign ahead: Finish.

5. _____ Dear Dr. Brooks:

6. _____ The host said: "Let's eat!"

7. _____ Maya decided to see the movie when the reviewer summed it up in one word: hysterical.

8. _____ The triathlon consisted of three events: swimming, biking, and running.

Lesson 2.16 Semicolons

A **semicolon** is a cross between a period and a comma. Semicolons can be used to join two independent clauses, to separate clauses containing commas, and to separate groups which contain commas.

Semicolons join two independent clauses when a coordinate conjunction is not used.
The city's sounds are loud; I love the excitement.

Semicolons are used to separate clauses when they already contain commas.
After the sun sets, the lights come on; the city is beautiful at night.

Semicolons are also used to separate words or phrases that already contain commas.
Billi's new apartment has a bedroom for her, her sister, and her brother; a laundry room; an exercise room; and a game room.

Rewrite It
Rewrite the following sentences adding semicolons where needed.

1. The insulation in the room wasn't very effective it was freezing.

_____

_____

2. Although we were relieved it didn't rain, we needed it a drought was upon us.

_____

_____

3. They needed equipment to start a business computer monitor printer and furniture, such as desks, chairs, and lamps.

_____

_____

4. Riana has the aptitude for science it is her favorite subject.

_____

_____

5. Since the opening is delayed, we'll shop on Tuesday I'm looking forward to it.

_____

_____

Lesson 2.17 Hyphens

Hyphens are used to divide words, to create new words, and are used between numbers.

Use a hyphen to divide the word between syllables.
>   *beau-ti-ful*   *per-form*

Do not divide one-syllable words with fewer than six letters.
>   *through*   *piece*

Do not divide one letter from the rest of the word.
>   *event-ful*   *not: e-ventful*

Divide syllables after the vowel if the vowel is a syllable by itself.
>   *come-dy*   *not: com-edy*

Divide words with double consonants between the consonants.
>   *swim-ming*   *mir-ror*

Hyphens can be used to create new words when combined with *self, ex,* and *great.*
>   *The pianist was self-taught.*

Hyphens are used between numbers.
>   *twenty-one*

Complete It
Choose the best word in parentheses to complete each sentence.

1. Next year I'll pick an (instru-ment, instr-ument) to play in the band.

2. Julia burned her (ton-gue, tongue) on the hot chocolate.

3. An (o-ceanographer, ocean-ographer) studies the oceans and the plants and animals that live in them.

4. My (ex-coach, excoach) won teacher of the year.

5. The glass holds (thirty two, thirty-two) ounces.

6. The students are raising money for their chosen (char-ity, chari-ty).

7. Armonite would like a (ch-air, chair) for her bedroom.

8. The clock seems to be (run-ning, runn-ing) fast.

9. Richard's (great aunt, great-aunt) bakes the best blackberry pie.

10. Her jersey number is (sixty-four, sixty four).

Lesson 2.18 Parentheses

Parentheses are used to show supplementary material, to set off phrases in a stronger way than commas, and to enclose numbers.

Supplementary material is a word or phrase that gives additional information.
> Theresa's mother *(the dentist)* will speak to our class next week.

Sometimes, words or phrases that might be set off with commas are set off with parentheses instead. It gives the information more emphasis for a stronger phrase.
> Leo's apartment building, *the one with the nice window boxes,* was voted prettiest in the neighborhood.
> Leo's apartment building *(the one with the nice window boxes)* was voted prettiest in the neighborhood.

Parentheses are also used to enclose numbers.
> Jacklyn wants to join the track team because *(1)* it is good exercise, *(2)* she can travel to other schools and cities, and *(3)* she can meet new friends.

Match It
Match the sentences in Column A with the reason why parentheses are used in Column B. Draw an arrow to make your match.

Column A

1. When cooking rice, don't forget to (1) rinse the rice, (2) steam the rice, and (3) eat the rice!

2. The preliminary findings (announced yesterday) are important to the study.

3. The dinosaur bones (a huge discovery) can be seen in the museum.

Column B

supplementary material

set-off with emphasis

enclose numbers

---

4. The orientation (for freshmen) is this weekend.

5. Mac must (1) wash the dishes, (2) do his homework, and (3) get ready for bed.

6. We're setting up our lemonade stand (the one that made $100 last summer) Memorial Day weekend.

supplementary material

set-off with emphasis

enclose numbers

Chapter 3

Lesson 3.1 Tricky Verb Usage

The irregular verbs *bring* and *take* are often confused with each other. When you *bring* something, it is coming in or toward you. When you *take* something, it is moving away.

The forms of *take* are *take* (present), *took* (past), and *taken* (past participle).
The forms of *bring* are *bring* (present), *brought* (past), and *brought* (past participle).

>   The teacher asked her students to *bring* in newspapers.
>
>   Jessica *took* magazines to her sick friend.
>
>   He *had taken* the tickets to the game.

The irregular verbs *lay* and *lie* are also easily confused.

The verb *lay* means *to place*. The forms of the verb *lay* are *lay* (present), *laid* (past), and *laid* (past participle).
The verb *lie* means *to recline*. The forms of the verb *lie* are *lie* (present), *lay* (past), and *lain* (past participle).

>   The teachers *lay* the papers on their desks.
>
>   The kittens *lie* by the window in the sun.
>
>   Yesterday, the kittens *lay* on the blankets in the laundry room.
>
>   Mother *has laid* her briefcase on the same table every night for years.

Complete It
Complete the following sentences by circling the best answers in parentheses.

1. Don't (bring, take) the library books out of the building.

2. Brian and Matt (take, taken) extra water to the baseball games.

3. Last year Lilly (bring, brought) cupcakes on her birthday.

4. Grover (brought, took) six cookies out of the box.

5. Yesterday, we (take, took) blankets and towels to the animal shelter.

6. The children were (bring, brought) home when it started to thunder.

7. Marv was (took, taken) to the hospital when he sprained his ankle.

8. Grandma said, "Aubrey, (bring, take) me a glass of water, please."

9. Charlie (brought, took) seeds from his own garden to plant new flowers in the park.

Lesson 3.1 Tricky Verb Usage

Identify It
Write whether the forms of *lay* and *lie* mean *to place* or *to recline*. Write a **P** for *place* and an **R** for *recline*.

1. _____ Don't lie in the sun without sunscreen!

2. _____ It was unusual that the papers were missing; he had laid them in the same spot every morning.

3. _____ Meagan and Ashley had lain in the sun too long.

4. _____ Jean laid the covers over the plates before the rain hit.

5. _____ Please lay the cups and plates at the end of the table.

6. _____ The toddlers lay down for a long nap earlier today.

7. _____ Don't lay your homework by your computer; you'll forget about it in the morning.

8. _____ Lie on the blanket on the sand.

9. _____ Barbara laid her blanket near the bed.

10. _____ Maggie lay down for a quick nap yesterday.

Try It
Write six sentences of your own. Use various forms of the verbs *lie, lay, bring,* and *take*.

1. _____

2. _____

3. _____

4. _____

5. _____

6. _____

Lesson 3.2 Adjectives and Adverbs

Adverbs modify verbs, adjectives, and other adverbs. Some adverbs are easily confused with adjectives.

Bad is an adjective, and *badly* is an adverb.

   That was a *bad* concert; the music was too loud. (*bad* modifies the noun *concert*)
   Tyler drives *badly*; he almost ran that stop sign. (*badly* modifies the verb *drives*)

Good is an adjective, and *well* is an adverb.

   We watched a *good* game. (*good* modifies the noun *game*)
   Both teams played *well*. (*well* modifies the verb *played*)

The word *already* is an adverb. It answers the question *when*.

   It was morning and *already* time to leave.

The phrase *all ready* means *completely ready*.

   The team was *all ready* to leave.

Complete It

Circle the correct word in parentheses. Then, underline the word it modifies (except for numbers 5 and 6) and write what part of speech it is on the lines after each sentence.

1. We threw out the (bad, badly) bruised orange. _____

2. Celina played (good, well) and won her match. _____

3. I just finished a really (good, well) book; I couldn't put it down. _____

4. The instructions were (bad, badly), and we got lost. _____

5. By the time the bus picked us up we were (all ready, already) late.

6. If everyone in the class is (all ready, already) to go, we'll line up at the door.

7. It was a (good, well) recipe; I'll make that again. _____

8. If our chorus sings (good, well), we'll advance to the semifinals. _____

9. Daryl (bad, badly) sang the last song. _____

10. Ally had a (bad, badly) excuse for not playing in the game. _____

Lesson 3.2 Adjectives and Adverbs

Rewrite It

Rewrite the following letter, correcting the use of the words *bad*, *badly*, *good*, *well*, *all ready*, and *already* as necessary.

Dear Grandpa,

    I'm sorry you couldn't make it to my soccer game last Saturday. I played very good. Our team had been playing bad until a couple of weeks ago. We all got together and watched the World Cup on television. Teams from all over the world compete to determine a world champion. The United States' women's team played so good in the first Women's World Cup that they won the tournament. Our team had all ready lost several games when we watched the World Cup. We needed some well motivation. It worked. We won our next three games. Now, we're already to go to the championships.

                Love,
                Hannah

_____

_____

_____

_____

_____

_____

_____

_____

_____

Try It

Write six sentences of your own. Write a sentence using each of the following words: *bad*, *badly*, *good*, *well*, *all ready*, *already*.

_____

_____

_____

_____

_____

_____

Lesson 3.3 Negatives and Double Negatives

A **negative** sentence states the opposite. Negative words include *not, no, never, nobody, nowhere, nothing, barely, hardly,* and *scarcely;* and contractions containing the word *not*.

Double negatives happen when two negative words are used in the same sentence. Don't use double negatives; it will make your sentence positive again, and it is poor grammar.

Negative: We *won't* go anywhere without you.
Double negative: We *won't* go *nowhere* without you.

Negative: I *never* like to ride my bike after dark.
Double negative: I *don't never* like to ride my bike after dark.

Negative: I can *hardly* wait until baseball season.
Double negative: I *can't hardly* wait until baseball season.

Rewrite It

Rewrite the following sentences. Correct the sentence if it contains a double negative.

1. I love breakfast; I can't imagine not skipping it.

_____

2. I can't scarcely believe I made it all the way down the slope without falling.

_____

3. Samantha doesn't never like to wear her coat outside.

_____

4. The class hasn't received their report cards yet.

_____

5. I'm not going nowhere until it stops raining.

_____

6. Paul has barely nothing to contribute to the argument.

_____

7. Sarah never reveals her secrets.

_____

8. I don't think nobody can make it to the event early.

_____

Lesson 3.4 Synonyms and Antonyms

Synonyms are words that have the same, or almost the same, meaning. Using synonyms can help you avoid repeating words and can make your writing more interesting.

clever, smart   *reply, answer*   *wreck, destroy*   *applaud, clap*

Antonyms are words that have opposite meanings.

wide, narrow   *accept, decline*   *break, repair*   *borrow, lend*

Find It

Think of an antonym for each word in the box. Then, find it in the word search puzzle. Words may be written horizontally or vertically, backward or forward.

disagree	war	north	wise
shallow	success	remember	absent

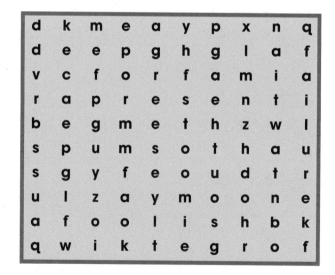

Lesson 3.4 Synonyms and Antonyms

Match It
Read each set of words below. Circle the two words in each set that are synonyms.

1. pardon   forget   forgive   ordinary

2. damage   mend   repair   mock

3. likely   unlikely   probable   rarely

4. depart   leave   arrival   mingle

5. heal   insist   injure   wound

6. accept   decline   formula   refuse

7. remorse   regret   replace   joy

8. thin   obese   slender   flexible

Rewrite It
Rewrite each sentence below. Use a synonym for **boldface** words and an antonym for underlined words.

1. The police officer had to **pursue** the **criminal**, who **hopped** in his car and sped away.

   _____

2. Harriet enjoys cooking with foods that have bold flavors.

   _____

3. When Enzo **finished** his book, he felt quite satisfied with the ending.

   _____

4. Dr. Williams asked the **nervous** little girl to exhale slowly.

   _____

Lesson 3.5 Analogies

An **analogy** is a comparison between two pairs of words. To complete an analogy, figure out how the pairs of words are related.

      Coop is to *chicken* as *hive* is to *bee.*
      A coop is a home for a chicken, just as a hive is a home for a bee.

      Petal is to *flower* as *wing* is to *bird.*
      A petal is part of a flower, just as a wing is part of a bird.

      Excited is to *bored* as *silence* is to *noise.*
      Excited is the opposite of bored, just as silence is the opposite of noise.

Complete It
Complete each analogy below with a word from the box.

fish	mice	forest	drive	ten
peddle	golf	necklace	page	apple

1. Spaghetti is to noodle as _____ is to fruit.

2. Neck is to _____ as finger is to ring.

3. _____ is to book as blade is to fan.

4. Pedal is to _____ as write is to right.

5. Sand is to beach as tree is to _____.

6. Six is to twelve as _____ is to twenty.

7. _____ is to mouse as horses is to horse.

8. Bat is to baseball as club is to _____.

9. _____ is to car as sail is to boat.

10. Flock is to geese as school is to _____.

Lesson 3.5 Analogies

Identify It
Underline the word from each pair that completes the analogy.

1. Teacher is to (school, books) as lifeguard is to pool.

2. (Bark, Tail) is to dog as neigh is to horse.

3. Shy is to (bold, timid) as guest is to visitor.

4. Orlando is to Florida as (Wisconsin, Detroit) is to Michigan.

5. King is to (queen, kingdom) as prince is to princess.

6. Stove is to (kitchen, cook) as tub is to bathroom.

7. Liz is to Elizabeth as Danny is to (Tommy, Daniel).

8. (Spring, Fall) is to winter as lunch is to dinner.

9. Copper is to penny as wool is to (sheep, sweater).

10. Four is to quarter as (one, five) is to fifth.

Try It
Follow the directions to write your own analogies.

1. Write an analogy in which the words are synonyms.

   _____

2. Write an analogy that shows a part-to-whole relationship.

   _____

3. Write an analogy that shows a numerical relationship.

   _____

Lesson 3.6 Homophones

Homophones are words that sound the same but have different spellings and different meanings. There are hundreds of homophones in the English language.

> *cereal* - food made from grain
> *serial* - of a series

If you are unsure about which homophone to use, look up the meanings in a dictionary.

Identify It
Circle the correct homophone in each sentence.

1. My teacher will (council, counsel) me on what subjects to take next year.

2. This material has a smooth texture but that one is more (course, coarse).

3. The television program is going to be shown as a (cereal, serial) once a week for six weeks.

4. The (council, counsel) meets every Wednesday evening to discuss city plans.

5. I like to ride my bike on the scenic (course, coarse) along the river.

6. My favorite breakfast is a big bowl of (cereal, serial).

Match It
Fill in the blanks in the sentences in Column A with a homophone from Column B.

Column A	Column B
1. I bid one _____ more and won the item.	overseas
2. Deb has a beautiful _____ on her finger.	oversees
3. The sailor was stationed _____.	ring
4. The flowers have a beautiful _____.	wring
5. _____ out the dish cloth over the sink.	cent
6. Mr. Morgan _____ metal production.	scent
7. David _____ the envelope yesterday.	sent
8. My oldest dog _____ feeding time for all of my pets.	overseas
9. I would like to travel _____ for a semester.	oversees
10. It was raining so hard I had to _____ out my shirt.	ring
11. Did I hear someone _____ the doorbell?	wring
12. The letter was _____ to the wrong address.	cent
13. The item costs three dollars and one _____.	scent
14. The perfume has a strong _____.	sent

Lesson 3.7 Multiple-Meaning Words

Multiple-meaning words, or **homographs**, are words that are spelled the same but have different meanings. They may also sometimes have different pronunciations.

The word *bow* can mean "a looped piece of ribbon or cloth," or it can mean "to bend at the waist."

> Lexi put a *bow* on top of her gift for Chandler.
> "Be sure you *bow* to the audience at the end of the performance."

Find It

Read each sentence. Then, circle the definition that describes the meaning of the underlined word as it is used in the sentence.

1. Before leaving the house, my mother always makes sure her <u>compact</u> is in her purse.

    a. dense and tightly packed

    b. a small case with a mirror

2. Juan added vanilla <u>extract</u> to the cookie dough.

    a. take out

    b. concentrated form

3. The <u>proceeds</u> from the auction will be used to provide art scholarships.

    a. money from a sale

    b. moves forward

4. Officer Wilkins talked calmly with the man who was <u>upset</u> about the accident.

    a. spilled or overturned

    b. distressed or anxious

5. The school board was <u>inclined</u> to agree with Mr. Radkey's ideas about a sales tax.

    a. tended to feel a certain way

    b. sloping

6. The nurse held a <u>compress</u> against the bruise on Nina's leg.

    a. a cloth pad

    b. push together

Lesson 3.7 Multiple-Meaning Words

Identify It

Read each pair of sentences. Circle **N** for noun or **V** for verb to identify the part of speech for the word in **boldface**. Each pair of sentences will have two different answers.

1. Horace dusted the **display** of books in the store's front window. **N   V**

   The schools in our district **display** student artwork throughout their halls. **N   V**

2. Please **number** your answer 1 through 10. **N   V**

   Dr. Patel analyzed the **number** of tadpoles living in the pond. **N   V**

3. After the movie, Preston and Kelly debated whether the **remake** was better than the original. **N   V**

   Sonja had to **remake** the pie after she discovered one of the kittens eating it.

   N   V

4. Louisa made the basket, **evening** the score and making the crowd go wild. **N   V**

   Later this **evening**, we will go to my grandparents' house for a party. **N   V**

5. The reporter explained that the **recall** only affected certain brands of baby food. **N   V**

   Do you **recall** that time when we got a flat tire on our way to zoo? **N   V**

Rewrite It

Read each sentence below. Then, write a new sentence using a different meaning for the underlined word. Use a dictionary if you need help.

1. The book's <u>content</u> is too difficult for children under five years old to understand.

   _____

2. The water contains <u>minute</u> amounts of chlorine and fluoride.

   _____

3. King Alfred ordered his <u>subjects</u> to work through the night to finish the bridge.

   _____

4. Brynna rides her <u>moped</u> near the curb so cars can safely pass her if they need to.

   _____

5. A <u>combine</u> moved slowly back and forth across the acres of wheat.

   _____

6. Several <u>inserts</u> fell to the floor as Mikki took a magazine from the rack.

   _____

Lesson 3.8 Connotations and Denotations

A word's **denotation** is its actual, literal meaning. It is the meaning you would find if you looked the word up in a dictionary.

A word's **connotation** is the meaning associated with the word. The connotation may be more emotional, or tied to an idea or feeling about the word. Connotations can be positive, negative, or neutral.

For example, the words *house*, *home*, *shack*, and *residence* all mean approximately the same thing. Their denotation is "a place where people live." The connotation of these words, however, is different. *House* and *residence* both have a neutral connotation. *Home* has a positive connotation—it sounds cozy and reassuring. *Shack*, on the other hand, has a negative connotation—it sounds rundown and shabby.

Identify It

For each set of words below, write the general denotation (or literal definition) on the top line. On the line beside each word, write **P** for positive connotation, **N** for neutral connotation, and **NG** for negative connotation.

1. denotation: _____

   ask _____   demand _____   request _____

2. denotation: _____

   confident _____   pushy _____

3. denotation: _____

   slender _____   skinny _____

4. denotation: _____

   odd _____   special _____   unique _____

5. denotation: _____

   curious _____   nosy _____   interested _____

6. denotation: _____

   borrow _____   steal _____

7. denotation: _____

   cheap _____   thrifty _____   stingy _____

Lesson 3.8 Connotations and Denotations

Match It

Match each word with another word that has a similar denotation but different connotation. Write the letter of the matching word on the line.

1. _____ mimic   **a.** scent

2. _____ childish   **b.** accumulate

3. _____ odor   **c.** depart

4. _____ limit   **d.** mock

5. _____ dog   **e.** hungry

6. _____ escape   **f.** restrict

7. _____ starving   **g.** mutt

8. _____ collect   **h.** childlike

Try It

Write a sentence for each word below. The words in each pair have similar denotations but different connotations.

1. inexpensive _____

    cheap _____

2. puny _____

    small _____

3. proud _____

    boastful _____

4. smile _____

    smirk _____

5. soggy _____

    moist _____

6. carefree _____

    irresponsible _____

Lesson 3.9 Figures of Speech: Similes, Metaphors, and Personification

Complete It

Complete each sentence below with a simile.

1. The jet soared through the air like _____ .

2. The kitten's fur felt soft as _____ .

3. Mr. Robinson's laugh rang out like _____ .

4. The rooster stood on the fence and crowed like _____ .

5. After the spring storm, the forest smelled as fresh as _____ .

6. Maya tripped as she stepped onto the stage, and her face turned as red as
_____ .

7. With each step, Rowan's boots crunched the snow, sounding like
_____ .

8. Hannah's new scissors cut through fabric like _____ .

Try It

Imagine you have been shipwrecked on a deserted island. Write a short paragraph describing the sights, sounds, smells, and feelings you might experience. Include at least two similes in your paragraph.

_____

_____

_____

_____

_____

_____

_____

_____

Lesson 4.1 Writer's Guide: Prewriting

The five steps of the writing process are **prewriting**, **drafting**, **revising**, **proofreading**, and **publishing**.

Prewriting, the first stage of the writing process, involves planning and organizing. This is the stage where you get the ideas for your paper and start plotting it out.

When you prewrite, you:

- Think of ideas for your topic that are not too narrow or too broad. Write down your chosen ideas.

- Select your favorite topic, the one you think you can write about the best.

- Write down anything that comes to your mind about your chosen topic. Don't worry about grammar and spelling at this stage. This is called *freewriting*.

- Organize your information the way you might organize it in your paper. Use a graphic organizer. Graphic organizers visually represent the layout and ideas for a written paper. Graphic organizers include spider maps, Venn diagrams, story boards, network trees, and outlines.

- Use your graphic organizer to find out what information you already know and what information you need to learn more about.

Prewriting Example

Assignment: biography of a hero

Topic ideas: Martin Luther King, Jr., Eleanor Roosevelt, Jesse Owens, Cleveland Amory, Lance Armstrong, Rachel Carson

Freewriting of selected topic: Cleveland Amory hero of animals. Author. Founder of the Fund for Animals. Wrote The Cat Who Came for Christmas. Read Black Beauty as a child and wanted a ranch for rescued animals. Established Black Beauty Ranch for rescued animals.

Graphic organizer:

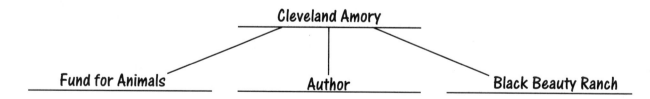

Lesson 4.2 Writer's Guide: Drafting

Drafting involves writing your rough draft. Don't worry too much about grammar and spelling. Write down all of your thoughts about the subject, based on the structure of your graphic organizer.

When you draft, you:

- Write an **introduction** with a topic sentence. Get your readers' attention by stating a startling statistic or asking a question. Explain the purpose of your writing.

- Write the **body** of your paper. Use your graphic organizer to decide how many paragraphs will be included in your paper. Write one paragraph for each idea.

- Write your **conclusion**. Your conclusion will summarize your paper.

Drafting Example

My hero was a hero: a hero to animals. Cleveland Amory (1917-1998) was an author, an animal advocate, and an animal rescuer. Reading Black Beauty as a child inspired a dream for Amory. Cleveland Amory made his dream a reality.

Amory founded The Fund for Animals. The Fund for Animals is an animal advocacy group that campaigns for animal protection. Amory served as its president, without pay, until his death in 1998. Cleveland Amory was an editor. He was an editor for The Saturday Evening Post. He served in World War II. After world war II, he wrote history books that studied society. He was a commentator on The Today Show, a critic for TV guide, a columnist for Saturday Review. Amory especially loved his own cat, Polar Bear, who inspired him to write three instant best-selling books: The Cat Who Came for Christmas, The Cat and the Curmudgeon, and The Best Cat Ever.

When Amory read Black Beauty as a child. When he read Black Beauty, he dreamed of place where animals could roam free and live in caring conditions. The dream is real at Black Beauty Ranch, a sanctuary for abused and abandoned animals The ranch's 1,620 acres serve as home for hundreds of animals, including elephants, horses, burros, ostriches, chimpanzees, and many more. Black Beauty Ranch takes in unwanted, abused, neglected, abandoned, and rescued domestic and exotic animals.

Cleveland Amory is my hero because he is a hero. He worked to make his dreams realities. His best-selling books, the founding of The Fund for Animals, and the opening of Black Beauty Ranch are the legacy of his dreams. Words from Anna Sewell's Black Beauty, the words that inspired Cleveland Amory, are engraved at the entrance to Black Beauty Ranch: "I have nothing to fear; and here my story ends. My troubles are all over, and I am at home." Cleveland Amory died on October 15, 1998. He is buried at Black Beauty Ranch, next to his beloved cat, Polar Bear.

Lesson 4.3 Writer's Guide: Revising

Revising is the time to stop and think about what you have already written. It is time to rewrite.

When you revise, you:

- Add or change words.
- Delete unnecessary words or phrases.
- Move text around.
- Improve the overall flow of your paper.

Revising Example (body of paper)

Cleveland Amory did more than just write about the animals he loved.
                                        in 1967   one of the world's most active
  ^Amory founded The Fund for Animals. The Fund for Animals is an animal advocacy
                    rights and
group that campaigns for animal protection. Amory served as its president, without
                  Amory extended his devotion to animals with Black Beauty Ranch.
                              started his writing career as
pay, until his death in 1998. Cleveland Amory was an editor. He was an editor for The
                                                    serving in
Saturday Evening Post. He served in World War II. After world war II, he wrote history
                                                      ^
books that studied society. He was a commentator on The Today Show, a critic for
                            Amory's love of animals, as well as great affection for
TV guide, a columnist for Saturday Review. Amory especially loved his own cat, Polar
            led
Bear, who inspired him to write three instant best-selling books: The Cat Who Came for

Christmas, The Cat and the Curmudgeon, and The Best Cat Ever.

        Cleveland Amory made his childhood dream come true in 1979 when he
              opened Black Beauty Ranch in Texas.   H
        When Amory read Black Beauty as a child. When he read Black Beauty, he
                                            ^
dreamed of place where animals could roam free and live in caring conditions. The
      for hundreds of
dream is real at Black Beauty Ranch, a sanctuary for abused and abandoned animals
                                      6
The ranch's 1,620 acres serve as home for hundreds of animals, including elephants,
                                          ^
                                                          animals
horses, burros, ostriches, chimpanzees, and many more. Black Beauty Ranch takes
                                                        ^
in unwanted, abused, neglected, abandoned, and rescued domestic and exotic

animals.

Lesson 4.4 Writer's Guide: Proofreading

Proofreading is the time to look for more technical errors.

When you proofread, you:

- Check spelling.
- Check grammar.
- Check punctuation.

Proofreading Example (body of paper after revision)

Cleveland Amory started his writing career as an editor for <u>The Saturday Evening</u>
<u>Post</u>. After serving in <u>w</u>orld <u>w</u>ar II, he wrote history books that studied society. He was
a commentator on <u>The Today Show</u>, a critic for <u>TV</u> <u>g</u>uide , a columnist for <u>Saturday</u>
<u>Review</u>. Amory's love of animals, as well as great affection for his own cat, Polar Bear,
led him to three instant best-selling books: <u>The Cat Who Came for Christmas</u>, <u>The Cat</u>
<u>and the Curmudgeon</u>, and <u>The Best Cat Ever</u>.

Cleveland Amory did more than just write about the animals he loved. Amory
founded The Fund for Animals in 1967. The Fund for Animals is one of the world's most
active animal advocacy group that campaigns for animal rights and protection.
Amory served as its president, without pay, until his death in 1998. Amory extended his
devotion to animals with Black Beauty Ranch.

Cleveland Amory made his childhood dream come true in 1979 when he opened
Black Beauty Ranch in Texas. He dreamed of place where animals could roam free
and live in caring conditions. The dream is real for hundreds of unwanted, abused,
neglected, abandoned, and rescued domestic and exotic animals at Black Beauty
Ranch. The ranch's 1,620 acres serve as home for elephants, horses, burros, ostriches,
chimpanzees, and many more animals.

Lesson 4.5 Writer's Guide: Publishing

Publishing is the fifth and final stage of the writing process. Write your final copy and decide how you want to publish your work. Here is a list of some ideas:

- Read your paper to family and classmates.

- Illustrate and hang class papers in a "Hall of Fame" in your class or school.

- Publish your work in a school or community newspaper or magazine.

Publishing (compare to the other three versions to see how it has improved)

Biography of a Hero: Cleveland Amory

My hero was a hero: a hero to animals. Cleveland Amory (1917-1998) was an author, an animal advocate, and an animal rescuer. Reading <u>Black Beauty</u> as a child inspired a dream for Amory. Cleveland Amory made his dream a reality.

Cleveland Amory started his writing career as an editor for <u>The Saturday Evening Post</u>. After serving in World War II, Amory wrote history books that studied society. He was a commentator on <u>The Today Show</u>, a critic for <u>TV Guide</u>, and a columnist for <u>Saturday Review</u>. Amory's love of animals, as well as great affection for his own cat Polar Bear, led him to three instant best-selling books: <u>The Cat Who Came for Christmas</u>, <u>The Cat and the Curmudgeon</u>, and <u>The Best Cat Ever</u>.

Cleveland Amory did more than just write about the animals he loved. Amory founded The Fund for Animals in 1967. The Fund for Animals is one of the world's most active animal advocacy groups that campaigns for animal rights and protection. Amory served as its president, without pay, until his death in 1998. Amory extended his devotion to animals with Black Beauty Ranch.

Cleveland Amory made his childhood dream come true in 1979 when he opened Black Beauty Ranch in Texas. He dreamed of a place where animals could roam free and live in caring conditions. The dream is real for hundreds of unwanted, abused, neglected, abandoned, and rescued domestic and exotic animals at Black Beauty Ranch. The ranch's 1,620 acres serve as home for elephants, horses, burros, ostriches, chimpanzees, and many more animals.

Cleveland Amory is my hero because he is a hero. He worked to make his dreams realities. His best-selling books, the founding of The Fund for Animals, and the opening of Black Beauty Ranch are the legacy of his dreams. Words from Anna Sewell's <u>Black Beauty</u>, the words that inspired Cleveland Amory, are engraved at the entrance to Black Beauty Ranch: "I have nothing to fear; and here my story ends. My troubles are all over, and I am at home." Cleveland Amory died on October 15, 1998. He is buried at Black Beauty Ranch, next to his beloved cat, Polar Bear.

Lesson 4.6 Writer's Guide: Evaluating Writing

When you are evaluating your own writing and the writing of others, being a critic is a good thing.

You can learn a lot about how you write by reading and rereading papers you have written. As you continue to write, your techniques will improve. You can look at previous papers and evaluate them. How would you change them to improve them knowing what you know now?

You can also look at the writing of others: classmates, school reporters, newspaper and magazine writers, and authors. Evaluate their writing, too. You can learn about different styles from reading a variety of written works. Be critical with their writing. How would you improve it?

Take the points covered in the Writer's Guide and make a checklist. You can use this checklist to evaluate your writing and others' writing, too. Add other items to the checklist as you come across them or think of them.

Evaluation Checklist

❑ Write an introduction with a topic sentence that will get your readers' attention. Explain the purpose of your writing.

❑ Write the body with one paragraph for each idea.

❑ Write a conclusion that summarizes the paper, stating the main points.

❑ Add or change words.

❑ Delete unnecessary words or phrases.

❑ Move text around.

❑ Improve the overall flow of your paper.

❑ Check spelling.

❑ Check grammar.

❑ Check punctuation.

❑ _____

❑ _____

❑ _____

Lesson 4.7 Writer's Guide: Writing Process Practice

The following pages may be used to practice the writing process.

Prewriting

Assignment: _____

_____

Topic ideas: _____

_____

_____

Freewriting of selected topic: _____

_____

_____

_____

_____

_____

_____

_____

_____

_____

_____

_____

_____

Graphic Organizer:

Lesson 4.7 Writer's Guide: Writing Process Practice

Drafting

_____

_____

_____

_____

_____

_____

_____

_____

_____

_____

_____

_____

_____

_____

_____

_____

_____

_____

_____

_____

_____

_____

_____

_____

_____

_____

_____

_____

Lesson 4.7 Writer's Guide: Writing Process Practice

Revising

_____

_____

_____

_____

_____

_____

_____

_____

_____

_____

_____

_____

_____

_____

_____

_____

_____

_____

_____

_____

_____

_____

_____

_____

_____

_____

Lesson 4.7 Writer's Guide: Writing Process Practice

Proofreading

_____

_____

_____

_____

_____

_____

_____

_____

_____

_____

_____

_____

_____

_____

_____

_____

_____

_____

_____

_____

_____

_____

_____

_____

_____

_____

_____

_____

_____

_____

_____

_____

_____

_____

Lesson 4.7 Writer's Guide: Writing Process Practice

Publishing

Final Draft: Include illustrations, photographs, graphic aids, etc.

_____

_____

_____

_____

_____

_____

_____

_____

_____

_____

_____

_____

_____

_____

_____

_____

_____

_____

_____

_____

_____

_____

_____

_____

_____

_____

_____

SPECTRUM®

Reading

JBall

Have you ever been to a baseball game in another country or watched one on television?

1 Alex and Emily Godfrey had been in Japan with their parents for nearly a week. They were there to visit their mother's old college roommate, who had moved to Japan after college to teach English. She had planned to come home after a few years, but she had fallen in love with the country and with the man who would eventually be her husband.

2 "What's our plan for the afternoon?" asked Alex after lunch one day.

3 "Well," said Mr. Ito, "we have tickets for a 4:00 baseball game. How does that sound?"

4 "I had no idea baseball was popular in Japan," replied Alex.

5 "Dad takes us to professional games a few times a year at home," said Emily. "Alex and I keep a list of cities we've visited where we have had a chance to go to a game. I had no idea that Tokyo would ever be on our list!"

6 The Itos and the Godfreys prepared for the afternoon's events. Just a few hours later, they found themselves standing inside the stadium among a crowd of excited fans.

7 "What are the names of the teams that are playing today?" asked Alex, looking around curiously.

8 "The home team is the Yakult Swallows. They will be playing the Hiroshima Toyo Carp," said Mrs. Ito. "Baseball isn't my cup of tea, but this promises to be a good game."

9 The two families found their seats in the bleachers. Alex and Emily grinned as they listened to all the noisemakers around them. Some people were hitting together plastic bats, and others were yelling through megaphones that looked as though they had been hinged together.

10 "Are those cheerleaders?" asked Emily. She was referring to a group of men on the ball field who led the crowd in chants and cheers.

11 Mrs. Ito nodded, "I forget that Americans don't have cheerleaders for baseball games. It also probably seems unusual that they're all men. That's just one of the differences between American and Japanese baseball culture."

12 Once the game began, Emily and Alex became quickly engrossed. The game itself didn't seem much different at all from the American baseball games they had attended. They were surprised, though, to see people waving American flags from time to time.

13 Mr. Ito explained, "Japanese teams are each allowed to have three foreign players. When American players come up to bat, their fans show support by waving your country's flag."

14 In between innings, Mrs. Ito bought Alex and Emily a snack. Some vendors sold pretzels, popcorn, and hot dogs, but Alex and Emily decided to try one of the Japanese alternatives. With Mrs. Ito's help, they selected *yakisoba*, noodles flavored with ginger and soy sauce.

15 At the end of the game, the Godfreys and the Itos piled back into the car to head home. Alex and Emily were tired, but their minds were racing with all they had seen that day.

16 "Did you have a good day, kids?" asked Mrs. Godfrey, turning to Alex and Emily.

17 They nodded. "I wish we could go to JBall games at home, too," said Emily. "After today, I have a feeling that American baseball may never be quite as interesting again."

I. Why were the Godfreys in Japan?

_____

2. What do you think Emily meant when she said, "American baseball may never be quite as interesting again"?

_____

_____

3. What is one way American and Japanese baseball are similar? What is one way they are different?

_____

_____

4. Do you think that Alex and Emily will go to another JBall game if they have a chance? Why or why not?

_____

_____

_____

Circle the word that best completes each sentence.

5. Alex and Emily decide to try food that they would not be _____ to find at an American game.
allowed   likely   impressed

6. The Godfreys are _____ to learn how American and Japanese baseball are different.
curious   refusing   apprehensive

7. Noisemakers are a popular _____ at Japanese baseball games.
explanation   resource   custom

An **idiom** is a group of words that has a special meaning. For example, the idiom *hit the hay* means *to go to bed*. Write the idiom from paragraph 8 on the line next to its meaning.

8. something of interest; something a person enjoys _____

9. Would you enjoy attending a sporting event in another country? Explain why or why not.

_____

_____

_____

Yakyu

Who is Sadahara Oh, and why is he so famous in the world of baseball?

1   What could be more American than baseball? It was one of the earliest sports played in America, created during the mid-1800s. But the Japanese have been playing for nearly as long. In fact, baseball's popularity in Japan rivals its popularity here in the United States.

2   In the early 1870s, Horace Wilson, an American professor living in Tokyo, introduced baseball to his students. They loved it, calling the game *yakyu*, which means *field ball*. It quickly caught on with students all over the country. Japanese leaders also embraced baseball because they thought that it contained elements that were already part of Japanese culture. For instance, baseball's focus on the mental competition between pitcher and hitter was similar to the one-on-one competitions of martial arts.

3   By the early 1900s, amateur baseball leagues had been established in secondary schools and colleges throughout Japan. To this day, the enthusiasm for college baseball in Japan is equivalent to the excitement people have for college football or college basketball's March Madness in the United States.

4   To make baseball even more popular, American teams regularly toured Japan in the early 1900s and played exhibition games against the local amateurs. Top American baseball stars like Babe Ruth and Lou Gehrig came to Japan in the 1930s and played against the top Japanese college teams. The Americans won all 17 games they played, but baseball fever swept the whole country. A professional Japanese baseball league was formed in 1936. The Great Tokyo baseball club—known today as the Yomiuri Giants—was the first team, but it was soon joined by six others.

5   Like so many other things around the world, World War II interrupted Japanese baseball when almost all of the players became soldiers. After the war, the United States occupied Japan. The military commanders who were in charge recognized that baseball was an important part of Japanese culture, so they encouraged the professional teams to reform and continue playing. By 1955, with the help of television, professional baseball in Japan became bigger than ever.

6   The Yomiuri Giants are not just the oldest pro team in Japan; they may also be the greatest. From 1965 through 1973, the Giants won nine consecutive national championships, partly because of the legendary player Sadahara Oh. The surname *Oh* means *king*, and he certainly was the king of baseball in Japan. Among his many incredible statistics, Oh holds the world record for career home runs—868! That is more than Hank Aaron, Babe Ruth, Mark McGuire, Barry Bonds, and Sammy Sosa.

7   Japanese professional players have also come to the United States and played in Major League Baseball, setting records here as well. Current players include the New York Yankees' Ichiro Suzuki. In 2004, Suzuki broke a baseball record for hitting that had stood for more than 80 years! Kazuhiro Sasaki, who played for the Seattle Mariners, was named the American League Rookie of the Year in 2000, and Hideo Nomo of the Los Angeles Dodgers was MLB's 1995 Rookie of the Year.

1. Check the sentence that best states the main idea of the passage.

_____ Although baseball is thought of as an American sport, there are many fans and talented players of Japanese baseball, or yakyu.

_____ American teams toured Japan in the early 1900s and played exhibition games against the local amateurs.

_____ Horace Wilson brought baseball to Japan in the 1870s.

2. Number the events below to show the order in which they happened.

_____ Horace Wilson introduced baseball to his students.

_____ World War II interrupted Japanese baseball.

_____ The Giants won nine consecutive national championships.

_____ Babe Ruth and Lou Gehrig played baseball in Japan.

3. Check the phrase that best describes the author's purpose.

_____ to inform

_____ to entertain

_____ to persuade

4. Why is Sadahara Oh's last name so appropriate?

_____

5. Why did Japan's leaders like baseball?

_____

_____

6. What is the literal meaning of *yakyu* in Japanese?

_____

7. During World War II, many of the players became _____

_____

Experimental Appetites

What kinds of foods from other cultures have you tried?

1   Alex and Emily sat at a table with their parents and Mr. and Mrs. Ito. Alex loved to try new foods. Alex had eaten at Asian restaurants at home several times, but he was sure that the meals he'd eat in Japan would be much more authentic.

2   Emily wasn't as confident as Alex was about trying new foods. Alex would eat practically anything and not think twice about it. Emily liked to be able to identify everything on her plate. She was willing to try new things, but she lacked Alex's enthusiasm for experimenting with new foods.

3   "Have you looked at the menu yet?" asked Alex and Emily's dad.

4   "Dad, it's in Japanese," said Alex.

5   Mr. Godfrey grinned. "That shouldn't stop you from looking at it," he said. "Maybe Mrs. Ito can give us some suggestions."

6   "Of course I can," she said, scanning the menu. "I thought we could start off with some sushi. Do you like fish?" she asked Alex and Emily.

7   "I do," replied Alex promptly.

8   Emily looked uncertainly at her parents. "I like some kinds of fish," she said.

9   "She likes fish that doesn't have a strong fishy taste to it," added her mom helpfully.

10   "We'll order several different kinds," decided Mrs. Ito. "Then, you'll have a chance to sample them and decide what you like." Mrs. Ito gave their order to the waiter. Then, she turned back to Alex and Emily.

11   "Do you know how sushi is made?" Mrs. Ito asked Alex and Emily. They shook their heads. "Well, the sushi chef begins with a very thin sheet of seaweed."

12   "We're going to eat seaweed?" asked Alex excitedly.

13   Mr. Ito smiled. "You wouldn't even know it was seaweed if we didn't tell you," he said.

14   Mrs. Ito continued, "The chef spreads a layer of sticky rice over the seaweed. Then, he adds different vegetables and fish. He rolls everything up inside the seaweed and slices it into little disks."

15   A few minutes later, the waiter returned with a wooden board that held several different types of sushi.

16   "You might want to try this kind first," Mr. Ito told Emily. "It has cucumber and avocado in it but no fish." The Itos showed the Godfreys how to pick up the sushi using chopsticks.

17   "What's this?" asked Alex, pointing to a small mound of something green.

18   "Sushi is often served with pickled ginger and a very spicy condiment called wasabi. The green stuff you were asking about is the wasabi. If you decide to try some, you'll probably want to use a very small amount at first."

19   No one at the table was surprised to learn that Alex loved the sushi. He even found that he liked wasabi, as long as he was careful to use only a small speck of it on each bite.

20   "What do you think, Emily?" asked Mrs. Godfrey after a few moments.

21   Emily picked up another piece of sushi with her chopsticks. "I love it," she said. "I think we're going to need to find a restaurant at home that serves sushi," she added.

22   Mr. and Mrs. Godfrey laughed. "Our kids are turning into very well-seasoned eaters!" said Mr. Godrey.

A fact is something that is known to be true. An opinion is what a person believes. It may or may not be true. Write **F** before the sentences that are facts. Write **O** before the sentences that are opinions.

1. _____ Sushi is delicious.

2. _____ The chef spreads a layer of sticky rice over the sheet of seaweed.

3. _____ Wasabi ruins the flavor of sushi.

4. _____ Mrs. Ito makes some suggestions about what to order.

5. Check the line beside the word or words that best describe what type of passage this is.

_____ informational text

_____ fiction

_____ tall tale

6. How are Alex and Emily different?

_____

_____

7. Why isn't everyone surprised that Alex likes sushi?

_____

_____

8. What holds everything together in a roll of sushi?

_____

9. What is *wasabi*?

_____

10. Why does Mr. Godfrey say, "Our kids are turning into some very well-seasoned eaters"?

_____

_____

Bonsai

Have you ever seen miniature trees, or bonsai, at a nursery or a botanic garden?

1   In Japan, the word *bonsai* means *tray plant*. It refers to the interesting combination of art and cultivation of miniature trees and plants. Bonsai originated in China more than 2,000 years ago. The tradition spread to Japan about 700 years ago, and it is still popular there today.

2   Some people believe that small, or dwarf, plants must be used in bonsai, but this is not true. Nearly any type of tree or plant can be used, as long as it is grown from a seed or small cutting. The owner must then prune, trim, and shape the plant as it grows so that it resembles, in miniature, a much larger tree. He or she must do this skillfully, however, because the plant must appear to have grown naturally, untouched by humans. It takes a great deal of care and patience to achieve this balance.

3   A bonsai is more than just a plant. It holds a special and significant place in Japanese culture. According to Japanese tradition, three elements are necessary to create a successful bonsai: truth, goodness, and beauty. When these three elements come together, a bonsai can live for hundreds of years! It may be passed down from one generation of a family to the next as a prized possession.

4   In Japan, bonsais are grown in containers outdoors but are brought into the home for special occasions. Inside, they are often placed in the *tokonoma*. This is a small area in traditional Japanese rooms intended for the display of artistic objects. In a Japanese garden, other items may be added to the bonsai. The addition of rocks, small buildings, and miniature people is called *bon-kei*. *Sai-kei* is a related art form in which entire landscapes are reproduced in miniature.

5   There are five basic styles of bonsai: the formal upright, informal upright, slanting, cascade, and semi-cascade. In the formal upright, the trunk of the tree should be perfectly straight, and the branches should be balanced. In the informal upright, the trunk should bend slightly to one side, but never toward the viewer. The trunk of a slanting tree leans to one side and may look similar to the informal upright.

6   Cascade and semi-cascade are similar because in both styles the leaves and the branches cascade down toward the base of the plant. The main difference is that in the cascade style, the leaves actually extend below the bottom of the container.

7   If you are interested in raising a bonsai of your own, there is no need to go all the way to Japan to find one. Today, bonsais are available in nurseries all over the United States. You will have to do a little research to make sure that you know how to properly care for your plant. You will also need to be prepared to spend time caring for your plant. But as any bonsai owner will tell you, your efforts are well worth the reward of being a part of this time-honored Asian tradition.

Write the words from the passage that have the meanings below.

1. the process of growing and caring for something

_____

2. to trim away the unwanted parts of a tree or bush

_____

3. copied; made again

_____

Write **T** before the sentences that are true. Write **F** before the sentences that are false.

4. _____ The tradition of raising bonsais was begun in Europe.

5. _____ Japanese bonsais are usually grown in containers outdoors.

6. _____ The owner of a bonsai must spend some time caring for the plant.

7. _____ There are three basic styles of bonsai.

8. What do you think the phrase *time-honored tradition* means?

_____

_____

9. What are the three elements needed to create a successful bonsai?

_____

10. How are the cascade and semi-cascade styles of bonsai similar?

_____

_____

11. What purpose would a reader have for reading this selection?

_____ for pleasure or entertainment

_____ for information

_____ to form an opinion about bonsai

A Schoolyard Garden

What are your favorite fruits and vegetables?

1 Have you ever eaten something that you grew in your own garden? Many people have not had the pleasure of this experience. Alice Waters, the owner of Chez Panisse Restaurant, set out to change all that for a special group of students at Martin Luther King Junior Middle School in Berkeley, California.

2 Waters worked with the school's principal, Neil Smith, to create a cooking and gardening program at the school. Waters believes in the importance of people knowing where their food comes from. She also believes that there is a strong relationship between food, health, and the environment. Her goal at the middle school was to show children the pleasure in gardening and in preparing the foods that they cultivated. She wanted to teach them that a healthy body and a healthy environment go hand in hand.

3 The project that Waters began took a lot of time and patience. She relied on the help of teachers, students, and community volunteers to turn an asphalt parking lot into a garden. At the same time, renovation was begun to turn an old, unused cafeteria into a kitchen where students could prepare foods and share meals with their teachers.

4 In the 1995–1996 school year, the first usable crops were planted. They included greens such as arugula and mustard, as well as lettuce, kale, bok choy, carrots, turnips, beets, and potatoes. The following year brought the addition of plants such as citrus trees, apples, plums, black currants, hazelnuts, figs, raspberries, runner beans, and hibiscus. Every year since then, new crops are added and old crops are evaluated to make sure that they are best suited for the environment and the needs of the school.

5 Students have found that they look forward to the time they spend in the garden each week. They have learned how to weed, prune, and harvest. They have learned about the life cycles of various plants. They also know how to enrich the soil through composting, a process in which leftover scraps of fruits and vegetables are used as fertilizer. Many have discovered that they like fruits and vegetables that they had never before been willing to try.

6 Alice Waters dreams that one day there will be a garden in every school in the United States. She hopes that school lunches can be prepared using the produce from the gardens and other locally-grown organic produce. If you are interested in learning more about Martin Luther King Junior Middle School's Edible Schoolyard, seeing pictures of the students and their garden, and finding out about how to start a garden at your school, visit www. edibleschoolyard.org.

1. What is *composting?*

_____

_____

2. Name four fruits or vegetables that are grown in the Edible Schoolyard.

_____

3. Do you think that other schools will create gardens based on Alice Waters's ideas? Why?

_____

4. Check the sentence that best states the **main idea** of the selection, or tells what the passage is mostly about.

_____ Alice Waters owns Chez Panisse Restaurant in California.

_____ Students look forward to the time they spend gardening each week.

_____ Alice Waters founded the Edible Schoolyard, a program in which students learn to grow and prepare their own foods.

5. Check the words that describe Alice Waters.

_____ generous

_____ unfriendly

_____ talented

_____ ambitious

_____ stingy

Write the idiom from paragraph 2 on the line next to its meaning.

6. goes together _____

7. Why does Alice Waters believe that students should know how to cook and garden?

_____

_____

8. Do you have a school garden at your school? If so, what do you grow there? If not, what could you do to help start one?

_____

A Growing Plan

Does your school have a garden?

1 Drew, Emilio, and Michi sat at a picnic table in the park on a beautiful, crisp fall afternoon. The air around them was filled with the sounds of children playing, dogs barking, and people laughing or calling to one another. But Drew, Emilio, and Michi ignored the sounds around them and focused on the task they had set out to complete.

2 They wanted to start a school garden at Jefferson Middle School. Initially, it had been Drew's idea. He had first seen a school garden when he went to visit his cousin P.J. in Washington. He was amazed at the variety of fruits and vegetables the students at P.J.'s school grew. "It's a lot of work," P.J. had warned. "But it's also my favorite part of the week. I love putting on my boots, getting outside, and seeing all the new things that have happened since I was last out there."

3 When Drew returned from his trip to Washington, he told Emilio and Michi all about what he had seen. Now the three of them were determined to come up with a plan to bring a school garden to Jefferson.

4 Drew opened his notebook and prepared to record any ideas they had for convincing Ms. Milano, the school principal, that the garden was a good idea.

5 "We're going to need an adult to supervise the whole operation," said Drew thoughtfully. "I know that Mr. Hasselbach gardens at home. Just last week he brought in a whole basket of tomatoes and zucchini from his garden. He might be willing to help." Drew jotted down Mr. Hasselbach's name in his notebook.

6 "We might need donations to get this project up and running," added Michi. "We could tell Ms. Milano that we would be willing to organize a bake sale or yard sale to raise funds."

7 "That's a great idea," said Emilio. "I think we need to be able to present her with a realistic plan. My aunt is the co-owner of a nursery. She could help us design the garden, select plants, and create a budget. That way, Ms. Milano wouldn't feel as though she were committing to something unknown."

8 Drew nodded and made some more notes. "P.J. mentioned that the students at his school cook meals with the produce from their garden. If we do something like that too, think of all the lessons we'd learn. We'd have to measure and weigh things and follow a recipe. Combine that with the science lessons we'd get from working in the garden, and there's no way Ms. Milano could turn us down!"

9 Michi and Emilio grinned. "If everything goes as planned, we'll be digging in the dirt in no time at all!"

The **point of view** tells the reader whose view of the story he or she is reading. In **first-person point of view**, the reader knows the thoughts and feelings of the person telling the story. In **third-person point of view**, the reader only knows what an outsider knows about a character. Mark each phrase below **F** for first-person and **T** for third-person.

1. _____ My cousin P.J. lives in Washington.

2. _____ Emilio's aunt is the co-owner of a nursery.

3. _____ Mr. Hasselbach has a vegetable garden.

4. _____ I hope Ms. Milano likes our idea.

5. What problem do Drew, Emilio, and Michi have at the beginning of the story?

_____

_____

6. Where did Drew get the idea to start a school garden at his middle school?

_____

7. How do Drew, Emilio, and Michi know that Mr. Hasselbach has a garden at home?

_____

_____

8. Name two ideas that the students have that they think will make Ms. Milano more likely to approve their plan.

_____

_____

_____

Write the idiom from paragraph 6 on the line next to its meaning.

9. to start something_____

10. What is the setting for this story?

_____

11. Would you like to have a garden at your school or at home? Why or why not?

_____

Garden Gourmet

Have you ever helped to prepare a meal for a large group of people?

1   Emilio and Michi spread the colorful tablecloth on the table. They made room for Drew, who was carrying a covered casserole dish with potholders. Small beads of water had condensed on the inside of the lid. "Watch out," Drew warned. "This is pretty hot."

2   A moment later, Kent and Alyssa added another steaming dish to the table. "That smells so good!" exclaimed Michi. "Are most of the parents here yet? I'm famished."

3   Kent peeked through the doors that led into the hallway. "I think Ms. Milano and Mr. Hasselbach just finished giving them the garden tour. They should be heading into the cafeteria next."

4   The students of Jefferson Middle School had spent all afternoon preparing for the evening meal. They did their best to transform the lunchroom into an elegant and beautiful dining area for their families. The gray metal tables were hidden beneath brightly-colored cotton tablecloths. Each table held a small glass vase with fresh flowers from the school's garden.

5   Only about half of the overhead lights were on. The rest of the lighting was provided by the small white lights that Michi and Alyssa had carefully wrapped around the columns that were scattered throughout the cafeteria. They thought that candles would do an excellent job of creating an elegant mood, but Ms. Milano would not be swayed from her conviction that candles were too risky to use in a school.

6   As the families found their seats, Ms. Milano motioned to Drew, Emilio, and Michi to join her at the front of the room. "Could I have everyone's attention?" asked Ms. Milano. "I know you can smell all the wonderful foods our students prepared, so I won't keep you from your dinners for long. I just wanted to take a moment to congratulate Drew, Emilio, and Michi for their wonderful idea."

7   Mrs. Milano continued, "A year ago, they first came to me with the plan for starting a garden at Jefferson. I was a bit skeptical at first, but they had thought through everything. Anytime I had a question about how we would make this work, they had an answer prepared. As you can see, they were absolutely correct. About three-quarters of the food you'll be enjoying tonight came from the school garden. The students prepared the entire meal themselves, with some guidance from Mr. Hasselbach."

8   Ms. Milano handed Drew, Michi, and Emilio each a tissue-wrapped package. They unwrapped their packages as Ms. Milano addressed the room. "As a thank-you to these students for their creative idea, hard work, and perseverance, they have each received a stepping stone for the garden. Their names and the date are engraved on the stones."

9   She turned to them. "Students for years to come will be enjoying the garden that you helped create," she said. "We thought it would be appropriate for them to have a reminder of our garden's ambitious founders."

10   Drew, Emilio, and Michi held up their stepping stones and grinned as the crowd clapped. "And now," said Ms. Milano, "please help yourselves to some of the mouthwatering food our young chefs have prepared. Dinner is served!"

Circle the word that best completes each sentence below.

1. The students put a great deal of _____ into the preparation of the meal.

   effort   guidance   transformation

2. Ms. Milano _____ Drew, Emilio, and Michi's contributions.

   regrets   appreciates   plans

3. The stepping stones are _____ with their names and the date.

   requested   remembered   engraved

4. Name two things the students did to transform the lunchroom.

   _____

   _____

5. Why did Ms. Milano give Drew, Michi, and Emilio stepping stones?

   _____

   _____

6. Why do you think Ms. Milano was skeptical when the students first presented her with the idea of starting a school garden?

   _____

   _____

7. About how much of the food the students served did they grow themselves?

   _____

   _____

8. In paragraph 8, what does perseverance mean?

   _____

9. List three adjectives that describe how you think Drew, Emilio, and Michi feel at the end of the story.

   _____

A Shriek in the Night

Have you ever been frightened by a sound in the night?

1   Savannah read under her covers with a flashlight until her eyes were closing. She switched off the flashlight and let her book drop to the rug beside her bed. She turned over and snuggled deeper into the soft flannel sheets.

2   It felt as though Savannah had been sleeping for only a few minutes when she awoke with a start to a terrible, bloodcurdling scream. She lay stiffly and silently in her bed waiting to see what would happen. Her clenched muscles had just begun to relax when she heard another scream coming from outside her bedroom window. This scream was followed by a series of wails and shrieks.

3   Savannah slipped from her bed and ran as quickly as she could to her parents' bedroom. "Mom," she whispered urgently. "Did you hear that screaming?"

4   Savannah's mom was already awake, sitting up and hunting for her slippers. Savannah's dad continued to snore. Neither Savannah nor her mother were surprised. Savannah's dad was notorious for being able to sleep through anything. When he lived alone before he got married, he had to set three alarm clocks every night. He positioned them in various places around his bedroom to make sure that he would get up in time for work.

5   Savannah's mom finally found her slippers and motioned Savannah toward the bedroom door. She shut the door behind them. "What do you think it is, Mom?" asked Savannah.

6   Before Mom could answer, she and Savannah heard the terrible shrieks again. They waited until it was over to speak. "I'm pretty sure it's an animal," said Mom. "Let's see if we can spot anything through the kitchen window."

7   Savannah and her mom scanned the dark backyard but couldn't see anything. They were getting ready to head back to bed when the noises began again. This time they both looked up into the large old oak trees that towered over the backyard. They could see two small eyes gleaming in the moonlight from one of the highest branches.

8   "I think it's an owl," said Mom, craning her neck to get a better look. "All I can see are its eyes, though."

9   "I feel so much better," said Savannah with relief in her voice. "Maybe we can look online in the morning and see if we can figure out what kind of owl it is," she suggested. "My teacher showed us a great Web site for wild animal identification."

10   Savannah and her mom both returned to bed. They heard the owl's cries one more time before they drifted back to sleep, but it didn't sound nearly as frightening anymore.

11   In the morning, Savannah and her mom were able to identify the owl from the night before as a barn owl. They used the Web site that Ms. Petrovic had recommended to listen to sound bites of different types of animals.

12   As they were listening, Savannah's dad came downstairs for breakfast. "What's all that racket?" he asked cheerfully, pouring himself a glass of orange juice.

13   "Doesn't that sound at all familiar, Dad?" asked Savannah, replaying the barn owl's call.

14   "Nope," said Dad. "Should it?"

15   Savannah and her mom just laughed.

Write the words from the story that have the meanings below.

1. causing fear

_____

2. held tightly together

_____

3. needing immediate attention

_____

4. well known for something unpleasant or unfavorable

_____

5. stretching the neck to see better

_____

6. Number the events below to show the order in which they happened.

_____ Savannah switched off her flashlight.

_____ Savannah and her mom saw the owl's eyes gleaming in the moonlight.

_____ Savannah's dad poured himself a glass of orange juice.

_____ Savannah ran into her parents' bedroom.

_____ Savannah's mom looked for her slippers.

7. Find one sentence that shows Savannah was frightened by the screaming she heard.

_____

_____

8. If Savannah hears a barn owl again someday, do you think she will be frightened? Why or why not?

_____

_____

9. What problem did Savannah have in the story?

_____

10. Why weren't Savannah and her mom surprised when the owl's cries didn't wake up Savannah's dad?

_____

_____

11. How were Savannah and her mom able to identify the owl's call?

_____

_____

Night Flyers

What other creatures are associated with the night?

1   Have you ever heard a hooting or screeching sound in the night and wondered if you were hearing an owl? It's more likely that you have heard an owl in the wild rather than seen one. Owls are nocturnal, which means that they are active mostly at night. Owls feed on live prey, and the darkness makes it harder for them to be seen by the small animals they hunt.

2   There are more than 175 species of owls, but they are generally divided into two categories--common owls and barn owls. Barn owls have a light-colored, heart-shaped face. Common owls are a diverse group with many different patterns and colorings, but all have a round face. The largest owls are as big as eagles. The smallest is the elf owl, which lives in Mexico and the southwestern United States. It measures only five inches and makes its home in the holes woodpeckers create in large cacti.

3   One attribute that is common to all owls is their sharp sense of hearing. Because they hunt at night, hearing is especially important to their survival. Owls have the ability to hear a rodent's movements from hundreds of feet away. In many species, the ear openings are positioned asymmetrically, or unevenly, on the owl's head. This is important to the owl's keen sense of hearing because it allows the owl to more accurately locate the source of the sounds.

4   Owls are farsighted, meaning they cannot see well at close distances. However, they can see well in dim light, which enhances their hunting skills. Unlike most animals, an owl's eyes do not move. Instead, the owl must turn its entire head to see anything that is not directly in front of it. For this reason, the owl has an extremely flexible neck. It is able to turn its head about 270 degrees. That is three quarters of a circle!

5   Another common attribute to all owls is their nearly silent flight. This keeps the owl's prey from hearing it approach, but it also permits the owl to use its hearing to locate the exact position of the animal. Owls' wings are a very soft, downy type of feather that muffles the sound in flight. A fringe of feathers along the edges of the wings is also thought to quiet the flapping sound of the owls' wings.

6   Owls are found in the myths, folklore, and legends of many cultures. In France, archaeologists discovered cave paintings between 15,000 and 20,000 years old that contain images of owls. Mummified owls have also been found in Egyptian tombs, which indicates they were respected in ancient Egyptian culture.

7   Owls symbolize wisdom in some cultures. In others, they are feared and thought to bring bad luck. It is likely that the negative associations with owls came about because they are nocturnal creatures. Things associated with night and darkness have often been feared throughout history.

8   The next time you are out at night, listen quietly for the sounds of an owl. You may be lucky enough to catch a glimpse of an owl's gleaming eyes or watch an owl soar across a field in nearly silent flight.

1. How are barn owls different from common owls?

_____

_____

2. Why is the owl's sense of hearing important to its survival?

_____

3. How do archaeologists know that ancient Egyptians respected owls?

_____

_____

4. What is unusual about the owl's neck and eyes?

_____

_____

5. In what part of the world does the smallest owl live?

_____

6. What is one reason that owls have been feared in some cultures?

_____

_____

7. A **summary** is a short sentence that tells the most important facts about a topic. Check the sentence below that is the best summary for paragraph 3.

_____ Owls hunt at night.

_____ Owls have a sharp sense of hearing, which helps them to be strong hunters.

_____ Some owls' ear openings are positioned asymmetrically.

8. What was the author's purpose in writing this selection?

_____

_____

9. In paragraph 4, enhances means

_____ makes weaker

_____ makes better or stronger

_____ changes

A Beacon of Light

Have you ever had the opportunity to visit a lighthouse?

1 Lighthouses can symbolize many different things. For tourists, they can be an interesting place to visit, explore, and photograph. For historians, they are a window to the past and a reminder of a different way of life. For sailors and ship captains, they are a sign of safety.

2 Lighthouses are structures located along the shorelines of large bodies of water. They project a strong beam of light that alerts sailors of their location. They can protect a boat from running aground at night or other times when visibility is poor because of fog or a storm. Lighthouses alert sailors that land is near and warn them of potential dangers, such as reefs or rocky harbors.

3 Originally, lighthouses were constructed with living quarters for the lighthouse keeper. It was the job of the keeper to maintain the lighthouse and make sure that it was always working properly. Although it could be lonely at times, it was an important job. Today, almost all lighthouses are automated, which means that there is no longer a need for lighthouse keepers.

4 No one is certain when lighthouses first came into existence. We do know that the concept of lighthouses is more than 3,000 years old. An epic Greek poem titled *The Iliad* was written by a man named Homer around 1200 B.C. In the poem, Homer refers to a lighthouse, giving modern scholars an idea of how long lighthouses have been a part of human life.

5 Early versions of lighthouses were quite different from today's lighthouses. They were usually made of iron baskets that were suspended from long poles. The baskets contained burning coal or wood. In the 1700s, these baskets were replaced with oil or gas lanterns. When electricity was invented, the lanterns were replaced with electric beacons.

6 In 1822, a French physicist named Augustin Fresnel invented a lens that would prove to be very important in lighthouse technology. The Fresnel lens uses glass prisms to concentrate light and send it through a very powerful magnifying lens. With the invention of the Fresnel lens, it became possible to project a beam of light as far as 28 miles from shore!

7 Lighthouse beams can be used in a variety of ways to help sailors identify the lighthouse and their own location. Different patterns and lengths of flashes are unique to a specific lighthouse. Sailors can observe a sequence and then look it up in a reference book that will tell them which lighthouse they have spotted.

8 During the day, sailors can identify lighthouses simply by their appearance. Some are short and fat, while others are tall and thin. They can be constructed of many different materials, such as wood, stone, brick, steel, and aluminum. The patterns also differ greatly. Some lighthouses are painted with stripes or a series of diamond shapes that distinguish them. Others are distinguished by their shape--round, square, rectangular, or conical (shaped like a cone).

9 Many lighthouses along America's coastlines are no longer functioning. Historical societies, concerned community members, and even the National Park Service have preserved them. They are sometimes converted into museums, inns, educational centers, or even private homes. If you ever have a chance to visit one, getting a glimpse of history is worth the trip.

1. How do we know that lighthouses have existed for at least 3,000 years?

_____

_____

2. How far can the Fresnel lens project light?

_____

3. Why aren't lighthouse keepers necessary for today's lighthouses?

_____

4. What are two ways in which lighthouses may be different from one another?

_____

_____

5. Why do you think that historians think it is important to preserve lighthouses?

_____

_____

6. What did early versions of lighthouses look like?

_____

_____

7. Check the phrase that best describes the author's purpose.

_____ to share the history of lighthouses

_____ to persuade the reader to visit a lighthouse

_____ to explain how lighthouses were built

8. In paragraph 3, what does the word automated mean?

_____

9. What is the main idea of this selection?

_____

_____

Lighthouse Life

Where will Paloma's imagination take her?

1   Paloma sat at a computer in the school library. She stared at the blank screen and the blinking cursor. She rummaged around in her backpack for a rubber band, and then she pulled her hair into a thick ponytail. Paloma looked at the computer screen. It was still blank. She sighed and flipped through her notebook to reread Mr. Molina's assignment. It was due in just two days, and Paloma knew that she couldn't procrastinate any longer.

2   *Write a creative short story using an experience that you have had recently,* Paloma read. *Your story should include two examples of figurative language. The finished story should be three to four pages long. Your first draft is due on Friday. Be prepared to share your story with the class and make notes for a revision, which you will have an additional week to complete.*

3   Paloma and her family had taken a trip to North Carolina's Outer Banks just before school began. They had visited four different lighthouses, and Paloma had wondered what it would be like to live in a lighthouse. She knew that before lighthouses were automated, they were run and maintained by a lighthouse keeper who lived on the premises. Paloma thought that would have been an interesting job to have, but she wanted to actually live in a lighthouse. Without thinking about it any longer, Paloma began to write the story.

4   I sat with Sadie curled on my lap and looked out the window at the crashing waves. The heavy rain beat against my lighthouse like a thousand footsteps racing up and down the walls. I held Sadie closer, and she let out a small meow of displeasure. I knew that the coming storm could not be too dangerous if Sadie was still acting normally. I have read that animals can sense changes in weather and will seek shelter from a tornado or hurricane. I was relying on Sadie's calmness to get me through my first hurricane on the island.

5   I knew that my lighthouse was sturdily built. It had survived more than one hundred years' worth of hurricanes and tropical storms. There was no reason to believe that the bricks and wood could not survive another. I looked up at the staircase that spiraled above me and shuddered as I felt the tower sway slightly in a gust of wind.

6   Paloma stopped and reread what she had just written. She smiled to herself, saved her story, and then settled into her chair to continue writing. She wasn't sure what was going to happen next, but she knew that if she just kept going, the story would continue to tell itself. Paloma couldn't wait to find out where it would take her.

1. What kind of animal is Sadie? How can you tell?

_____

2. What problem does Paloma have at the beginning of the story?

_____

_____

3. Find an example of a sentence or phrase Paloma uses to create tension in her story.

_____

4. The next time she has to write a story for school, do you think Paloma will put it off again? Why or why not?

_____

_____

5. Where does Paloma get her story idea?

_____

_____

Mark each sentence below **F** if it is in first-person point of view and **T** if it is in third-person point of view.

6. _____ I was relying on Sadie's calmness to get me through the hurricane.

7. _____ Paloma reread Mr. Molina's assignment.

8. _____ I looked up at the staircase and shuddered.

Find the simile in paragraph 4 and write it on the line below.

9. _____

_____

10. If you were given the same assignment as Paloma, what would you write about?

_____

_____

Lighthouse on the Move

How would you move a building that is 193 feet tall?

1   There are certain things that people just don't expect to see move. We expect structures like houses, schools, and office buildings to be stationary objects. That is why many people were surprised to learn that the tallest lighthouse in the United States, the Cape Hatteras Lighthouse in Buxton, North Carolina, was going to be moved in June of 1999.

2   Why would anyone want to move a lighthouse? The 193-foot-tall lighthouse was built between 1868 and 1870. It weathered countless storms, as well as many hurricanes. It guided sailors away from the Diamond Shoals, a dangerous, shallow area about 14 miles off the coast of Cape Hatteras.

3   The coastline around the Outer Banks is known as the Graveyard of the Atlantic. It is estimated that more than 230 ships sank there between 1866 and 1945. The Cape Hatteras Lighthouse faithfully did its duty in protecting sailors from harm. This is exactly why it was determined that the lighthouse would have to be preserved. Experts were worried that continued erosion by the pounding waves of the ocean would destroy the lighthouse. They wanted to move it before it collapsed and was swept out to sea.

4   Moving the 4,800-ton lighthouse was no small project. Many people protested the move. They believed that the lighthouse was not strong enough to withstand it. They felt that it should be allowed to remain in the place it had always been. Others thought that moving the lighthouse was not important enough to justify spending the 9.8 million dollars the move would cost. After much debate, it was decided that the project could proceed as planned.

5   The new location for the lighthouse was chosen. It would move a total of about 2,900 feet. In the new location, the Cape Hatteras Lighthouse would stand 1,600 feet from the ocean that threatened to destroy it. The planners estimated that it would take between four and six weeks to move the lighthouse. In reality, it took only about three weeks to complete the job.

6   The lighthouse was moved using the power of seven hydraulic jacks. It sat on pads of rollers that rested on a set of rails, similar to train tracks. After the lighthouse had moved from one set of tracks to the next, the first set of tracks was moved in front of the lighthouse so that it could pass over them again. The process was extremely slow. Many people came to watch what they figured would be a dramatic moment in North Carolina history. But the lighthouse only moved an average of about two inches per minute, which wasn't all that exciting to watch.

7   The Cape Hatteras Lighthouse survived the move and has settled into its new home. Some people still look at the vacant spot on the beach where it stood for so many years and feel a sense of sadness. Others are just relieved that the lighthouse was saved so that future generations could appreciate its bold, spiral stripes and proud history.

1. Number the events below to show the order in which they happened.

_____ People were worried that the lighthouse would collapse.

_____ The relocation was a success.

_____ The Cape Hatteras Lighthouse was completed in 1870.

_____ The lighthouse was removed from its existing foundation.

_____ Onlookers watched the slow progress of the lighthouse's move.

2. Check the line beside the word or words that best describe what type of passage this is.

_____ biography   _____ fiction

_____ historical nonfiction

3. Check the sentence that best states the main idea of the passage.

_____ The Cape Hatteras Lighthouse in Buxton, North Carolina, is the tallest lighthouse in the United States.

_____ The process used to move the Cape Hatteras Lighthouse was very slow.

_____ In 1999, the Cape Hatteras Lighthouse was moved further inland to prevent its destruction due to erosion.

4. What are the Diamond Shoals?

_____

_____

5. What is one reason that some people protested moving the lighthouse?

_____

_____

6. What is the Graveyard of the Atlantic?

_____

_____

7. Do you agree with the decision to move to the lighthouse? Explain.

_____

_____

Keeping the Light

What would it be like to live in a lighthouse?

1 Imagine living in an isolated place where bad weather was not uncommon and people's lives depended on you doing your job. This was the life of a lighthouse keeper before lighthouses became automated. Lights that had mirrors and lenses had to be cleaned and polished regularly. The keepers had to be watchful at night to make sure that the lamps stayed lit and there was enough fuel to last the night. When ships wrecked in nearby areas, lighthouse keepers were expected to help with the rescue effort.

2 Because the work was physically demanding and women rarely worked outside the home, the job of lighthouse keeper was most often given to men. However, the job often fell to the daughters or wives of lighthouse keepers when the men were called to war, became ill, or died. Women proved themselves to be equally capable of holding this difficult job that was as much a way of life as it was a career.

3 One of the most famous female lighthouse keepers was Ida Lewis of Newport, Rhode Island. Her father was the keeper of Lime Rock Lighthouse, but after only a few months at the job he had a stroke. Because Hosea Lewis was no longer able to perform his duties as keeper, 15-year-old Ida and her mother took over in 1853. Captain Lewis lived about 20 years longer, but Ida and her mother performed all the required duties of a keeper.

4 Ida was known as the best swimmer in Newport. She was also skilled at handling a rowboat, something that was not seen as particularly appropriate for a woman of that time. However, during her 39 years keeping the light at Lime Rock, Ida rescued between 18 and 25 people. That certainly made it seem less important whether or not Ida's behaviors were appropriate!

5 People were intrigued by this woman who appeared to make her own rules for living. Thousands of visitors came to Lime Rock in hope of seeing Ida Lewis in person. Ida was used to the quiet solitude of a lighthouse keeper's life, and she was uncomfortable with all the attention. Even so, she couldn't help being honored by the awards she received for her service. President Ulysses S. Grant made a trip to Rhode Island to visit Ida and to commend her on her heroism.

6 In 1924, Lime Rock was renamed Ida Lewis Rock in honor of the keeper who had died in 1911. The lighthouse service of Rhode Island also renamed Lime Rock Lighthouse the Ida Lewis Lighthouse. It is the only lighthouse to be named for its keeper.

1. Check the words that best describe Ida Lewis.

_____ hardworking   _____ strong-willed

_____ determined   _____ unpredictable

_____ nosy

Write **T** before the sentences that are true. Write **F** before the sentences that are false.

2. _____ It was more common for women than for men to be lighthouse keepers.

3. _____ After his stroke, Captain Lewis was able to resume his job as lighthouse keeper.

4. _____ Ida kept the light at Lime Rock for 39 years.

5. _____ President Ulysses S. Grant visited Ida in Rhode Island.

6. _____ Today, Lime Rock Lighthouse is called Ida Lewis Lighthouse.

7. Why did all the attention make Ida uncomfortable?

_____

_____

8. Why do you think that we don't know for sure how many people Ida rescued?

_____

9. How old was Ida when she began tending the lighthouse? _____

10. What were two jobs of lighthouse keepers before lighthouses became automated?

_____

_____

11. Do you think you would have enjoyed being a lighthouse keeper? Why or why not?

_____

_____

_____

A Picture Perfect Day

Have you ever taken any photographs?

1 "Hold that pose!" said Dante, snapping a photo of his mother.

2 Dante's mom looked up in surprise and spilled some of the orange juice she was pouring. "Dante, what are you doing?" she asked, setting the carton of juice on the counter.

3 "It's a project I'm doing for school," Dante explained, sitting down at the table. "For the next two days, I'm going to keep a photo diary of my life."

4 Mrs. Carter smiled at her son. "It sounds interesting," she said. "I'm just not sure that a picture of me in my pajamas pouring orange juice at 7 o'clock in the morning is the most interesting part of your day."

5 "I'm not supposed to leave anything out," replied Dante. "It doesn't really matter if it's interesting. This diary should be a realistic narrative of my day. You and breakfast are both a part of my day, so I wanted to make sure they were captured on film."

6 Mrs. Carter nodded and bit into a slice of toast. "What will you do with your photographs when you're done? Do you have to present them to your class?"

7 "I'm going to mount the photos on a piece of posterboard in chronological order," Dante said. "Then, the class will try to write a brief summary of my day based on the pictures I took."

8 "Do your dad and brother know about your photo diary project?" asked Mrs. Carter. "You might want to give them a bit of advance warning if they're going to be part of it."

9 Just then, Wesley came pounding down the stairs into the kitchen. He was carrying a basketball under one arm and grabbed a piece of toast as he sat down at the table.

10 "Wesley," said Dante, peering through the camera lens at his brother, "I'm doing a photo diary for school."

11 Wesley grinned directly at the camera as Dante snapped the photo. Mrs. Carter laughed. "I forgot who I was talking about here," she said, giving Wesley a quick squeeze on the shoulder. "I guess no explanation is necessary for your brother, Dante," she said.

12 "I don't blame him for wanting to get a picture of me," said Wesley. "When I make it into the NBA, those pictures will probably be pretty valuable," he joked.

13 Dante laughed as he got up from the breakfast table. "There are some things you just can't capture in pictures," he said, shaking his head. He took his dishes to the sink and then managed to get a picture of his dad adjusting his tie as he walked into the kitchen with the newspaper tucked under his arm.

14 He grabbed Mrs. Carter around the waist as she got up to get another cup of coffee. He waltzed her across the kitchen and then dipped her deeply as she laughed. "Isn't this going to make it into your diary?" he asked Dante.

15 Dante grinned. "I'm just not sure that my class would be able to work it into the narrative of my day. Like I said, there are some things you just can't capture in pictures."

Write **F** before the sentences that are facts. Write **O** before the sentences that are opinions.

1. _____ Keeping a photo diary is a difficult assignment.

2. _____ Dante's brother's name is Wesley.

3. _____ Dante's classmates will find it easy to create a narrative from his photos.

4. _____ Mrs. Carter spilled some orange juice.

5. _____ Mr. Carter has a good sense of humor.

6. The **protagonist** is the main character in a story, or the person the story is mostly about. Who is the protagonist in this story?

_____

_____

7. Why doesn't Dante want to leave out any details of his day?

_____

_____

8. Why does Wesley joke that photos of him will be valuable one day?

_____

_____

9. During what time of day does the story take place? How can you tell?

_____

_____

10. What is the setting for this story?

_____

11. If you were to make a photo diary of an average day in your life, describe four photos you would want to be sure to include.

_____

_____

_____

_____

Point and Click

Do you know how a camera works?

1   Cameras might seem almost unbelievable if you do not know how they work. Point a camera at something, push a button, and you end up with a realistic image of what you saw. How does that happen? The camera's ability to reproduce what you see is not actually all that complicated, once you understand a few basic elements. In fact, the camera itself is just a box that controls how much light reaches the film inside. The original Latin term *camera obscura* means *dark chamber*, and it is a perfect description.

2   Traditional film is a plastic strip that has been coated with light-sensitive chemicals. Like the rods and cones in our eyes, these chemicals change according to how much light enters the camera. The image that enters through the camera's lens creates a unique pattern in the chemicals that will be used when the photograph is developed in a lab. Instead of chemical film, a digital camera contains a light-sensitive electrical device that records the image.

3   Having just the right amount of light reach the film is crucial to taking a good picture. The two main devices that control light are the shutter and the aperture. The shutter is a small door inside the camera that opens and closes when you take a picture. It affects how long the film is exposed to light.

4   On a typical sunny day, the shutter speed might be as fast as 1/125 of a second to keep too much light from getting in. A quick shutter speed is also needed when you want to capture something that is moving. If the film is exposed too long, the moving object will be a blur in the developed photo.

5   Sometimes, slow shutter speeds are needed. For example, if you want to take a picture at night or in low light, you need to leave the shutter open longer so that enough light can reach the film and

create an image. To take photographs of stars or the moon, you would need to have the shutter open for a very long time.

6   The aperture is a circular opening behind the lens that can be adjusted to let in more or less light, similar to the iris in an eye. The aperture also determines the depth of field, or how much of the photo will appear to be in focus. When the aperture is open widely, the focus will only be on a narrow range of objects, but when the aperture is small, things both near and faraway will look sharp.

7   The aperture and shutter speed work together to get just the right amount of light to the film. For instance, if you want to photograph a fast-moving object, you need a fast shutter speed, but that may not let in enough light. To compensate, you need to open the aperture wider so that the proper amount of light reaches the film. Of course, a camera with an automatic setting will do all of the adjustments for you, so all you have to do is just "point and click."

Write the words from the passage that have the meanings below.

1. make a copy of

_____
Par. 1

2. a piece of equipment used for a specific purpose

_____
Par. 2

3. allowed to be reached by light

_____
Par. 3

4. to make up for something

_____
Par. 7

5. How is a camera's aperture similar to the iris in a human eye?

_____

_____

6. What is one example of a time you might want to use a slow shutter speed?

_____

7. What does the Latin term _camera obscura_ mean?

_____

8. How are digital cameras different from traditional cameras?

_____

9. What are the two main devices that control light in a camera?

_____

10. Why do you think it is easier to use an automatic camera than a manual camera?

_____

11. Check the phrase that best describes the author's purpose.

_____ to persuade

_____ to entertain

_____ to inform

Talking Photos

What will Dante learn in his interview with Mr. Salinas?

1   "Thanks for taking the time to meet with me, Mr. Salinas," said Dante, reaching out to shake the photographer's hand.

2   "I'm happy to do it," replied Mr. Salinas. "I love to talk about my work, and as patient as my family is, I'm sure they still get a little tired of hearing about it all of the time."

3   "I brought a voice recorder with me," said Dante, holding up the small black box. "Would it be all right with you if I recorded our conversation?" he asked. "That way, I won't be distracted by taking notes, and I can transcribe it later."

4   "That sounds good to me," said Mr. Salinas. He settled into his chair and took a sip of bottled water. "I'm ready when you are," he said.

5   *Dante Carter:* When did you first know that you wanted to be a photographer?

6   *Edward Salinas:* It wasn't until I had already graduated from college. I was teaching high school English, and I decided to take a photography class just for fun. The class was at a community arts center in downtown Seattle, Washington. It completely changed my life. I went back to school a year later to begin working on a degree in photography.

7   *DC:* Who has been your greatest influence?

8   *ES:* Well, I have been lucky to have had several wonderful mentors who encouraged and inspired me. After I completed my photography degree, I had a year-long internship with a very talented photographer named Elizabeth Chu. For the most part, she documented people's lives through photography. She had an amazing ability to capture so much character and personality in a single image.

9   *DC:* What other photographers do you admire?

10   *ES:* There are so many, I'm not even sure where to begin. The work of Walker Evans is extraordinary. He is probably best known for his photographs showing the poverty of life in the South during the 1930s. There is a very timeless and human aspect to his work. Alfred Stieglitz was influential in promoting the work of photographers as artists. His images of New York during the first part of the 20th century are stunning.

11   *DC:* What do you find most rewarding about your job?

12   *ES:* I suppose I'm most grateful that it doesn't feel like a job to me, even though it can often be hard work. There are plenty of frustrations when photos don't turn out the way I had anticipated. But documenting life and nature and beauty is very gratifying. I can't imagine anything else I'd rather do.

13   *DC:* Mr. Salinas, this has been really helpful. Thank you for meeting with me and sharing so much about your experiences. I'd like to be a photographer one day myself. Your comments were inspiring.

14   *ES:* I wish you the best of luck, Dante. From what I've seen, you have the motivation and ability to succeed at just about anything you put your mind to.

1. Why does Dante want to record his interview with Mr. Salinas?

_____

_____

2. What job did Mr. Salinas have before he became a photographer?

_____

_____

3. Name two people who have influenced Mr. Salinas's work.

_____

_____

4. What does Mr. Salinas like about his job?

_____

_____

Circle the word that best completes each sentence below.

5. Mr. Salinas was _____ with the work of Alfred Stieglitz and Walker Evans.

uninterested   impressed   disappointed

6. Dante's questions for Mr. Salinas were _____.

irritating   encouraging   thoughtful

7. Mr. Salinas _____ that his work can be frustrating at times.

mentioned   aspired   demanded

8. After his interview with Mr. Salinas, do you think that Dante will still want to become a photographer? Explain your answer.

_____

_____

9. List three adjectives you could use to describe Dante in this story.

_____

_____

_____

The World of Ansel Adams

How did Ansel Adams become one of the most well-known nature photographers?

1   The name Ansel Adams may not ring a bell with you, but there is a good chance that you would recognize his photographs. Adams's work includes some of the most beautiful and famous black-and-white nature photographs ever taken.

2   Ansel Adams was born in 1902 near San Francisco, California. Adams's interest in photography began on a trip to Yosemite National Park when he was 14 years old. His parents had given him a camera as a gift. Adams found that he was mesmerized by the scenery at Yosemite and fascinated by his ability to capture it on film.

3   Although Adams had already shown much promise as a pianist, photography became a hobby that was just as fulfilling for him. It turned out that his talent for photography was perhaps even greater than that for music.

4   The photographs for which Adams is best known are those that depict the beauty of wild areas. Many of his photos were taken in Yosemite National Park, the site of his first experience with a camera. Others captured images of wild places in the American West, as well as the California coast, near the area where Adams was raised.

5   One of the things that makes Adams's work so distinctive is the contrast that is present in so many of his photographs. Although Adams worked in black and white, there is an amazing amount of variety in tone. The darker shades are deep and rich, while the whites are crisp and bright.

6   Adams was able to achieve this through a system he developed called *zone exposure*. He divided the light in an image into ten different zones. This allowed him to accurately predict what the different shades of gray would look like in a photograph.

7   Through his photographs and the time that he spent in nature, Adams became an avid environmentalist. He became involved with the Sierra Club, a conservation group. The photography he did for them brought publicity to many issues they believed were important. His photographs serve as a record of wild areas of the American West—such as Sequoia, Mount Rainier, and Glacier National Parks—before humans had done much to disturb them.

8   Although his prints were often sold to collectors for large sums of money, Adams wanted to make sure that his photographs were available to everyone. Posters were created of several of his best-loved images. They are still available today, in addition to many books on Adams's work and even calendars that feature his photography. Ansel Adams died in 1984, but his photographs will continue to bring the joy and wonder of the natural world to people for many years to come.

1. Check the line beside the word or words that best describe what type of passage this is.

_____ historical fiction

_____ biography

_____ persuasive

2. Check the sentence below that is the best summary for paragraph 7.

_____ Adams was an environmentalist who was able to help the cause he believed in through his photographs of natural places.

_____ Adams visited Sequoia, Mount Rainier, and Glacier National Parks.

_____ The Sierra Club is a conservation group.

3. Check the words that best describe Ansel Adams.

_____ talented

_____ anxious

_____ enthusiastic

_____ creative

_____ suspicious

Write **T** before the sentences that are true. Write **F** before the sentences that are false.

4. _____ Adams was born on the East Coast.

5. _____ Adams received his first camera from a teacher.

6. _____ Adams was also a talented musician.

7. _____ The majority of Adams's photographs are black and white.

8. _____ Adams is still alive and lives California today.

Write the idiom from paragraph 1 on the line next to its meaning.

9. to sound familiar _____

10. In paragraph 7, it says that Adams was an "avid environmentalist." What does this mean?

_____

_____

Photographing History

Who was Margaret Bourke-White, and why is her work still so respected today?

1   What do the following people and places have in common—the Indian leader Gandhi, the survivors of the World War II concentration camps, the Great Depression, the steel mills of Cleveland, Ohio, and the Arctic Circle? Margaret Bourke-White photographed them all during her career as a photojournalist. She was present for many monumental events of the 20th century, and she recorded them with courage and sensitivity.

2   Margaret Bourke-White was born in New York in 1904. In college, she studied biology and planned to be a herpetologist, a scientist who studies reptiles and amphibians. Then, she took a class in photography and discovered a new passion.

3   After graduating from college, Bourke-White headed to Cleveland, where she photographed the steel mills that were so prevalent in that city. In the 1920s, American industry was booming and the country was growing. Bourke-White documented much of this growth and the factories where it was taking place. Although the material she was covering was cold and industrial, Bourke-White managed to make the photographs of machinery and factories both artistic and beautiful.

4   A publisher named Henry Luce was very impressed with Bourke-White's photographs of American industry and hired her to work at his magazine, *Fortune*. When he began a new magazine called *LIFE* in 1936, Bourke-White was one of Luce's first four photographers. In fact, her picture of a Montana dam was featured on the cover of the magazine's first issue.

5   Bourke-White's work with *LIFE* magazine led her on adventures all across the globe. She was the first foreign photographer to be allowed to take pictures in the Soviet Union in 1930. She took photos of the German

siege on Moscow in 1941. As the first female war correspondent of World War II, Bourke-White faced danger on a regular basis. This was at a time when it was still customary for women to work mostly in the home, taking care of a family and a household.

6   One of Bourke-White's closest brushes with danger occurred when she was assigned to cover the U.S. armed forces at the start of the war. On her way to North Africa, the ship she was traveling in was struck by a torpedo and sank. Bourke-White survived the attack and went on to follow and photograph the action of the war. When the concentration camps were liberated several years later at the end of World War II, Bourke-White was there. Wth her camera, she captured some of the most disturbing and moving images ever recorded.

7   As stressful and difficult as her work must have been, Margaret Bourke-White loved what she did. She was the eyes and ears of the world in places most Americans had never visited and never would. Although Bourke-White died at the relatively early age of 67, she had traveled the world and photographed much of what she saw. Her pictures are a permanent record of both her life and the world during the 20th century.

1. Check the sentence that best states the main idea of the selection.

_____ Margaret Bourke-White photographed Cleveland's steel mills in the 1920s.

_____ Margaret Bourke-White was a talented photojournalist who traveled the world and broke new ground for women.

_____ Margaret Bourke-White was one of *LIFE* magazine's first four photogrphers.

2. Is this selection a fantasy, or does it take place in reality? How can you tell?

_____

_____

3. Why was Bourke-White's job unusual for a woman?

_____

_____

4. What did Bourke-White plan to be before she discovered photography?

_____

5. What was unusual about Bourke-White's industrial pictures?

_____

6. Number the events below to show the order in which they happened.

_____ Bourke-White photographed the liberation of the concentration camps.

_____ Bourke-White began working for *LIFE* magazine.

_____ Henry Luce hired Bourke-White to work at *Fortune*.

_____ Bourke-White graduated from college.

7. What do you find most interesting about Margaret Bourke-White's life?

_____

_____

Reality Check

What will Ari and his mom find out about owning an exotic pet?

1   Through the kitchen's glass doors, Ari could see his mom sitting on the back deck. The pale green baby blanket she was knitting was pooled at her side, and she held it up every once in a while to check on her progress.

2   Ari slid open the door and pulled up a chair across from his mom. "Well, hi there," said Mrs. Stein, smiling at Ari. "What have you been up to this afternoon?"

3   Ari took a sip of his mom's iced tea. "I was watching this amazing animal show," he said. "It was about people who have all kinds of exotic pets. Did you know that you can buy Bengal tiger cubs and raise them yourself?" asked Ari excitedly.

4   "I'm not sure that's such a good idea," said Mrs. Stein, her knitting needles clicking along busily. "Tigers are beautiful, wild creatures," she added. "I hate to see people trying to domesticate animals that are meant to live in the wild."

5   Ari nodded. "A tiger would be a lot of responsibility. It would be almost impossible to give it the space it would need to feel free.

6   "There are other exotic animals that wouldn't be so dangerous or need a lot of space, though," said Ari. "I wrote down a few Web addresses where we could find some more information. Could we go look at them?" Ari looked hopefully at his mother.

7   Mrs. Stein sighed and grinned at Ari. "Let me finish this row, and I'll come inside and take a look at the sites with you. I'm not promising anything, though."

8   A few minutes later, Ari and his mom sat side by side in the glow of the computer screen. They saw pictures of miniature foxes with enormous ears, bristly hedgehogs, and boa constrictors. They read advertisements for lion cubs, piranhas, and warthogs.

9   Then, they found a Web site that discussed some of the problems with importing exotic pets. "They didn't talk about any of this on the show I watched," said Ari, looking confused. "I had no idea that there were so many abandoned or mistreated exotic pets in this country."

10   Ari's mom shook her head. "I didn't know either," she said. "It sounds like the show you saw only presented one side of the story. That's too bad, isn't it? I'm sure lots of people see advertisements or shows like the one you saw and don't really know what they are getting into."

11   Ari looked thoughtful, "Mom, do you think I could write a letter to the show I watched? Now that we've done some more research, I've changed my mind about owning an exotic pet. They should have explained both sides of the story."

12   Mrs. Stein patted Ari on the shoulder. "That's a wonderful idea," she said. "You've made a really mature decision. Someone that responsible could probably handle taking care of a dog or a cat. Do you want to check out a few of the local animal shelters while we're online?"

13   Ari couldn't think of what to say. He hugged his mom hard and turned back to the computer to begin searching for a cat or a dog that needed a good home.

1. What kinds of exotic animals did Ari and his mom see when they were online?

_____

2. Why did Ari decide to write a letter to the television show he watched?

_____

_____

3. Why did Mrs. Stein say that Ari was mature and responsible?

_____

_____

4. Do you think that Ari will be a good pet owner? Why or why not?

_____

_____

Mark each sentence below **F** if it is in first-person point of view and **T** if it is in third-person point of view.

5. _____ I can't believe we're going to get a dog or cat!

6. _____ Mrs. Stein put down her knitting.

7. _____ Ari turned on the computer.

8. _____ I think that writing a letter is an excellent idea.

9. Tell about a time when you read something or watched something that presented only one point of view. How did you feel about it? Did you want to learn more about the other point of view?

_____

_____

_____

_____

An Exotic Dilemma

Learn how exotic pets are turning up in unexpected places in Florida.

1   Would you know what to do if you saw a python slithering across your backyard? What about an anteater looking for dinner in your bushes or a seven-foot-long African monitor lizard running across your patio? People who live in most areas of the United States do not have encounters like these. But if you happen to live in southern Florida, there is a chance that you could run into a number of nonnative species that have settled in your hometown.

2   Exotic pets have become more and more popular in recent years. People often purchase an animal as a baby without realizing how difficult it may be to care for that animal when it is fully-grown.

3   For example, Burmese pythons are easy to buy at exotic pet stores or online. When the snake is young, it does not require much more work than any other pet reptile. But Burmese pythons can grow to be more than 20 feet long and can weigh about 250 pounds. There is not much space in the average American home or yard to care for such a creature! When the snake outgrows its cage and its owner tires of caring for and feeding such a large animal, the snake may be abandoned in a wild area.

4   In other parts of the country, it is likely that many of these exotic creatures would not be able to survive long in the wild. But the climate in southern Florida is wet and warm—not unlike the tropical areas where many of the animals are naturally found. Not only can many exotic pets adjust to living in Florida's natural areas, but if enough of them are released, they can start breeding.

5   The problem with invasive species is that scientists don't always know in advance which ones will alter the environment or harm native populations. In the last few years, people visiting Florida's Everglades National Park have watched fights between alligators and pythons.

6   It is not hard to imagine the impact of aggressive creatures. But even animals like vervet monkeys or Cuban tree frogs, which seem harmless, can change the delicate balance of the environment. They may compete with other animals that eat the same plants or insects. If their presence or behavior causes a change in the habits of other animals, the overall changes could be far-reaching.

7   Think about dominos lined up next to one another. None of them may be touching, but as soon as you tip one over, the whole row will tumble. This is not unlike the way plants and animals in the environment react to one another. One small change can set off a whole series of changes that not even scientists can predict.

1. Check the phrase that best describes the author's purpose.

_____ to entertain   _____ to instruct

_____ to inform

2. An **analogy** is a comparison between two things that may seem to be unalike but that have at least one similarity. An analogy is used to compare two things in paragraph 7. What are they?

_____

3. Name two animals that are nonnative species in southern Florida.

_____

4. Why is it hard to care for a full-grown Burmese python?

_____

_____

5. Why are exotic pets more likely to survive in the wild in a state like Florida than they are in a state like Ohio or Montana?

_____

_____

6. Do you think that abandoned exotic animals will continue to be a problem in Florida? Explain your answer.

_____

_____

7. How would you define the term _invasive species_?

_____

_____

8. In paragraph 2, _exotic_ means

_____

9. Would you ever purchase an exotic pet? Why or why not?

_____

_____

_____

The Everlasting Beauty of the Everglades

Why is the Everglades considered to be such a unique area of the country?

1   The Florida Everglades is one of the most diverse areas of the country. Within the Everglades you can find swamps, marshes, grasslands, and dense forests. Hundreds of species of plants and animals make their homes in the Everglades. Some are found in few other places in the world. About 1.5 million acres of the Everglades are National Park land. Within the park, there are more than 350 species of birds, 40 species of mammals, and 50 species of reptiles!

2   Scientists believe that the Everglades formed about eight to ten thousand years ago at the end of the last ice age. When the glaciers began to melt, they caused the sea level to rise and turned the low-lying area of the Everglades into swampland. When nearby Lake Okeechobee floods after heavy rains, the water level in the Everglades rises as well.

3   The weather is characterized by hot, wet summers and warm but dry winters. The temperature in the Everglades rarely drops below 60 degrees, and the average rainfall is often more than 50 inches per year. This wet, mild weather is the primary reason that plant and animal life is so abundant there.

4   As prevalent as living creatures appear to be in this lush landscape, the ecosystem of the Everglades must maintain its delicate balance. During the 20th century, canals were built which lowered the level of Lake Okeechobee. The lake overflowed much less frequently, which affected the water levels in the Everglades.

5   People also began looking for ways to farm the land surrounding the Everglades. This required using much of the Everglades' water supply. In addition, the pollution from fertilizers and pesticides used in farming began to run off into the water.

6   New types of flora were introduced, which also affected the balance of the ecosystem. The tiny seeds of the melaleuca tree were sprinkled from salt shakers into the Everglades from low-flying airplanes because melaleuca trees consume a great deal of water. People hoped that the trees would dry up the land and make the Everglades suitable for development. They also planned to use the trees for timber. The wood turned out to be difficult to harvest, so the trees just continued to grow, crowding out other species that are indigenous to the Everglades.

7   The Everglades National Park was founded in 1947 in an attempt to preserve the land and the plant and animal life. The area was not large enough to make a significant impact, so in 1989, the government expanded the park. In 1996, an act was passed allowing the government to purchase farmland, which could then be returned to natural swampy marshland.

8   These efforts are important because there are so many species to protect within the Everglades. It is the only place in the world where crocodiles and alligators coexist. It is also the home of the endangered Florida panther, as well as many other endangered species. Black bears, otters, pelicans, turtles, bats, deer, and manatees all make their home in the Everglades. Without a doubt, the Everglades are worth saving and preserving. Where else in the world can you find such lush diversity?

Write **F** before the sentences that are facts. Write **O** before the sentences that are opinions.

1. _____ The Everglades National Park covers about 1.5 million acres.

2. _____ Melaleuca trees consume a great deal of water.

3. _____ Everyone should visit the Everglades at least once.

4. _____ The Everglades are most beautiful in the summer.

5. _____ The Everglades are the only place in the world where crocodiles and alligators coexist.

6. What is the author trying to persuade the reader of in this passage?

   _____

7. Think about what you know about rain forests. Name two ways in which rain forests and the Everglades are similar.

   _____

   _____

8. About how many species of birds are there in Everglades National Park?

   _____

9. Why were melaleuca trees planted in the Everglades?

   _____

Circle the word that best completes each sentence.

10. Many people believe it is important to _____ our nation's wild places.

    destroy   investigate   preserve

11. It can be difficult to _____ the balance of an ecosystem.

    explain   maintain   cancel

12. What would you find most interesting about a trip to the everglades?

    _____

    _____

Moving Mountains

Where are most of the world's volcanoes located?

1   Have you ever heard of the Ring of Fire? It might sound like something straight out of science fiction, but it is a real place. The Ring of Fire is the name used by scientists to describe an area where frequent volcanic eruptions and earthquakes take place. In fact, about 75 percent of the world's 1,900 active and dormant, or inactive, volcanoes are located there.

2   In some parts of the world, giant pieces of Earth's crust, called *plates*, are constantly in motion. They collide and slowly slide over, under, and past one another. The Ring of Fire is located at the juncture of the Pacific plate with several other plates. The Ring of Fire is an arc-shaped region that runs along the coast of North and South America, along the eastern edge of Asia, across Alaska's Aleutian Islands, and along the coast of New Zealand in the South Pacific.

3   Sometimes, plates move past one another without creating much of a disturbance. Other times, when two plates collide, an earthquake occurs. This is exactly what happens at the well-known San Andreas Fault in California, and it is why earthquakes are so common in that part of the country.

4   Even though the plates move relatively slowly, at about the same rate that human fingernails grow, the friction they create as they slide into one another produces a great deal of energy. The heat from inside Earth is strong enough to melt rock and turn it into magma, or molten rock. Eventually, the magma rises because it is lighter, or less dense, than the rocky material that surrounds it. When it reaches the surface, it becomes known as lava and forms volcanoes.

5   The presence of dissolved gases in the magma determines whether or not the eruption will be explosive. Picture a bottle

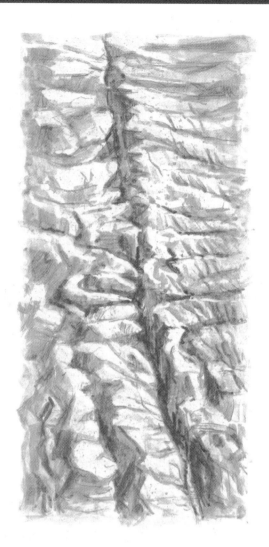

of soda that has been shaken. When the bottle is opened, the gases cause the liquid to explode from the bottle with force. In the same way, volcanoes that have a high concentration of gases will also explode with greater force.

6   Although most people view volcanoes as enormous and potentially dangerous mountains, scientists see them as temporary structures on Earth's surface. They may not change much over the course of a lifetime, or even several lifetimes. Still, scientists know that over time volcanoes will move and shift, rise and fall with the movement of Earth's plates.

1. What is one difference between the way that scientists view volcanoes and most other people view them?

_____

_____

_____

2. For what reason is the San Andreas Fault well known?

_____

_____

3. The author compares the rate at which Earth's plates move with something that is more familiar. What is the other element in the comparison?

_____

4. Name two continents that border the Ring of Fire.

_____

5. What percentage of the world's volcanoes are located in the Ring of Fire?

_____

6. Why does magma rise to the surface?

_____

_____

_____

7. What purpose would a reader have for reading this passage?

_____ for pleasure or entertainment

_____ for information

_____ to learn how to solve a problem

8. In paragraph 4, which word means "the rubbing together of two objects or surfaces"?

_____

Watery Giants

What are the oceans' most destructive waves, and what causes them?

1   If you have ever gone swimming in an ocean or in one of the Great Lakes, you may have some idea how powerful waves can be. Waves that are only a few feet tall hold enough energy to knock you off your feet. Now, try to imagine the power of a wave that is 50 feet tall and more than 100 miles wide, traveling at speeds of as much as 500 miles per hour. It's easy to see how such a wave could devastate an entire town.

2   The name for these enormous waves is *tsunami*, which means *harbor wave* in Japanese. Tsunamis are caused by a disturbance in the ocean, such as an earthquake or undersea volcanic eruption. Although underwater disturbances are the most common cause of tsunamis, they can also occur if a large meteorite crashes into the ocean.

3   Tsunamis may be relatively small when they are far out at sea. However, as they draw closer and closer to shore, they gather power. One sign of an approaching tsunami is water that recedes at the shore. This occurs because so much of the ocean water is sucked into the wave as it gathers strength.

4   Tsunamis do not consist of a single wave. One wave follows another in a series that may last several hours. A *period* is the length of time in between waves. For average wind-powered waves, a period may be about ten seconds long. Because a tsunami is so much larger, its period may be as long as an hour.

5   Tsunamis have destroyed homes, schools, and entire coastal towns in minutes. The force of a wave as it breaks can be strong enough to travel several hundred feet inland. That is exactly what happened to Hilo, a town on the island of Hawaii, in 1946. At that time, there was not yet an accurate warning system in place.

6   An earthquake registering 7.1 on the Richter scale occurred in Alaska's Aleutian Islands on April 1. About four hours later, Hawaii was struck with the first of seven waves. The waves measured between 24 and 32 feet in height and arrived at 15 to 20 minute intervals. By the time the tsunamis had run their course, 159 lives had been taken.

7   The devastation of the 1946 tsunamis led a team of scientists and government officials to create the Pacific Tsunami Warning System. They hoped that people would never again suffer such great losses because they were unaware of a tsunami's approach. They set up a system to monitor earthquakes that could cause tsunami. They also determined ways to predict the time of arrival of tsunamis so that people would have a chance to evacuate.

8   Unfortunately, there was no such warning system covering the Indian Ocean on December 26, 2004. An enormous earthquake took place and triggered the deadliest tsunami in history. Countries like Thailand, India, and Indonesia were especially hard hit. The loss of life was devastating, and people all around the world reached out to help the victims.

9   Plans are being made to create a global tsunami monitoring system. No system is perfect, but as technology advances, humans will learn better ways to protect themselves against some of the most incredible and powerful forces of nature.

I. Check the line beside the word that best describes what type of passage this is.

_____ biography

_____ informational

_____ fiction

2. What does the word *tsunami* mean in Japanese?

_____

3. What are two possible causes of tsunamis?

_____

4. What is one way in which tsunamis are different than other waves?

_____

5. What is one positive effect of the 1946 tsunamis?

_____

6. Name three countries that were affected by the tsunami of 2004.

_____

7. Why didn't the Pacific Tsunami Warning System alert people of the 2004 tsunami?

_____

Circle the word that best completes each sentence below.

8. Tsunamis can cause great _____.

accuracy   destruction   earthquakes

9. Scientists are looking for ways to be able to better _____ the arrival of tsunamis.

explain   control   predict

10. Tsunamis are not _____ caused by meteorites.

frequently   oddly   powerfully

Creatures of the Night

Do you have bats in your neighborhood? If you do, at what times of day have you seen them?

1   Charley and Mattie Rosen helped their parents clean up after dinner. Charley rinsed the dishes in a tub of clean water and then handed them to his mom to be dried. Mattie gathered firewood so that they could make s'mores and tell scary stories. Mattie loved the smell of wood smoke and the taste of gooey marshmallows melting the chocolate between crisp graham crackers.

2   "How much more wood do we need, Dad?" asked Mattie, setting a small stack beside her father.

3   "I think that should last us for a while, Mattie," replied Mr. Rosen. Mattie brushed her hands on her jeans and crouched beside her dad to watch as the fire grew larger and hotter.

4   "Look at those birds!" exclaimed Charley, pointing a soapy finger at the sky. His parents and Mattie followed his finger and saw what appeared to be a flock of birds swooping out of a tree into the deep blue sky of twilight.

5   "I don't think those are birds, Charley," said Mrs. Rosen, drying her hands on a dishtowel. "I'm pretty sure they're bats. You can tell by the way they fly. See how jerky their movements are? Birds seem to fly more gracefully than bats do."

6   "Shouldn't we get into the tent?" asked Charley nervously. "Vampire bats can suck your blood, can't they?"

7   Mr. Rosen chuckled. "I don't think we have to worry too much about that. There are only a few species of vampire bats in the world, and none of them live in North America. Besides, even vampire bats don't feed on human blood."

8   "What about rabies?" asked Mattie, leaning in closer to her dad.

9   "Bats can carry rabies, but it's quite unusual," said Mrs. Rosen. "We're not going to have close contact with the bats, so it's not anything we need to worry about.

10   "Didn't I ever tell you kids about my trip to Bracken Cave when I was in college?" Mrs. Rosen asked. Mattie and Charley shook their heads, but they kept an eye on the sky.

11   "Well," said Mrs. Rosen, "I was visiting a classmate from school who lived in San Antonio, Texas. She had told me all about a place called Bracken Cave. About 20 million Mexican free-tailed bats go there every year to give birth and raise their young."

12   "Twenty million bats?" said Mattie and Charley incredulously.

13   Mrs. Rosen nodded. "Watching them come out of the cave at night was one of the most remarkable things I have ever seen. The entire sky seemed to fill with them. Conservationists say that the bats from Bracken Cave eat about 200 tons of insects each summer evening."

14   The Rosens sat quietly, looking up at the sky as it darkened. The fire gave off a gentle glow as they patiently waited, hoping to catch another glimpse of the bats as they set out on their evening's activities.

Mark each sentence below **F** if it is in first-person point of view and **T** if it is in third-person point of view.

1. _____ I love making s'mores!

2. _____ Charley rinsed the dishes in a tub of clean water.

3. _____ I went to San Antonio to visit a friend from college.

4. _____ Mr. Rosen said that vampire bats don't live in North America.

Write **F** before the sentences that are facts. Write **O** before the sentences that are opinions.

5. _____ Mattie gathered wood for the fire.

6. _____ Everything is more enjoyable when you are camping.

7. _____ Mexican free-tailed bats come to Bracken Cave to give birth and raise their young.

8. _____ The sky is most beautiful at dusk.

9. How do you think Mattie and Charley will feel the next time they see a bat? Why?

_____

_____

10. What ingredients are used to make s'mores?

_____

11. Find one sentence that shows that Mattie enjoys camping. Write it on the lines below.

_____

_____

12. Where is Bracken Cave located?

_____

Write the idiom from paragraph 10 on the line next to its meaning.

13. watched or observed _____

Going Batty

Keep reading to learn why many people try to attract bats to their yards and neighborhoods.

1   Some animals have good reputations. Most people think of dogs as being friendly and reliable. Kittens are sweet and cuddly. Everyone loves dolphins, seals, and chimpanzees. Other animals, such as bats, do not have nearly as positive a reputation. Many people are frightened of bats and believe that the small flying creatures will become tangled in their hair or give them rabies. There are many myths and superstitions surrounding bats. All of this makes it difficult for educators to get out the word that bats are actually wonderful, useful, and amazing creatures.

2   More than 1,100 species of bats can be found in almost every region of the world, except for the extreme polar and desert regions. Bats, the only flying mammals in the world, vary in size, coloring, and habits. The smallest bat in the world has a wingspan of only two inches and weighs less than a penny. The largest bat has a wingspan of about six feet. Most bats eat insects, but some species feed on fruit, pollen, and nectar, and others eat small animals like fish, frogs, and rodents. Although many scary stories tell of vampire bats, in reality, only three species out of more than one thousand survive on the blood of other animals.

3   Bats are useful creatures. They consume large quantities of insects every evening. A single common brown bat can eat as many as 2,000 insects a night. Imagine how many more mosquito bites you would have each summer if bats were not busy patrolling the night sky.

4   In addition, some bats pollinate plants and flowers. They suck the nectar from one plant and then transfer the plant's pollen when they move on to feed from another plant. In rain forests, bats drop plant seeds as they move, which allows new plants to grow. In regions where the rain forests are in danger, bats perform a very important task, because they insure that new growth will replace plants and trees that have been cut down or destroyed.

5   Because bats are nocturnal creatures, they have the difficult task of flying and catching all their meals in total darkness. This does not present much of a problem for them, though, because they use a special technique called *echolocation*. Bats emit very high-pitched sounds that bounce off objects, no matter how small they are. Bats use the reflected sounds to form pictures in their brains of where things are located. It might not sound like a simple process, but it is obviously very effective. After all, they can find a mosquito flying through the air in complete darkness.

6   The next time you see the flutter of wings in the sky at dusk, there is no need to run for cover. Instead, think about the good deeds that bats perform for human beings and think about their incredible diversity. Maybe you'll even decide to build a bat house in your backyard to encourage the furry flying creatures to take up residence nearby.

1. Explain how *echolocation* works.

_____

_____

_____

2. What is the author trying to persuade the reader of in this selection?

_____

3. How can you encourage bats to live near your home?

_____

4. Why do you think some people are afraid of bats?

_____

5. Write two ways in which species of bats may differ from one another.

_____

Write **T** before the sentences that are true. Write **F** before the sentences that are false.

6. _____ Some bats pollinate plants and flowers.

7. _____ More than 3,000 species of bats exist.

8. _____ Bats are nocturnal creatures.

9. _____ The smallest bat in the world weighs less than a penny.

10. _____ Bats feed only on insects.

11. Check the phrase that best describes the author's purpose.

_____ to instruct _____ to inform _____ to entertain

12. In paragrah 6, the author mentions bats' "incredible diversity." What does this mean?

_____

_____

13. After reading the article, has your opinion of bats changed? Explain.

_____

_____

The Racing Gloves

What special equipment do you think a wheelchair athlete needs?

1 Julio and Tasha sat on the porch drinking lemonade and eating pretzels that Julio's Uncle Jorge had made earlier that morning. Tasha popped the last bite of pretzel in her mouth and dusted the salt from her hands. "Your pretzels are great," Tasha told Uncle Jorge when she saw him wheel into the doorway. "I've never eaten homemade soft pretzels before."

2 "They're easy to make," said Uncle Jorge. "Next time you come over, I'll show you and Julio how to make them," he added, maneuvering his wheelchair down the ramp that led from the front door to the porch.

3 A mail truck pulled up in front of the house, and a moment later, the postal carrier came up the front walk carrying a stack of mail and a small brown package.

4 "Who is the package from, Uncle Jorge?" asked Julio eagerly.

5 Uncle Jorge opened the box and removed a pair of odd-looking gloves from the crumpled brown wrapping paper. "I've been waiting for these," he said, trying on the gloves. He flexed his fingers back and forth several times. "I'm going to be racing in the Boston Marathon this spring," he told Tasha and Julio.

6 "I don't think I knew that the race in Boston was a marathon," said Julio, inspecting one of his uncle's gloves. "You haven't raced in a marathon before, have you?"

7 "This will be my second," said Uncle Jorge. "I've completed plenty of shorter races during the past ten years. Last year, I did my first marathon, and I qualified for the Boston Marathon. My best friend, who is a wheelchair racer too, placed third in his age group in last year's Boston Marathon. We have a friendly competition going, so that's given me incentive to stick to my training schedule."

8 "Is your racing chair very different from your everyday chair?" asked Tasha.

9 Uncle Jorge nodded. "It has two large wheels like this chair does," he said, gesturing to his wheelchair, "but it also has a third, smaller wheel in front. Sports tires are also different than my everyday tires." He grinned. "It's kind of like the difference between wearing running shoes and loafers."

10 "Do a lot of wheelchair racers compete in the Boston Marathon?" asked Julio, dipping a piece of pretzel in some spicy mustard.

11 "It's considered one of the most prestigious races," replied Uncle Jorge. "Other than the Olympic and Paralympic Games, the Boston Marathon is the only race in the world for which you have to meet a qualifying time in order to participate."

12 Tasha and Julio exchanged glances. "I wish it was closer to home so we could go along and cheer for you," said Julio.

13 Uncle Jorge looked at him thoughtfully. "Let me talk to your parents," he said. "Maybe you can drive up with Aunt Amelia and me the night before the race." He smiled at Julio and Tasha. "I'm going to need the biggest cheering section I can get!"

1. What analogy does Uncle Jorge make when he is talking about his everyday tires as compared to his racing tires?

_____

_____

2. How is a racing wheelchair different from a regular wheelchair? How are they similar?

_____

_____

_____

Write **F** before the sentences that are facts. Write **O** before the sentences that are opinions.

3. _____ Uncle Jorge has completed a marathon before.

4. _____ Uncle Jorge will probably complete the marathon in less time than his friend.

5. _____ Tasha and Julio ate the pretzels Uncle Jorge baked.

6. _____ The package contained Uncle Jorge's racing gloves.

7. _____ Uncle Jorge makes the best soft pretzels.

8. Check the words that best describe Uncle Jorge.

_____ impatient

_____ competitive

_____ determined

_____ lonely

_____ enthusiastic

9. How is the Boston Marathon different from most other races?

_____

_____

10. What kind of relationship do Uncle Jorge and his best friend have?

_____

A Reason to Run

Have you ever participated in a charity event?

1   Julio and Tasha sat on the sun-warmed grass at the park. They were stretching before they set out on their afternoon run. As they stretched, they spoke about the upcoming race. Neither Julio nor Tasha had raced before, but they had been training together for nearly three months and felt prepared.

2   "Do you have any sponsors yet?" asked Tasha. Her voice was a bit muffled as she bent over and gripped her ankles in a deep stretch.

3   "Not really," replied Julio. He stood up and leaned to one side, reaching as far as he could over his head with the opposite hand. "My parents and my grandma have both signed up. I know my aunts and uncles will help out, too, but I haven't actually asked them yet. What about you?"

4   Tasha took a quick drink from her water bottle and stood up. "I haven't asked anyone but my parents yet," she said. "I'm really nervous about asking other people to sponsor me for this race," she confessed. "I really want to run, and I want to help support the Leukemia Society, but I'm dreading the whole process of asking for sponsors."

5   Tasha and Julio started down the bike path at a medium jog. "What are you worried about?" asked Julio. "I think that people will be willing to help out a good cause. We're not asking them to buy anything. All we want is a donation to the Leukemia Society in exchange for the time and effort we put into training."

6   "I know," agreed Tasha. "It shouldn't be a big deal, but I'm just afraid that no one will want to participate, or that they'll pledge to support me and I won't be able to finish the race for some reason."

7   Julio and Tasha ran single file for a few seconds as they passed a family on roller blades. When Julio caught up to Tasha, he said, "Listen, I completely understand why it's hard for you to ask people you don't know for donations. I can help you with that part. But you have to have a little more confidence in yourself about the race. We've both been able to run the entire three miles for the last month. You're practically not even out of breath anymore when we finish. This race is going to be a piece of cake for you."

8   The two runners were quiet for a moment. The only sound was the gentle thudding of their shoes hitting the path. "You're right," said Tasha finally. "Running the race isn't going to be the hard part for me. Do you have any ideas about whom we could ask for pledges?"

9   Julio, who was starting to become a bit short of breath, nodded. "Could you ask the parents of the players on your soccer team?" he asked. "Also, the neighborhood block party is going to be next weekend. That could be a great time to ask our neighbors. Everyone will be in a good mood, so they'll probably be pretty receptive to helping us out."

10   Tasha smiled. "We make a good team, Julio," she said. "I definitely feel like I can do this now."

11   Julio smiled back. "Good," he said, picking up the pace, "because the last one to make it to the finish today has to buy ice cream on the way home!" Tasha laughed as the two friends sprinted toward the park's gates.

1. What problem does Tasha have in the story?

_____

_____

2. How does Julio help her resolve the problem?

_____

_____

3. Name one way in which Tasha and Julio are similar.

_____

4. Name one way in which Tasha and Julio are different.

_____

5. What charitable organization will Julio and Tasha help by running the race?

_____

6. Why does Julio think that it would be a good idea to ask their neighbors to pledge money during the block party?

_____

7. The **theme** of a story is its subject. It tells what idea the story is mostly about. Check the word below that best describes the theme of "A Reason to Run."

_____ fitness   _____ friendship   _____ loyalty

Circle the word that best completes each sentence below.

8. Tasha feels that she can _____ with Julio's support.

win   succeed   apply

9. Julio _____ Tasha to have more confidence in herself.

encourages   discourages   requests

Write the idiom from paragraph 7 on the line next to its meaning.

10. easy; simple to do _____.

Getting Up to Speed

Where can you go running safely in your neighborhood?

Before you begin training:

- Find a running "buddy" to train with you. Ask a friend from school or from your neighborhood, your brother or sister, or a parent or other relative.

- Make sure you have a good pair of running shoes that fit you properly.

- Stay hydrated! Even if you aren't perspiring visibly, exercise uses up a great deal of your body's water. Be sure to drink water frequently to keep your energy level up and your body working.

- Snack on healthful foods. Fruits and vegetables, whole grains, and low-fat dairy products all help maintain a healthy body. Have an apple and a piece of cheese, some yogurt sprinkled with granola, or an orange and a handful of whole-grain pretzels. You'll find that you have plenty of energy to complete the goals you set for yourself.

- Get in the habit of taking a few minutes to stretch before you begin running. Stretching helps you stay flexible. It can also help protect your body from injury.

1   The best way to begin training is by alternately walking and running. This allows your body to become accustomed to the challenge of running without overdoing it. Begin your first week with running for two minutes and walking for four minutes. Do this sequence five times in a row, four times a week.

2   If you feel comfortable doing this sequence after a week, you're ready to progress to the next level. If it still feels challenging, continue with it for another week.

3   When you decide to move to the next level, you'll run three minutes and walk for three minutes. Continue to progress each week, increasing the time you spend running and decreasing the time you spend walking, until you reach 30 minutes of continuous running.

4   When you are running, you should be able to comfortably talk with your running buddy. If you are pushing yourself too hard, talking will be difficult because you'll be short of breath.

5   The days of the week that you don't run, try some different kinds of fitness activities, like hiking, ice skating, jumping rope, or playing basketball. You'll find that these activities use different muscles than running does. This kind of cross-training can help you get into even better shape than only repeating a single activity. Don't forget to schedule at least one day of rest every week. It's always a good idea to give your body a chance to recover from your daily workouts.

6   Consider keeping a runner's log or journal. You can record the weather, your route, the distance you ran, and how you felt. You might notice that you prefer running early in the day or that eating an orange before you go for a run gives you a good boost in energy.

7   Most of all, remember to have fun. Running is just one of many different activities you can do to stay in shape. Vary your routine enough to keep it interesting, and bring along a friend to keep you company.

1. What are some types of fitness activities mentioned in the selection besides running?

_____

2. What do you think cross-training is?

_____

_____

3. What is the best way to begin training?

_____

_____

4. What purpose would a reader have for reading this selection?

_____ for pleasure or entertainment   _____ to learn how to become a runner

_____ to form an opinion about running

5. Write a summary sentence for paragraph 5.

_____

_____

6. What kind of information could you record in a runner's log?

_____

_____

7. Do you think the author is trying to persuade the reader of anything in this selection? Explain.

_____

_____

8. In bullet 3, what does *hydrated* mean?

_____

9. Are you a runner? If so, explain what you like about it. If not, would you like to take up running? Why or why not?

_____

_____

A Mysterious Glow

Have you ever seen an organism that glows? Where were you?

1 It was the Taylors' first night at the beach. Miles, Sophie, and their parents sat outside and enjoyed a big seafood dinner that included fresh fish, scallops, crab, coleslaw, and corn on the cob. The sun was a ball of fire as it slipped into the ocean and left a peach-colored glow in the sky. They played several board games, and by nine o'clock, everyone had caught their second wind.

2 "How does an evening stroll along the beach sound?" asked Mrs. Taylor, stretching as she stood up. "It's a beautiful night, and I don't think you kids have ever seen stars the way they look over the ocean at night."

3 "Sounds good to me," said Mr. Taylor, collecting the game pieces on the coffee table and putting them back in the box.

4 Sophie used a flashlight to guide the group down the sandy path in between the cottages, and in just a few minutes the Taylors found themselves on the beach. Miles and Sophie took off their flip-flops and let the sand squish between their toes.

5 "The sand is so much cooler than it was earlier today!" exclaimed Sophie, remembering how she had danced across the beach to the water to keep from burning the soles of her feet.

6 Mrs. Taylor nodded. "The sand absorbs the sun's heat during the day, but it cools off quickly as soon the sun goes down."

7 Miles and Sophie walked ahead of their parents, wading in the gentle waves along the shore as they tried to pick out constellations in the cloudless sky. "Miles," said Sophie after a few minutes, "do you notice anything weird about the water? Doesn't it seem like it's almost glowing?" She stopped walking and kicked her bare foot in the water. There was an explosion of milky-green light where Sophie kicked. Miles and Sophie looked at one another. "This is totally bizarre," said Sophie.

8 She and Miles crouched at the water's edge and ran their hands back and forth rapidly in the cool water. Swirls of light traced the pattern their hands had made.

9 Their parents had finally caught up to Miles and Sophie. "Did you find something?" inquired Mrs. Taylor, kneeling beside Sophie. Before Sophie even had time to answer, Mrs. Taylor gasped. "This is incredible," she said swirling her hands in the water. "I've read about it, but I've never seen it myself. Ian, did you see this?" she asked Mr. Taylor.

10 He nodded, and even in the dim light Sophie and Miles could see the look of amazement on their dad's face. "What is it, Mom?" asked Sophie. "Why is the water glowing?"

11 "It's called *bioluminescence*," said Mrs Taylor. "You're not actually seeing the water itself glow. There's just a high concentration of tiny organisms in it that create light. It's similar to the type of light that fireflies produce."

12 "I think we were all too busy looking at the stars in the sky to see the ones in the ocean," marveled Mr. Taylor.

1. Write one sentence from the story that indicates how the Taylors felt about discovering the bioluminescence.

_____

2. What happened when Sophie kicked the water?

_____

3. What explanation does Mrs. Taylor have for why the water is glowing?

_____

_____

4. Why do you think the Taylors didn't notice the glowing water right away?

_____

5. Do you think that Sophie and Miles will try to learn more about bioluminescence when they get home? Why or why not?

_____

Read the sentences below. Write **B** next to the sentence if it tells about something that happened before Miles and Sophie noticed the water was glowing. Write **A** if it describes something that happened after.

6. _____ Mrs. Taylor swirled her hands in the water.

7. _____ Mr. Taylor collected the game pieces from the coffee table.

8. _____ Miles and Sophie picked out constellations in the night sky.

9. _____ Miles and Sophie took off their flip-flops.

10. _____ Mrs. Taylor knelt beside Sophie.

Write the idiom from paragraph 1 on the line next to its meaning.

11. felt refreshed _____

A metaphor is a comparison of two things without using the word _like_ or _as_. For example, _Her fingers were icicles_. Find the metaphor in paragraph 1, and write it on the line.

12. _____

Living Lights

What would it be like to glow in the dark?

1   Very few organisms that live on land have the ability to glow in the dark, but it is a surprisingly common characteristic among deep-sea marine creatures. In fact, about 90 percent of animals that live 200 to 1,000 meters below the surface of the ocean are bioluminescent.

2   The word *bioluminescence* (bahy-oh-loo-muh-nes-uhns) comes from the Greek word *bios*, which means *living*, and the Latin word *lumen*, which means *light*. It refers to organisms that produce light as a result of a chemical reaction. Bioluminescence is a cool light. In a lightbulb, about 97 percent of the energy is used to create heat, and only 3 percent is used to create light. When bioluminescence is produced, very little energy is used to create heat. This is one reason that scientists are so interested in learning about bioluminescence and how it might be used to create more efficient, less wasteful light sources.

3   Ocean animals use bioluminescence in various ways. You might think that light would not be very effective as camouflage because it would draw attention to an animal instead of helping it hide. However, if you were a predator hunting a bobtail squid and you looked up at the squid's belly, its bioluminescence would allow it to blend with the stars of the night sky.

4   Other animals use bioluminescence to attract mates. This is the case with fireflies on land, who use light signals to attract others of the same species. It is also true of ocean animals like the Bermuda fireworm.

5   One species of squid uses bioluminescence to confuse predators. If it feels threatened, it spews a cloud of bioluminescent chemicals. While the predator is surprised and confused, the squid has time to quickly escape.

6   Another possible use of bioluminescence is to lure prey. The cookie cutter shark is one animal that uses its light in this way. Patterns of bioluminescence on the shark's underside may resemble small fish to predators like tuna or mackerel. When they come closer to investigate, the shark attacks. The anglerfish uses a similar method to capture prey. It extends a glowing lure from an appendage on its head. Other fish mistake the glowing lure for a meal and venture closer. When they do, the anglerfish moves quickly and snaps them up.

7   Because many bioluminescent animals live deep underwater, most people don't have the opportunity to observe them. However, tiny one-celled creatures called *dinoflagellates* (din-uh-flaj-uh-leyt) live in the sea and produce much of the visible bioluminescence near the ocean's surface. In areas that have large numbers of dinoflagellates, the motion of waves, a boat, a porpoise, or even a hand can easily disturb them and cause them to glow. On a dark night, this eerie but beautiful sight can create quite a light show in the ocean!

1. Write a sentence that tells the main idea of the passage.

_____

2. Explain one way in which an animal can use bioluminescence to lure prey.

_____

_____

3. What kind of creature produces much of the visible bioluminescence near the ocean's surface?

_____

4. How does bioluminescence help camouflage the bobtail squid?

_____

_____

5. How is bioluminescence different from the light produced by a lightbulb?

_____

_____

6. What can cause dinoflagellates to glow?

_____

_____

7. Check the line beside the word or words that best describe what type of selection this is.

_____ science fiction   _____ informative   _____ fantasy

8. The Latin root **mar** means *sea*. Find a word in paragraph 1 with the root **mar**.

_____

9. The Latin root **fic** means *make* or *do*. Find a word in paragraph 2 with the root **fic**.

_____

10. The Latin root **tract** means *pull* or *drag*. Find a word in paragraph 4 with the root **tract**.

_____

A Stinging Surprise

What happens when Miles has an unexpected encounter with a jellyfish?

1   Sophie, Miles, and Mr. Taylor walked along the beach. The late afternoon sun reflected off the water and made it sparkle like a sea of diamonds.

2   "Quick, kids, look at the seagull!" exclaimed Mr. Taylor. He pointed toward a gull that had just swooped down and plucked a large fish from the water. The fish wriggled, and they could see that it was a struggle for the seagull to hold its catch firmly without dropping it.

3   "I can't believe that a bird that size can carry such a...ouch! Dad, help! I think I stepped on something!" Miles hopped on one foot, trying to shake the stinging sensation from his other foot. Mr. Taylor reached him quickly and helped Miles take a seat on the warm sand.

4   "I think that's what you stepped on," said Sophie, pointing to a sand-covered, jelly-like blob on the beach. "Is it a jellyfish, Dad?"

5   Mr. Taylor nodded. Then, he looked at Miles who was wincing in pain. "You're all right, Miles," he said, giving his son a gentle squeeze on the shoulder. He turned to Sophie. "Do you see that lifeguard tower down the beach?" he asked. Sophie nodded. "Can you run over there and tell the lifeguard that we think your brother was stung by a jellyfish?"

6   Sophie nodded and headed for the tower. Meanwhile, Mr. Taylor emptied the bucket of seashells and used it to gently rinse the sand from Miles's foot with seawater.

7   "How does that feel?" he asked Miles. [8] "About the same," replied Miles. "It burns and stings."

9   In just a few minutes, Sophie returned with the lifeguard, a friendly-looking man with deeply tanned skin and curly black hair.

10   He opened a small red and white box and removed some rubbing alcohol. "First, we're going to clean the area with a bit of alcohol," he began. "Vinegar works too, just in case you're ever stung again."

11   "Now what are you going to put on it?" asked Sophie curiously.

12   "Well, it might sound funny, but I'm making a paste using meat tenderizer and water." He smeared the paste on the heel of Miles's foot, which had become red and slightly swollen. "Meat tenderizer is an enzyme that breaks down protein. Jellyfish poison is a protein, so it works on the poison the same way it does on meat."

13   "It actually feels better already," said Miles in surprise.

14   The lifeguard smiled. "If you don't have any meat tenderizer at home, a paste made of baking soda and water will also soothe it. If the area becomes any more irritated in the next couple of hours, I'd suggest seeing a doctor. Otherwise, you'll probably be feeling much better by morning."

15   "Thank you for all your help," said Mr. Taylor, shaking the lifeguard's hand. "Come on, Miles. This is probably the last piggyback ride you're going to get before you get taller than me!"

1. Number the events below to show the order in which they happened.

_____ Mr. Taylor shook the lifeguard's hand.

_____ The Taylors watched a seagull catch a fish.

_____ The lifeguard cleaned the sting with alcohol.

_____ Sophie pointed to the sand-covered jellyfish.

_____ The lifeguard smeared meat tenderizer on Miles' foot.

2. If you don't have alcohol and meat tenderizer at home, what else can you use to treat a jellyfish sting?

_____

3. Under what circumstances does the lifeguard recommend that Miles see a doctor?

_____

4. Why does meat tenderizer soothe a jellyfish sting?

_____

5. What were the Taylors looking at when Miles was stung?

_____

6. How did the Taylors determine what Miles had stepped on?

_____

7. The **climax** of a story is the point of highest excitement. What is the climax in "A Stinging Surprise"?

_____

Find the simile in paragraph 1, and write it on the line below.

8. _____

9. Have you ever been stung by something, like a bee or some fire ants? How did you react? How did you treat it?

_____

_____

_____

Curious Creatures

Have you ever seen a jellyfish in the wild or at a zoo or an aquarium?

1   What kind of animal has no brain, no bones, and no circulatory system? This might sound like a riddle, but it isn't. The jellyfish is one of the ocean's most unusual creatures. Instead of having all the organs that are typical of most animals, jellyfish have specialized tissues that carry out the various functions they need to survive.

2   The term *jellyfish* is inaccurate because these animals are neither fish nor made of jelly. They are invertebrates, which means that they do not have backbones. They are also relatives of corals and sea anemones. Scientists believe that there may be as many as 2,000 types of jellyfish in the world's oceans. Most species are found in saltwater, though a few freshwater varieties do exist.

3   Because there are so many different species of jellyfish, it is not surprising that there is such variety in their appearance. The smallest jellyfish are less than an inch in length, while the largest may grow to be 200 feet long! Shape and color are two more ways in which jellyfish differ. Typically, jellyfish have little color because their bodies are composed of 95 to 99 percent water. Some species are more colorful and may be brown, pink, white, or blue.

4   Most jellyfish have the same basic shape. From the top, they look similar to an umbrella or a mushroom, with long thin tentacles that extend below their "heads." The tentacles are lined with stinging cells called *nematocysts* that the jellyfish uses to capture food such as small fish, plankton, and other small sea creatures.

5   These same stinging cells are what cause people such pain if they accidentally step on a jellyfish that has washed up on shore or brush against a tentacle as they swim in the ocean. The sting from most species of jellyfish is relatively harmless, though it can be painful. However, there are several

species of jellyfish whose sting can be fatal.

6   For the most part, jellyfish are transported by ocean currents and the wind. They have some ability to move through the water by contracting muscles in the main part of the body. These contractions can push the jellyfish vertically through the water at a slow pace. For the most part, though, jellyfish are content to float through the waves, waiting for the next potential food source to become tangled in their tentacles.

7   The next time you go to the beach, keep your eyes open for a colorless blob gently floating on the water's surface. If you're lucky, you'll get a close-up view of one of the ocean's strangest creatures.

1. Why does the author say that the description of a jellyfish might sound like a riddle?

_____

2. How much of a jellyfish's body is composed of water?

_____

3. What are nematocysts?

_____

4. Check the phrase that best describes the author's purpose.

_____ to entertain

_____ to inform

_____ to persuade

Write **T** before the sentences that are true. Write **F** before the sentences that are false.

5. _____ All species of jellyfish are totally harmless to humans.

6. _____ Jellyfish do not have most of the organs that are common in other animals.

7. _____ Jellyfish can move only where the wind and the tides take them.

8. _____ Only about one-third of a jellyfish's body is water.

9. _____ A few freshwater species of jellyfish do exist.

10. What three things is a jellyfish lacking that most animals have?

_____

11. An invertebrate has no _____.

12. How do jellyfish move?

_____

_____

Tune in to History

Do you know who invented television?

1   Television is such a familiar part of our daily lives that you probably never think about its history or the fact that as recently as 70 years ago many people had never even heard of it. The word *television* comes from the Greek word *tele*, which means *far*, and the Latin word *visio*, which means *sight*. It's the perfect description for this electronic device that receives images and sound transmitted from another place.

2   Early in the 20th century, many experiments were attempted to transmit moving images from one place to another. Because there were so many contributors, it is hard to pinpoint exactly who gets credit as the inventor of TV. However, television as we know it today was developed in the 1920s by two men working separately.

3   Philo Taylor Farnsworth, a farm boy from Idaho, demonstrated the first electronic television in 1927. It was a prototype of the TVs we use today. During the late 1920s, a Russian-born scientist named Vladimir Zworykin worked with the electronics company RCA to develop the first marketable televisions. Because of this pivotal role in bringing TV to the public, he was regarded for many years as the "inventor" of television. Historians disagree about which man deserves more credit, but today, Farnsworth's contribution is seen as the crucial first step in the technological developments made by Zworykin.

4   The first TVs were not too impressive by our standards. In fact, they were actually radios with an extremely small television device attached. The screen was lit by a reddish neon light, and the image was only the size of a postage stamp.

5   By the 1930s, TVs became available to the public, but they were very expensive— about $7,000 each in today's money. After World War II, however, the price dropped significantly and televisions became a much more common sight. By the late 1950s, color televisions became available, and the Western series *Bonanza* became the first TV show to be regularly shown in color.

6   Television is similar to radio in the way that it uses an antenna to pick up signals sent over the airwaves. Local TV stations still send signals that can be picked up by your TV's antenna, but increasing numbers of people use cable to receive their television broadcasts.

7   In 1949, John Watson, a television salesman in rural Pennsylvania, was having a hard time selling his TVs. Television signals were weak by the time they reached his town, and people did not think it was worthwhile to buy a TV. Watson put up a giant antenna to get better reception and offered his customers a free connection to the stronger signal. Eventually, he started to charge for the service, and cable TV was born.

1. What was the first TV show to be regularly shown in color?

_____

2. Who are the two people that are often given credit for inventing television?

_____

3. What Latin and Greek roots are found in the word *television*? What do they mean?

_____

4. About how much would a 1930s television have cost in today's dollars?

_____

5. Check the phrase that best describes the author's purpose.

_____ to entertain

_____ to inform

_____ to persuade

Circle the word that best completes each sentence below.

6. Televisions became _____ priced after World War II.

significantly   reasonably   highly

7. John Watson's _____ thinking led to the invention of cable TV.

creative   unimaginative   selfish

8. Farnsworth and Zworykin both _____ the invention of the modern television.

developed   requested   contributed to

9. In paragraph 3, which word means "an original model"?

_____

10. When did televisions first start becoming more common?

_____

Moving Images

What is the most important event you have seen on TV?

1   With at least one television in nearly every home in the United States, TV has become the major source for news. September 11, 2001, and the days that followed kept people glued to their television sets for information and comfort. During the more recent war in Iraq, Americans turned on their TVs for similar reasons. Many historical events from the past 50 years would not be remembered the same way without the televised images. Some events were even shaped by the powerful influence these images have on the public.

2   The "Checker's Speech" by vice-presidential candidate Richard Nixon was an early example of how television can change the public's perception of someone. Nixon had been accused of accepting gifts for his campaign and was viewed negatively by the public.

3   On September 9, 1952, Nixon went on TV to defend himself. He claimed that the only questionable gift he had received was the family dog, Checkers, and he was not about to give the pet back. The public was moved to tears by Nixon's speech, and he redeemed himself. However, television would not be so kind to Nixon in the future.

4   In 1959, television played an important role in the presidential debate between Richard Nixon and John F. Kennedy. Viewers saw a younger, smiling Kennedy trading viewpoints with Nixon, who was scowling and looked uncomfortable. Radio listeners, who had heard only the words and ideas, thought that Nixon had won the debate. However, television viewers declared Kennedy the winner. The power of televised images in politics was never underestimated again.

5   During the tragedy of JFK's assassination, television allowed the citizens of our nation to grieve together. People across the country saw Kennedy's coffin as it was loaded onto *Air Force One* while Jackie Kennedy, the First Lady, stood by watching. Millions who were still in shock over these unbelievable events viewed JFK's funeral procession. Many citizens were also reassured about the power of our democracy as they watched Vice-President Lyndon Johnson quickly sworn in as the new president.

6   Not all historical moments on television involve politics. For instance, the Beatles' appearance on the *Ed Sullivan Show* on February 9, 1964, changed American pop culture. Viewers across the nation saw their goofy grins and goofier haircuts, as well as the crowd's frenzied cheering, and "Beatlemania" was born.

7   In July of 1969, 94 percent of Americans who owned televisions watched a live broadcast and saw Neil Armstrong and Buzz Aldrin become the first humans on the moon. Around the world, nearly one billion people watched this event on TV.

Write the words from the passage that have the meanings below.

1. the way in which one is viewed or perceived

_____

2. changed for the better; reformed

_____

3. felt comforted and less anxious

_____

Write **T** before the sentences that are true. Write **F** before the sentences that are false.

4. _____ Nixon stated that he did not receive any questionable gifts.

5. _____ About 75 percent of Americans who owned televisions watched Armstrong and Aldrin walk on the moon.

6. _____ The Beatles appeared on the *Ed Sullivan Show* in 1964.

7. _____ Lyndon Johnson became president after Kennedy's assassination.

8. Do you think that television as a source of news will be as important in the future as it has been in the past? Explain.

_____

_____

9. How did the "Checker's Speech" change the way people thought of Richard Nixon?

_____

_____

10. Do you think it is fair for people to base their opinions on what they see as well as what they hear? Explain.

_____

_____

11. What kind of effect did television have on the popularity of the Beatles?

_____

12. How did Kennedy and Nixon appear to be different from one another during their televised debate?

_____

Book Fair Brainstorming

Does your school hold an annual book fair?

1 "This is a lot of responsibility, Caleb," said Tanika, twirling her pen. "I don't have much experience planning an event like this. I'm glad Mr. Rutledge trusted us to work out all the details, but I'm still worried that we'll forget something important."

2 Caleb leaned back in his chair. "I'm not worried, Tanika," he said. "We just have to be organized. I have no doubt that this will be the best annual book fair George Washington Middle School has ever seen. We'll raise so much money for the library that they'll have to build a new room to accommodate all the books they'll be able to buy," he joked.

3 Tanika grinned at Caleb. "You might be just a bit too optimistic, but I agree with you that somehow we'll manage to make this book fair a success."

4 Caleb took out a pad of paper. "Do we have the list of books the librarians ordered?" he asked.

5 Tanika handed Caleb some papers that he quickly leafed through. "We should think of some interesting display ideas," he said thoughtfully. "The book fairs that we've had in the last few years have been kind of dull. I want this one to make everyone feel excited about reading."

6 "What if we set up areas with different themes?" suggested Tanika. "We can borrow different kinds of sports equipment from Ms. Spisak and make a display near the sports books."

7 Caleb was sitting up in his chair writing furiously. "That is a fantastic idea, Tanika!" he said excitedly. "We can have a different exhibit for each area. My class has a turtle and some fish that we could display in the area with books about animals."

8 "The librarians ordered quite a few winter and holiday books, as well," said Tanika, consulting the list again. "We could make a festive winter scene in one area. I know where there are some little white lights from the school play. I can bring in my ice skates and a few pairs of mittens for the display."

9 "What about trying to see if we could get a few writers to come in on the day of the book fair? They could sell autographed copies of their books and answer questions students have about being a writer."

10 "Rachael Weinstock's mom wrote a picture book a few years ago," said Tanika. "She's done several author events around town, and there's a good chance she'd be willing to help us."

11 "And Carson Davies's dad used to be an editor for a children's book publisher. He might know some local authors, too," added Caleb. He made a few more notes on his pad of paper. "Are you still worried about being able to pull off this book fair, Tanika?" he asked.

12 Tanika shook her head. "Now I just can't wait for it to get here," she said. "I think a little of your optimism has started to rub off on me!"

1. The Latin root **ann** means *year*. Find a word in paragraph 2 with the root **ann**.

_____

2. The Greek root **graph** means *write*. Find a word in paragraph 9 with the root **graph**.

_____

3. The Latin root **loc** means *place*. Find a word in paragraph 11 with the root **loc**.

_____

Write **F** before the sentences that are facts. Write **O** before the sentences that are opinions.

4. _____ Tanika worries too much.

5. _____ This year's book fair will be better than previous fairs.

6. _____ Rachael Weinstock's mom is the author of a picture book.

7. _____ Caleb's class has a turtle and some fish.

Mark each sentence below **F** if it is in first-person point of view and **T** if it is in third-person point of view.

8. _____ I think this book fair will be a success.

9. _____ Caleb looked through the list books the librarians ordered.

10. _____ My sister might have some sports equipment we could use.

11. What are two ideas that Tanika and Caleb have to make this year's book fair more exciting?

_____

_____

12. Why does Caleb think that Mr. Davies might be able to help?

_____

_____

Read the descriptions below. Write **C** next to the phrase if it describes Caleb.
Write **T** if it describes Tanika.

13. _____ feels calm and confident about the success of the book fair

14. _____ suggests setting up areas with different themes

15. _____ offers to bring in ice skates and mittens for the winter display

Book Fair Funds

How will Tanika and Caleb decide to spend the proceeds from the book fair?

1 Tanika and Caleb sat at a large round table in the library with their teacher, Mr. Rutledge, and one of the school librarians, Mrs. Angley. The adults were grinning widely at Tanika and Caleb, who smiled back uncertainly.

2 "You are probably wondering why we asked you both to stay a few minutes after school today," began Mr. Rutledge. "We have the totals from last weekend's book fair, and we wanted to share them with you," he continued. "Mrs. Angley, will you do the honors?" he asked, turning to the librarian.

3 Mrs. Angley nodded. "This has been the most successful book fair in the nine years that Washington has held book fairs," she said, passing out a sheet of paper that showed the results of previous book fairs. "Much of the credit goes to you two," she added, gesturing to Tanika and Caleb, who still had expressions of awe on their faces. "Mr. Rutledge is also deserving of some credit since it was his idea to involve such creative and motivated students in planning the fair."

4 "This is great news," said Caleb. "We could see that people were enjoying themselves at the fair, but we had no idea how that would translate into profits."

5 "The planning required a lot of work," added Tanika, "but we had so much help. It really was a team effort."

6 "Because you both put so much energy and enthusiasm into this event," said Mr. Rutledge, "we've decided that we could use your help in allocating the money we raised. The principal and the library staff have already set aside funds for items that are necessities. However, it has not yet been decided how the remaining money will be used. Do you have any ideas?"

7 Caleb and Tanika were quiet for a moment as they thought about the possibilities. Then, Caleb spoke up. "I agree with what Tanika said about the fair being a team effort. Students from every class contributed, and it would be nice if there was a way we could show our appreciation. Could they help decide which books will be added to the library's collection?" he asked.

8 "That's an excellent idea," agreed Mr. Rutledge.

9 "If there's any money left over," said Tanika, "do you think we could use it to bring authors and illustrators to the school more often? Everyone I talked to seemed to think that was the best part of the fair."

10 Mrs. Angley nodded. "We've already put some money aside for that," she said. "The school received several donations from parents during the fair, and the principal thinks that the money would be well spent just as you've suggested."

11 "There's just one more thing," said Mr. Rutledge, turning to Tanika and Caleb. "Would you consider helping to plan next year's book fair? We could use your expertise."

12 Tanika and Caleb exchanged glances. "With an invitation like that, how could we resist?" said Caleb.

I. Why do Caleb and Tanika think that the students should be able to vote on the books that will be added to the library?

_____

_____

2. Do you think that Caleb and Tanika work well together as a team? Why or why not?

_____

_____

3. Why did Mr. Rutledge and Mrs. Angley decide to ask for Caleb and Tanika's help?

_____

_____

4. What is the setting for this story?

_____

5. Do you think that Caleb and Tanika will choose to work together on future projects? Explain.

_____

_____

6. Check the line beside the word or words that best describe what type of selection this is.

_____ a tall tale   _____ realistic fiction   _____ historical fiction

7. In paragraph 6, what does *allocating* mean?

_____

8. If you were in Caleb or Tanika's place, how would you choose to spend the money?

_____

_____

A Writer's Life

Who are your favorite authors? Do you know how they became writers?

1   Louis Sachar is one of the most well-known writers of children's books today. He is the author of more than 20 books that are loved by children, parents, teachers, and critics alike. You might recognize Sachar's name from the series of *Wayside School* books or *Marvin Redpost* books. You might also know him as the author of the Newbery Award-winning book *Holes*.

2   As successful as Louis Sachar is at writing funny, touching books that kids can relate to, he didn't always know he wanted to be a writer. Sachar remembers enjoying his writing assignments in school, but writing wasn't something he did on his own. When he was in college, he studied economics, and even briefly studied Russian language and literature.

3   Sachar spent time as a teacher's aide when he was in college because he thought it would be an easy way to earn class credit. Although the work was not as easy as he thought it would be, Sachar found that he really enjoyed working with young people. In fact, Hillside Elementary, where Sachar worked as an aide, eventually became the inspiration for his popular *Wayside School* books. The kids in the books are even named after students that Sachar worked with in real life!

4   Even after his experiences teaching and working with children, Sachar still hadn't made a decision about what career path to follow. After college, he decided to go to law school. He graduated several years later with a law degree. By this time, Sachar had published his first children's book, but he didn't feel confident about making a living as a writer.

5   About ten years later, after the publication of several more books, Sachar finally felt that his books were successful enough for him to devote himself to writing full time. In 1989, Sachar quit his job as an attorney and became a writer.

6   Sachar spends about two hours writing each morning, when he feels most fresh and sharp. He likes to be alone when he writes, except for the company of his two dogs, Tippy and Lucky. Some writers base their stories closely around the people and events in their lives, and others create characters and places that are entirely fictional. Sachar uses a combination of the two. He tries to remember what it was like to be a child and to use those memories and feelings in his novels. He also uses his teaching experiences, as well as moments from his daughter's life.

7   Sachar doesn't sit down with an organized plan or outline when he starts a new book. Instead, he begins with just a seed of an idea––maybe a character trait or a funny event. He starts writing and finds that the act of writing produces more ideas. Those ideas branch out into other ideas, and before he knows it, a new book is well on its way.

8   Sachar doesn't worry too much about perfecting his story, plot, characters, and setting the first time around. In fact, he may rewrite his story five or six times before he even sends it to his publisher. That might seem like a lot of work, but one thing is for sure—Louis Sachar seems to have hit on a winning formula for writing!

1. Check the words that best describe Louis Sachar.

_____ creative   _____ intelligent

_____ humorous   _____ nosy

_____ unpredictable

2. What purpose would a reader have for reading this selection?

_____ for information about the life and work of Louis Sachar

_____ to learn how to solve a problem

_____ to form an opinion about the work of Louis Sachar

3. Check the line beside the word or words that best describe what type of selection this is.

_____ autobiography   _____ historical nonfiction   _____ biography

4. Name two series of books that Louis Sachar has written.

_____

5. Why didn't Sachar become a full-time writer as soon as his first book was published?

_____

_____

6. What happens after Sachar has completed the first draft of a book?

_____

_____

7. Name two sources of ideas for Sachar's stories and characters.

_____

_____

8. If you were to write a short story or a novel, what sources of ideas could you use? Be specific.

_____

_____

So, You Want to Be a Writer?

What are some tips on becoming a writer?

1. Read everything you can. Most writers are voracious readers. They read because they love to lose themselves in books. They like the sounds of language and the way that reading a good description can feel as satisfying as winning a baseball game or eating a banana split.

As you read, pay attention to what speaks to you. Do you like stories that are fast-paced and full of unexpected twists? Do you prefer to read books with characters who seem like someone you might know? Do you like tales that take you on faraway adventures, or ones that explain the mysteries of the natural world? Do you like to feel scared when you read under the covers, or do you like a story that makes you laugh until you cry? Think about the types of writing you like best, and try to identify the qualities that appeal to you.

2. Keep a notebook. It's easy to forget a good idea if you do not record it immediately. If you get in the habit of carrying a notebook or journal with you everywhere you go, you can write down anything you want to remember. When you are talking to friends in the cafeteria or waiting for the bus, something might spark an idea for a character or a scene in a story. You might have a dream you don't want to forget, or you might just write down the lyrics of a song you love. These everyday thoughts and observations can be material for a story, poem, or essay that you write one day.

3. Write every day. One piece of advice that nearly all writers agree on is that writers must write. It doesn't matter if you feel like you have nothing to say; the important thing is that you write every single day. Sometimes, you need to give yourself permission to write things you know won't be your best work. Once you start writing, you'll see that this is a good way to clear your mind and make room for more of the "good stuff."

4. Join or start a writing group. Do you have any friends who enjoy writing? Think about starting a writing group with other people who have similar interests. It helps to have the support of other writers. You will also receive valuable feedback, or suggestions, about how to make your work better.

5. Do your homework. If you decide that you would like to submit your work for publication, make sure to do your research. If you are sending your writing to a magazine, look through old issues. Does it seem like your writing fits in with the other stories or articles? If you are submitting to a book publisher, explore their Web site to make sure your material is similar to (but not exactly the same as) other books they publish.

Also make sure that you pay attention to the guidelines. Present your work to them exactly the way they have requested it. If your work doesn't conform to their guidelines, the publisher may not even look at it.

6. Stay positive. A writer's life can be frustrating. Sometimes it's hard to sit down and write. You may get many rejections before you receive a single acceptance. This is why perseverance is an important quality for a writer to have.

Writing can also be one of the most satisfying jobs in the world. Most writers feel lucky to do what they do and wouldn't trade their career for any other. You could be one of them someday.

1. Check the phrase that best describes the author's purpose.

_____ to instruct

_____ to entertain

_____ to inform

2. Name three things you might record in a writer's notebook.

_____

_____

3. What does the author mean by "Do your homework"?

_____

_____

4. Why is perseverance an important quality for a writer to have?

_____

_____

5. Why do you think that most writers like to read?

_____

6. On the lines below, write a summary of Step 3.

_____

_____

7. Why do you need to write every day?

_____

_____

8. What do you think the author's feelings about writing as a professional are? Why?

_____

_____

A Lone Adventure

Will Tyler be able to survive all alone on a faraway island?

1   When I woke up, my mouth was full of sand and the sun was glaring angrily at me from high in the cloudless sky. I sat up and spit the sand from my mouth. I could feel every sore muscle as I walked the few feet to the water. The salt stung my dry, cracked lips, but the water helped remove the last bits of sand that lay gritty and unpleasant below my tongue and in my teeth.

2   As I stood in the water to soothe my sunburned skin, I tried to piece together the events of the past few days. Try as I might, I could remember very little. I knew that my boat had capsized because I could see its remains lying not far down the beach. I knew that the crew had escaped in the lifeboats when they became sure the ship was sinking. They had begged me to come with them, but I insisted that a captain must always remain with his ship.

3   A few minutes later, I decided to walk down the beach and see what remained of my beloved vessel. My stomach was an animal, growling and rumbling hungrily. As bright as the day was, I knew that night would fall quickly. I needed to build a shelter for myself before dark, and I would need a source of fresh water and food.

4   It would be hard to call the bits of wood that were strewn about the beach a boat. Luckily, I found a canvas bag that was tied to a large, flat piece of wood that I must

have used as a makeshift raft. I worked at the knot for a few minutes before I was able to loosen it enough to untie the bag.

5   Inside, I was pleased to find a knife, a wool blanket, a small bottle of water, and four cans of food--fish, beans, corn, and stewed tomatoes. There was also a box of matches, but my heart sank when I saw how soggy they were. I would place them on the beach to dry in the sun, but I was skeptical that they would be of much help in producing fire.

6   I chose a spot just off the beach to make my shelter. The sandy ground would provide a bit more comfort than the land farther up in the wooded area, which was knotted with the roots of trees and covered with twigs and branches. I used my knife to split pieces of bamboo that I planned to use as the walls and roof of my hut.

7   I was sweating with the effort of my work when I felt a cool breeze that chilled my damp skin. I stood quietly, enjoying a moment of relief from the sun's glare, when I noticed dark clouds gathering in the sky. I quickly resumed my task, hoping that the storm would not move in too rapidly. Another gust of wind caught the edge of my blanket and carried it down the beach. I raced after it as the first sounds of thunder rumbled around me.

8   The garbage truck growled and rumbled as it chugged down the street. Tyler lay on his bed with his eyes open for a moment before he could identify the sound. He sat up quickly, and the book that had been resting on his covers dropped to the floor with a thud. The bearded face of Robinson Crusoe stared up at Tyler from the cover of the book as he fumbled for his glasses. He glanced at his bedside clock. Eight o'clock! He had overslept again. Tyler jumped out of bed and headed for the bathroom.

1. Why didn't the narrator escape from the sinking ship on one of the lifeboats?

_____

2. Name three items the narrator found in the canvas bag.

_____

_____

3. Personification is a literary device in which human characteristics are given to inanimate objects. In the sentence *Sam's bed beckoned to him invitingly,* Sam's bed is personified. Find an example of personification in the story, and write it on the line below.

_____

4. What do you think the book Tyler was reading when he fell asleep was about?

_____

_____

5. From what point of view are the first seven paragraphs of the story told?

_____

_____

6. From what point of view is the last paragraph told?

_____

_____

7. What purpose would a reader have for reading this selection?

_____ for information

_____ to answer a specific question

_____ for entertainment

Find the metaphor in paragraph 3, and write it on the line.

8. _____

9. Why is most of this selection in italics?

_____

The Real Crusoe

How long do you think you could go without human company?

1   *Robinson Crusoe* by Daniel Defoe is one of the most well-known and widely-read books ever written. It was published in 1719, and by the end of the next century, more than 700 versions, translations, sequels, and imitations had been published.

2   *Robinson Crusoe* is a fascinating adventure tale of a man who is shipwrecked on an island and survives until his rescue 28 years later. There is no doubt that Defoe was an imaginative and gifted storyteller, but the idea for the fictional character of Crusoe didn't come solely from Defoe's imagination. That is why it is believed that the story of Robinson Crusoe was actually based on the real life adventures of Alexander Selkirk.

3   Selkirk was a Scottish sailor on a ship called the *Cinque Ports*. He had had frequent disagreements with the ship's captain, William Dampier, about the safety of the craft and the decisions the captain had made during the expedition. Selkirk demanded to be left ashore at the Juan Fernández Islands (about 400 miles off the coast of Chile) when he became convinced that the *Cinque Ports* was no longer seaworthy.

4   Captain Dampier was not sorry to see Selkirk go and happily left him on one of the islands. Selkirk seemed to have had a moment of regret as the ship left, but it was too late; no one heard his cries for the ship to return.

5   Selkirk quickly learned what he needed to do to survive on the uninhabited island. He had brought several items with him from the ship, including a musket, gunpowder, a knife, carpenter's tools, clothing, and a few books.

6   Selkirk used native trees and his tools to construct two huts for shelter, which he then covered with long grasses. There were plenty of goats on the island, so he was assured a steady supply of milk and meat. There were even vegetables that had been planted by Spanish sailors who had stopped at the island in years past.

7   At first, Selkirk had a serious problem with the island's rats, which gnawed at him at night while he slept. However, sailors had also left cats on the island. Selkirk found that he could easily control the rat population by using meat to entice the cats to remain nearby.

8   Selkirk managed to survive on the island for four years. Loneliness and depression were as much a problem for him as food and shelter. Eventually, though, Selkirk came to enjoy living alone with only his books, cats, and goats for company.

9   When he was finally rescued by a ship called the *Duke*, Selkirk found that it was difficult to adjust to being around people again and that he had lost some of his language skills. He became accustomed to living in society again, but a part of him always missed the peace of the island.

10   In 1712, Woodes Rogers, captain of the *Duke*, published *A Cruising Voyage Round the World*, which included an account of Alexander Selkirk's experiences in the Juan Fernández Islands. This book, as well as Defoe's *Robinson Crusoe*, has given readers a chance to experience the life and adventures of an island castaway—adventures they could otherwise only imagine.

1. What nationality was Selkirk?

_____

2. Why do you think Selkirk called out to the *Cinque Ports* as it sailed away from the island?

_____

_____

3. How do we know so many details about Selkirk's experiences on the island?

_____

_____

5. What is one difference between Robinson Crusoe and Alexander Selkirk?

_____

_____

_____

6. Is *Robinson Crusoe* fantasy, or does it take place in reality?

_____

7. Is *A Cruising Voyage Round the World* fantasy, or does it take place in reality?

_____

Circle the word that best completes each sentence below.

8. Selkirk's use of _____ thinking allowed him to survive on the island.

optimistic   creative   frequent

9. It was difficult for Selkirk to _____ to life in society.

readjust   communicate   accustom

10. Woodes Rogers's book _____ Selkirk's experiences.

neglected   ridiculed   detailed

11. After reading this article, would you be interested in reading *Robinson Crusoe?* Why or why not?

_____

_____

A Desert in Bloom

Will Chiara and her mom be able to make themselves feel at home in their new house?

1 Chiara made her way down the hallway, past the neatly stacked cardboard boxes, and into the kitchen, where the early morning sunlight streamed through the windows. She stepped over another stack of boxes and slid open the glass door that led to a small deck. Chiara's mom was sipping a cup of coffee, wisps of steam drifting into the air.

2 "What are you doing, Mom?" asked Chiara, staring out at the turquoise sky and clumps of plants that dotted the backyard.

3 "Well," began Mrs. Giardini, "I was just noticing how strange and unfamiliar the landscape is here. Arizona and Massachusetts could be different planets, as far as the landscape is concerned. I was missing all the greenery in our backyard at home, but I was also appreciating how blue the sky is here. It really contrasts with the red earth, doesn't it?" she asked, taking a sip of coffee.

4 Chiara nodded. "I see what you mean," she said. "It doesn't look like we could grow much here, does it?" she said gesturing to the few dusty looking plants in the yard.

5 "I have an idea," said Mrs. Giardini suddenly. "Have you had your breakfast yet?" she asked. Chiara shook her head. "Grab a muffin and some fruit, and come with me."

6 Half an hour later, Chiara and her mom pulled into a nursery on the outskirts of town. As they entered the greenhouse, both Chiara and her mother took a deep breath, inhaling the familiar green, damp scent of growing plants. "Can I help you?" asked a man wearing a tag with the nursery's logo and the name *Joseph* printed on it.

7 Mrs. Giardini smiled. "We've just moved here from Massachusetts," she began. "We need some help starting a desert garden."

8 "Welcome to Arizona!" said Joseph. "The weather and the landscape here might take a little getting used to, but once you fall in love with it, you won't want to live anywhere else.

9 "My first recommendation is that you primarily plant native plants. They thrive in this climate for a reason, and you won't have to spend all your time watering plants that were meant to live somewhere else."

10 "That makes sense," said Mrs. Giardini. "I've never grown cacti or other succulents before, but I think that it could be fun to experiment with them."

11 Joseph nodded in agreement. "You can create some beautiful cacti gardens, but you aren't limited to planting only succulents in the desert." He pointed to several nearby pots. "I'll show you a few of my favorites. The desert willow has beautiful blooms that some people think resemble orchids. Indian paintbrush can provide bright bursts of color in your garden."

12 Chiara and her mom grinned at each other. "I don't think we had any idea what a lush, colorful garden we could have in the desert!" exclaimed Mrs. Giardini. "I'm not even going to worry about our stacks of boxes until we get a good start on the garden."

13 "I can't wait to begin," said Chiara, already loading plants into the cart.

1. Number the events below to show the order in which they happened.

_____ Joseph showed Chiara and her mom several of his favorite desert plants.

_____ Chiara ate her breakfast in the car.

_____ The Giardinis moved to Arizona from Massachusetts.

_____ Mrs. Giardini said she missed the greenery in her old backyard.

_____ Chiara found her mother sitting on the deck sipping coffee.

2. What problem do Chiara and her mom have at the beginning of the story?

_____

3. Do you think that planting a garden will help the Giardinis feel more at home in Arizona? Why or why not?

_____

_____

4. What is one way in which Massachusetts and Arizona are different?

_____

5. What does Mrs. Giardini mean when she says, "Arizona and Massachusetts could be different planets"?

_____

_____

6. Name the two different settings in this story.

_____

7. Why were Chiara and her mom surprised to hear that they could plant colorful, blooming plants?

_____

_____

8. Why does Joseph recommend that Chiara and her mom plant native plants?

_____

_____

A Dry, Hot Land

Where is the world's largest desert?

1   Unless you live in the western part of the United States, you may consider deserts to be exotic, rare places. Actually, deserts are very common, covering nearly one-third of Earth's land surface. Although lack of precipitation is the most obvious characteristic of desert regions—they receive less than ten inches per year—deserts also have high rates of evaporation. What little precipitation does fall is quickly absorbed back into the atmosphere.

2   Because of this lack of moisture, deserts can be very hot during the day. Water has a natural cooling effect, but without it, the sun cooks the land. In some deserts, temperatures are regularly as high as 130 degrees Fahrenheit. However, after the sun goes down, all that heat escapes from the desert ground and the temperatures drop quickly, sometimes all the way to freezing!

3   Some deserts are not hot, even during the day. Areas with low precipitation and high evaporation rates located in the extreme Northern Hemisphere are called *tundras,* a type of frozen desert. Because of the tundra's extremely low temperature, any moisture that is present remains frozen.

4   Sandy deserts are the most familiar, probably because they are filmed and photographed so often for their natural beauty. Looking like giant, frozen ocean waves, sand dunes reach up to meet the brilliant blue sky. In fact, the dunes are not frozen at all. They are constantly moving and act more like the ocean than you might think.

5   Winds in the desert are very powerful because there is so little in the landscape to slow them down. The sand gets pushed around, just like water in the sea, and shifted and shaped into constantly changing wave-like forms. However, only about 20 percent of Earth's deserts are made of sand. Most deserts consist of larger rocks like pebbles and stones.

6   The largest desert on Earth is the Sahara in northern Africa. Covering more than three-and-a-half million square miles, the whole United States could fit within this arid region. The Sahara is one of the driest places on Earth. It receives almost no rainfall during the year and has basically no surface water. However, there is water flowing underground that occasionally reaches the desert surface. An area of moisture and plant life within a dry desert is called an *oasis.* Although there are some natural oases, most of them are artificially created by irrigation or wells.

7   The Gobi is a major desert found in Asia. It sits on a plateau that stretches between two higher mountains. Even though part of the Gobi is as harsh as any desert, most of it is covered in a thin layer of bushes and grass that allows people to live there. The famous Venetian (*və'neSHən*) traveler Marco Polo made his way across the Gobi in 1275, becoming the first explorer to describe this arid region to Europeans.

8   The largest desert in the United States is the Mojave Desert, which covers parts of California, Utah, Nevada, and Arizona. An area of the Mojave, called *Death Valley,* is the lowest and hottest point in North America. Despite its reputation for hot temperatures, the Mojave does get quite cold during the winter, regularly dropping to 20 to 30 degrees Fahrenheit, and it sometimes even snows there.

Write the words from the passage that have the meanings below.

1. the process by which liquid changes into vapor or gas

_____

2. water that falls to Earth in the form of rain or snow

_____

3. hills of sand that are pushed into shape by the wind

_____

4. dry; having little rainfall

_____

5. an area of flat land that is higher than the surrounding land

_____

6. How much of Earth's land surface do deserts cover?

_____

7. Who was Marco Polo?

_____

8. Why do some people compare sand dunes to ocean waves?

_____

_____

9. What is an oasis? What is the plural form of oasis?

_____

_____

Write **T** before the sentences that are true. Write **F** before the sentences that are false.

10. _____ Most of Earth's deserts are made of sand.

11. _____ The Sahara receives almost no rainfall.

12. _____ The Mojave Desert is the largest American desert.

13. _____ The Gobi is located in northern Africa.

Calling Nowhere

Why would there be a phone booth in the middle of the desert?

1   At some point following World War II, a phone booth was installed in the Mojave Desert, 12 miles from the nearest interstate. It seems like an odd location for a phone booth, but there are two mines in the area, and the phone was originally installed for use by the miners and their families.

2   Godfrey Daniels, a computer programmer from Arizona, heard about the phone from a friend. He had the number and decided to call it one day, just to see if anyone might answer. He didn't really expect a response, and sure enough, there was no answer when he called.

3   After dialing the number periodically, he was shocked to hear a busy signal one day. He assumed that there was a problem with the line, but he kept calling anyway. After several tries, someone actually answered the phone. Daniels spoke with a woman who worked at one of the mines. She lived in a remote area without phone service and used the phone for making calls.

4   Daniels loved the idea of a phone in the middle of nowhere. He was even more fascinated with the idea that someone might actually be available to answer the phone in such a remote place. He posted the phone's number on the Internet, and people began calling it. Just as Daniels was intrigued by the idea of the phone booth in the middle of the desert, so were the callers who had visited his Web site.

5   Daniels eventually traveled to Southern California to visit the booth himself. Evidently, he wasn't the only person to have that idea. As more people heard about the Mojave Desert phone booth, tourists decided to visit the secluded location. People who called the phone began to frequently hear a busy signal. When someone answered the phone, he or she had the opportunity to speak with callers from all around the United States, as well as Germany, England, Italy, France, Australia, and South Africa.

6   What did strangers find to talk about during these unusual calls? They usually identified themselves and discussed where they were calling from and how they had heard about the phone booth. One thing people love about the Internet is how it seems to make the world feel smaller. Maybe in some small way, the Mojave Desert phone booth accomplished the same thing.

7   In May of 2000, the National Park Service and Pacific-Bell, the owner of the phone booth, made the decision to remove the booth. The National Park Service felt that the area was receiving too much traffic as a result of all the publicity surrounding the booth. They were worried that it might somehow damage the environment, and they felt that it was their responsibility to protect the land of the Mojave Desert National Preserve.

8   Today, the place where the booth once stood is marked by a simple tombstone. People who don't know that it was removed still call the number. There is no disconnect message on the line. The number just rings and rings, as the caller waits patiently for someone to answer.

1. How did Godfrey Daniels publicize the Mojave Desert phone booth?

_____

_____

2. Do you think the National Parks Service and Pacific-Bell made the right decision to remove the phone booth? Explain.

_____

_____

3. What happens if someone calls the phone booth today?

_____

4. Why was the phone booth originally installed?

_____

_____

5. On the lines below, write the main idea of paragraph 6.

_____

_____

Write **T** before the sentences that are true. Write **F** before the sentences that are false.

6. _____ The phone booth was originally intended to be used by miners.

7. _____ The phone booth is still in working order today.

8. _____ Godfrey Daniels posted the number of the booth on the Internet.

9. _____ The phone booth was located in Arizona.

10. _____ People seemed to like the idea of connecting with others in faraway places.

11. If the phone booth was still in place today, would you want to call the number? Explain.

_____

_____

Math Grade 6 Answers

Chapter 1

Lesson 1.1, page 6

	a	b
1.	Commutative	Associative
2.	Identity	Commutative
3.	Associative	Property of Zero
4.	Identity	Commutative
5.	3 + (5 + 2)	7 × 5
6.	4	(3 × 2) × 5
7.	9 + 7	2 + (5 + 4)
8.	7	37
9.	0	0

Lesson 1.2, page 7

	a	b
1.	multiply	add
2.	add	multiply
3.	(4 × 6) + (4 × 2)	2 × (5 + 4)
4.	5 × (1 + 6)	(4 × 2) + (4 × 6)
5.	(8 × 4) + (8 × 3)	5 × (0 + 1)
6.	5	2
7.	6	5
8.	2	4
9.	16	16
10.	21	25

Lesson 1.2, page 8

1a.	(22 × 100) + (22 × 2) = 2,244
1b.	(40 × 25) − (1 × 25) = 975
2a.	(146 × 30) + (146 × 3) = 4,818
2b.	(30 × 16) − (2 × 16) = 448
3a.	(30 × 35) + (6 × 35) = 1,260
3b.	(50 × 106) + (1 × 106) = 5,406
4a.	(20 × 256) − (1 × 256) = 4,864
4b.	(40 × 17) + (5 × 17) = 765
5a.	(57 × 40) − (57 × 2) = 2,166
5b.	(48 × 40) + (48 × 5) = 2,160
6a.	(80 × 80) + (2 × 80) = 6,560
6b.	(50 × 82) + (1 × 82) = 4,182
7a.	(40 × 142) + (3 × 142) = 6,106
7b.	(264 × 70) − (264 × 3) = 17,688
8a.	(10 × 39) + (2 × 39) = 468
8b.	(60 × 35) − (2 × 35) = 2,030

Lesson 1.3, page 9

	a	b	c	d
1.	8,748	13,056	11,220	49,795
2.	113,300	86,184	227,664	284,886
3.	331,364	471,534	342,042	440,295
4.	747,612	901,550	955,192	2,070,672

Lesson 1.4, page 10

	a	b	c	d	e
1.	5 r4	2 r14	4	4 r2	2 r14
2.	2 r2	7	27 r1	32	29 r14
3.	30 r5	13 r23	19 r25	26 r17	18

Lesson 1.5, page 11

	a	b	c	d
1.	8,624	14,340	71,687	13,888
2.	10,615	16,399	52,125	90,396
3.	138	359	83	151
4.	318	158	117	694

Lesson 1.6, page 12

1.	1, 2, 4, 8 1, 2, 3, 4, 6, 12	1, 2, 4	4
2.	1, 2, 3, 6 1, 2, 3, 6, 9, 18	1, 2, 3, 6	6
3.	1, 2, 3, 4, 6, 8, 12, 24 1, 3, 5, 15	1, 3	3
4.	1, 2, 4 1, 2, 3, 6	1, 2	2
5.	1, 5 1, 2, 3, 4, 6, 12	1	1
6.	1, 2, 4, 8, 16 1, 2, 3, 4, 6, 12	1, 2, 4	4

Lesson 1.7, page 13

	a	b		a	b
1.	306	1976	5.	224	48
2.	1728	260	6.	405	630
3.	4290	126	7.	21624	14620
4.	92	75			

Lesson 1.8, page 14

	a	b	c	d	e
1.	5.6	0.04	0.0975	13.44	17.5
2.	0.0918	0.0486	28.105	2.1087	275.04
3.	19.8468	206.703	303.986	20.4102	563.85
4.	95.934	58.734	15.036	2.2382	0.6724
5.	0.1698	9.434	0.1909	0.09	12.532

Lesson 1.9, page 15

	a	b	c	d
1.	2.2	85	0.4	1.5
2.	40	5.3	40	65
3.	3000	30	0.25	1.2
4.	0.4	40	5	6

Chapter 2

Lesson 2.1, page 16

	a	b	c	d
1.	$\frac{4}{15}$	$\frac{5}{8}$	$\frac{5}{8}$	$\frac{3}{10}$
2.	$\frac{7}{16}$	$\frac{16}{27}$	$\frac{3}{10}$	$\frac{9}{35}$
3.	$\frac{1}{9}$	$\frac{11}{18}$	$\frac{4}{25}$	$\frac{9}{28}$
4.	$2\frac{5}{6}$	$4\frac{3}{8}$	$6\frac{33}{40}$	4
5.	$18\frac{2}{15}$	$20\frac{1}{4}$	$7\frac{7}{12}$	$8\frac{3}{4}$
6.	14	$5\frac{4}{9}$	$3\frac{21}{32}$	$3\frac{5}{6}$

Lesson 2.2, page 17

| 1. 2 | 2. 4 | 3. 9 |

Lesson 2.3, page 18

	a	b	c	d
1.	$\frac{5}{6}$	$\frac{9}{16}$	$\frac{5}{6}$	$1\frac{1}{15}$
2.	$\frac{4}{7}$	$1\frac{1}{15}$	$2\frac{2}{9}$	$\frac{5}{6}$
3.	$2\frac{5}{8}$	$1\frac{1}{6}$	$\frac{1}{2}$	$2\frac{1}{2}$

Math Grade 6 Answers

4. $\frac{9}{10}$ $1\frac{1}{27}$ $\frac{4}{5}$ $\frac{6}{7}$

Lesson 2.4, page 19

	a	b	c	d
1.	$\frac{3}{4}$	$\frac{1}{2}$	$2\frac{2}{7}$	$\frac{7}{15}$
2.	$3\frac{6}{7}$	$2\frac{1}{72}$	$\frac{13}{18}$	$\frac{12}{25}$
3.	$2\frac{2}{5}$	$\frac{1}{2}$	$1\frac{1}{3}$	$\frac{17}{24}$
4.	$\frac{9}{10}$	$1\frac{23}{57}$	$\frac{3}{13}$	$5\frac{2}{5}$

Chapter 3

Lesson 3.1, page 20

	a	b		a	b
1.	$\frac{5}{12}$	$\frac{1}{7}$	**6.**	$\frac{7}{11}$	$\frac{1}{3}$
2.	$\frac{4}{5}$	$\frac{4}{7}$	**7.**	$\frac{1}{2}$	$\frac{1}{6}$
3.	$\frac{1}{2}$	$\frac{8}{11}$	**8.**	$\frac{9}{25}$	$\frac{7}{10}$
4.	$\frac{5}{6}$	$\frac{7}{10}$	**9.**	$\frac{8}{9}$	$\frac{2}{19}$
5.	$\frac{1}{4}$	$\frac{3}{4}$	**10.**	$\frac{21}{62}$	$\frac{1}{12}$

Lesson 3.1, page 21

	a	b		a	b
1.	$\frac{15}{2}$	$\frac{4}{5}$	**4.**	$\frac{5}{16}$	$\frac{7}{12}$
2.	$\frac{3}{1}$	$\frac{8}{7}$	**5.**	$\frac{2}{1}$	$\frac{8}{7}$
3.	$\frac{7}{11}$	$\frac{4}{5}$	**6.**	$\frac{3}{5}$	$\frac{3}{2}$

Lesson 3.2, page 22

	a	b	c
1.	8	16	1
2.	9	1	10
3.	21	2	21
4.	64	11	15
5.	15	36	10

Lesson 3.2, page 23

	a	b	c
1.	1	9	8
2.	4	16	5
3.	8	6	6
4.	49	5	10
5.	70	9	10

Lesson 3.3, page 24

1. Cans, 4, 8, 12; Cost, $2.25, $4.50, $6.75
2. Ice Cream, 180, 360, 540, 720, 900, 1,080; Hours, 2, 4, 6, 8, 10, 12
3. Distance, 650, 1300, 1950; Hours, 3, 6, 9
4. Bagels, 640, 1280, 1920, 2560; Hours, 4, 8, 12, 16

Lesson 3.4, page 25

1. 5   **3.** 24 minutes   **5.** 12
2. $\frac{1}{2}$ hour   **4.** $\frac{1}{2}$ day   **6.** $130

Lesson 3.5, page 26

	Fraction	Decimal		Fraction	Decimal
1.	$\frac{1}{50}$	0.02	**8.**	$\frac{11}{100}$	0.11
2.	$\frac{2}{25}$	0.08	**9.**	$\frac{3}{100}$	0.03
3.	$\frac{27}{100}$	0.27	**10.**	$\frac{11}{50}$	0.22
4.	$\frac{13}{100}$	0.13	**11.**	$\frac{17}{100}$	0.17
5.	$\frac{17}{25}$	0.68	**12.**	$\frac{83}{100}$	0.83
6.	$\frac{18}{25}$	0.72	**13.**	$\frac{97}{100}$	0.97
7.	$\frac{14}{25}$	0.56	**14.**	$\frac{43}{100}$	0.43

Lesson 3.6, page 27

	a	b		a	b
1.	$5\frac{1}{5}$	76	**7.**	$31\frac{1}{2}$	$8\frac{1}{10}$
2.	$9\frac{3}{5}$	7	**8.**	$3\frac{17}{25}$	$14\frac{2}{5}$
3.	18	$7\frac{1}{2}$	**9.**	54	$21\frac{1}{2}$
4.	$1\frac{24}{25}$	$3\frac{4}{5}$	**10.**	$4\frac{4}{5}$	$5\frac{2}{5}$
5.	8	$6\frac{3}{4}$	**11.**	36	19
6.	64	15	**12.**	$10\frac{1}{2}$	$\frac{3}{4}$

Lesson 3.7, page 28

	a	b		a	b
1.	20.48	10.4	**7.**	5.88	38
2.	2.225	4.62	**8.**	9	31.24
3.	6.96	20	**9.**	5.796	64
4.	6.132	42.14	**10.**	7.84	27.9
5.	2.048	3.19	**11.**	2.56	24
6.	42	4.5	**12.**	4.32	2.7

Lesson 3.8, page 29

	a	b		a	b
1.	60%	20%	**6.**	20%	150%
2.	15%	64%	**7.**	30%	200%
3.	15%	40%	**8.**	37.5%	125%
4.	10%	90%	**9.**	50%	25%
5.	75%	40%	**10.**	120%	80%

Chapter 4

Lesson 4.1, page 30

	a	b
1.	-8 0 8	-25 0 25
2.	-10 0 10	-7 0 7
3.	-12 0 12	-9 0 9
4.	-6 0 6	-2 0 2
5.	-11 0 11	-14 0 14

6.

	a	b
7.	-10	-1
8.	3	-7
9.	4	8
10.	-13	15
11.	32	-27
12.	-17	20

Lesson 4.2, page 31

	a	b			a	b
1.	-45	8		**7.**	-10	7
2.	528	62		**8.**	60	-95
3.	345	-8		**9.**	-97	-34
4.	7500	-80		**10.**	-100	15
5.	10	-250		**11.**	-25	390
6.	3	-8		**12.**	95	$6,000$

Lesson 4.3, page 32

	a	b	c
1.	4	13	-10
2.	-7	11	2
3.	-12	-5	1
4.	14	-8	-13
5.	3	7	-4
6.	-15	9	12
7.	16	6	-20
8.	-40	-24	17
9.	33	-41	19
10.	26	18	-35
11.	-53	21	30
12.	25	-21	47

Lesson 4.4, page 33

	a	b	c
1.	-2	-7	1
2.	6	3	-5
3.	$2 < 7$	$-1 > -4$	$5 > 0$
4.	$-4 < 1$	$0 > -8$	$-8 > -10$
5.	$7 > -7$	$-2 < 0$	$4 < 6$
6.	$1 > -1$	$6 > 3$	$-6 < -3$
7.	$4 > -2$	$-6 < -4$	$3 > -3$
8.	$-5, -3, 0$	$-8, 2, 8$	
9.	$-7, -3, 0, 5$	$-2, -1, 2, 4$	
10.	$-6, -3, -2,$	$-8, -3, -2,$	
	$2, 5$	$0, 5$	

Lesson 4.5, page 34

1.	$(-7, 8)$	**4.**	$(2, -2)$	**7.**	I	**10.** D
2.	$(3, 9)$	**5.**	$(-9, -6)$	**8.**	K	
3.	$(-4, -4)$	**6.**	J	**9.**	F	

Lesson 4.6, page 35

1.	11	**2.**	15	**3.**	15	**4.**	12	**5.**	4

Chapter 5

Lesson 5.1, page 36

	a	b	c
1.	3×10^1	4×10^3	5×10^4
2.	6×10^5	7×10^2	9×10^1
3.	4×10^4	1×10^5	4×10^2
4.	$3 \times 3 \times 3$	$5 \times 5 \times 5 \times 5 \times 5$	$1 \times 1 \times 1 \times 1 \times 1 \times 1$
5.	12×12	$8 \times 8 \times 8$	$6 \times 6 \times 6$
6.	$7 \times 7 \times 7 \times 7$	$4 \times 4 \times 4 \times 4$	$11 \times 11 \times 11 \times 11$
7.	3^3	8^2	7^5
8.	24^2	4^3	6^6
9.	2^4	38^3	5^5
10.	16	64	1
11.	64	81	125
12.	243	216	121

Lesson 5.2, page 37

	a	b	c
1.	expression	equation	expression
2.	equation	expression	equation
3.	$3; x$	$4; y$	
4.	$1; z$	$5; n$	
5.	$7; b$	$1; m$	
6.	$1; r$	$6; d$	
7.	$n + 5$	$8 - x$	
8.	$x + 7$	$n \times 11$	
9.	$6n = 18$	$70 - n = 29$	
10.	$\frac{8}{n} = 2$	$7 \times 12 = 84$	

11. six decreased by a number is equal to three

12. the product of five and thirteen is equal to 65

Lesson 5.3, page 38

	a	b
1.	$x + 5$	$12 \div n$
2.	$7n$ or $7 \times n$	$7 - c$
3.	$n + 15 = 23$	$x \div 4$ or $\frac{1}{4} x$
4.	$6 + p$	$15m$ or $15 \times m$
5.	$11 - n = 7$	**8.** a number decreased by 5
6.	$8n + 4 = 84$	**9.** three times a number divided by 6
7.	$n \div 5 = 6$	

Lesson 5.4, page 39

1.	$28z + 56b$		**9.**	$30a + 54b$
2.	$16x + 72$		**10.**	$27x + 5,625$
3.	$4 \times 4r$		**11.**	$7(3c)$
4.	$27 + 72x$		**12.**	$18 + 63f$
5.	$48 + 96t$		**13.**	$67,228g - 134,456d$
6.	$\frac{3t}{4}$		**14.**	$\frac{3e}{5}$
7.	$8s^3 + 4$		**15.**	$15z^6 + 15$
8.	$90x + 120$		**16.**	$10y + 20$

Lesson 5.5, page 40

	a	b	c
1.	addition	subtraction	
2.	subtraction	addition	
3.	6	4	17
4.	11	12	0
5.	12	10	0

Math Grade 6 Answers

	a	b	c
6.	3	21	9
7.	0	20	4
8.	30	15	10
9.	$x + \$6 = \$20; x = \$14$		
10.	$g + 12 = 27; g = 15$		

Lesson 5.5, page 41

	a	b	c
1.	7	6	15
2.	14	2	22
3.	33	13	0
4.	23	0	15
5.	14	24	1
6.	6	6	24
7.	$21 + n = 37; 16$		
8.	$n - 9 = 33; 42$		
9.	$2 + 5 + n = 25; 18$		

Lesson 5.6, page 42

	a	b	c
1.	divide	multiply	
2.	multiply	divide	
3.	3	25	12
4.	9	1	8
5.	2	16	5
6.	3	$2\frac{1}{2}$	10
7.	$\frac{1}{4}$	20	81
8.	2	40	3
9.	36	6	10
10.	40	16	1
11.	6	150	3
12.	4	4	8

Lesson 5.6, page 43

	a	b	c
1.	9	5	6
2.	12	27	15
3.	8	1	6
4.	50	36	48
5.	5	0	16
6.	19	28	63
7.	$6 \times n = 12$ or $12 \div 6 = n; 2$		
8.	$48 \div n = 12$ or $48 \div 12 = n; 4$		
9.	$25 \times n = 150$ or $150 \div 25 = n; 6$		

Lesson 5.7, page 44

1. $8 > z$
2. $g < -19$
3. $d < 12$
4. $13 > k$
5. $x > -17$
6. $y < -17$
7. $0 \leq r$

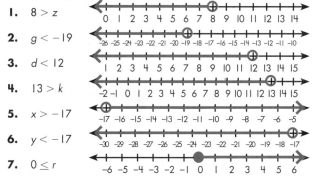

8. $w \geq 3$

Lesson 5.7, page 45

1. $x < 14$
2. $y > 18$
3. $p < -15$
4. $v < -10$
5. $s \geq -12$
6. $f \geq 6$
7. $w < -9$
8. $g \leq 12$

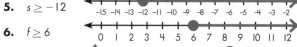

Lesson 5.8, page 46

1. total cost = $\$1.25 \times$ weight

Dependent Variable	Cost (Dollars)	$1.25	$2.50	$3.75
Independent Variable	Weight (Pounds)	1	2	3

2. height = $6 + (2 \times \text{time})$

Dependent Variable	Height (Feet)	12	18	54
Independent Variable	Time (Months)	3	6	24

Lesson 5.8, page 47

1. time = $150 \div$ reading speed

Dependent Variable	Time	10	7.5	5
Independent Variable	Speed (pgs./day)	15	20	30

2. height = $12 - (\text{time} \times 2)$

Dependent Variable	Height (Inches)	10	8	6
Independent Variable	Time (Hours)	1	2	3

3. height = $1 + 1.5(\text{time})$

Dependent Variable	Height (Inches)	2.5	4	5.5
Independent Variable	Time (Days)	1	2	3

4. temperature = $250° + (8° \times \text{time})$

Dependent Variable	Temperature (°F)	258	266	274
Independent Variable	Time (Minutes)	1	2	3

Chapter 6

Lesson 6.1, page 48

	a	b
1.	40 sq. in.	$27\frac{1}{2}$ sq. ft.
2.	$12\frac{1}{2}$ sq. ft.	36 sq. yd.

Lesson 6.1, page 49

	a	b	c
1.	27.5 sq. ft.	48 sq. yd.	104.5 sq. in.
2.	10 sq. ft.	123.25 sq. cm	32 sq. m

Math Grade 6 Answers

Lesson 6.2, page 50

	a	b	c
1.	18 sq. yd.	324 sq. m	276 sq. cm
2.	216 sq. km	529 sq. in.	48 sq. ft.
3.	9 in.	13 ft.	9 m

Lesson 6.2, page 51

	a	b	c
1.	624	450	651
2.	306	157.5	137.5

Lesson 6.3, page 52

	a	b	c
1.	80	56	26
2.	57	20	28

Lesson 6.3, page 53

	a	b	c
1.	52 sq. ft.	48 sq. m	24 sq. cm
2.	185 sq. yd.	12 sq. mi.	20 sq. in.

Lesson 6.4, page 54

	a	b	c
1.	420 cu. yd.	512 cu. in.	12,000 cu. ft.
2.	336 cu. ft.	100 cu. in.	648 cu. in.

Lesson 6.4, page 55

	a	b	c
1.	576 cu. cm	1,728 cu. cm	2,112 cu. m
2.	144 cu. mm	1,620 cu. mm	3,600 cu. cm
3.	1,280 cu. mm	12,000 cu. cm	7,800 cu. mm

Lesson 6.4, page 56

	a	b		a	b
1.	$\frac{30}{343}$ cu. in.	$\frac{4}{243}$ cu. ft.	2.	$\frac{160}{729}$ cu. cm	$\frac{40}{1331}$ cu. ft.

Lesson 6.5, page 57

	a	b	c
1.	862	144	1,720
2.	90	248	1,270

Lesson 6.5, page 58

	a	b	c
1.	62 sq. in.	48.7 sq. ft.	172 sq. yd.
2.	856 sq. cm	104 sq. m	248 sq. in.
3.	85.5 sq. ft.	2970 sq. mm	81.44 sq. cm

Lesson 6.6, page 59

	a	b	c
1.	240	540	217
2.	459	260	1254

Lesson 6.7, page 60

1. (0, 4)   2. (−2, −4)

Lesson 6.8, page 61

1. (3, 6) or (−5, 2)   2. (−4, 2) or (5, −6)

Chapter 7

Lesson 7.1, page 62

	a	b			a	b
1.	statistical	not		4.	not	statistical
2.	statistical	statistical		5.	not	statistical
3.	not	not				

Lesson 7.2, page 63

Answers may vary.

1a. The data spreads over 7 points.
1b. The center value of the data is 67.
1c. The lowest value in the data is 62.
2a. Some values in the data set are equal to 0.
2b. The highest value in the data set is 100.
2c. 0 appears the most in the data set.
3a. The data spreads across 92 points.
3b. 45 appears the most frequently in the data set.
3c. 45 is the middle value in the data set.

Lesson 7.3, page 64

	a	b			a	b
1.	60	78		4.	62	78
2.	106	98		5.	108	83
3.	111	92		6.	70.5	49.5

Lesson 7.4, page 65

	a	b			a	b
1.	34	19		4.	32	19
2.	19	2		5.	5	77
3.	34	6		6.	78	36

Lesson 7.5, page 66

	a	b			a	b
1.	4	40		4.	277	21
2.	28	108		5.	73	4
3.	26	24		6.	14 and 93	32

Lesson 7.6, page 67

	a	b			a	b
1.	$35\frac{3}{5}$	14		3.	68	51
	35	12			71	49
	43	12			79	37
2.	13	$20\frac{1}{6}$				
	12	$18\frac{1}{2}$				
	12	15				

Lesson 7.7, page 68

	a	b			a	b
1.	median	mean		3.	median	mean
2.	mean	mode		4.	median	mode

Lesson 7.8, page 69

	a	b			a	b
1.	3	5		4.	11	6
2.	10	10		5.	7	9
3.	8	4				

Lesson 7.9, page 70

	a	b
1.	5; 2; 7; 5	85; 75; 92.5; 17.5
2.	90; 72.5; 97.5; 25	12; 5; 43; 38
3.	16.5; 4; 39; 35	29; 16; 64; 48

Lesson 7.10, page 71

1a. 15.29; 5.29, 5.29,0.29,0.29, 0.71, 2.71, 7.71; 3.18
1b. 48.29; 10.29, 7.29, 3.29, 2.71, 3.71, 6.71, 7.71; 5.96
2a. 17.57; 7.57, 6.57, 5.57, 0.43, 4.43, 7.43, 7.43; 5.63
2b. 45.1; 34.1, 23.1, 23.1, 12.1, 1.1, 9.9, 9.9, 9.9, 20.9, 42.9; 18.7

Math Grade 6 Answers

Lesson 7.11, page 72
1. 37; 16.5; 9   3. 76; 37; 19.1   5. 62; 16; 13.08
2. 35; 14; 8   4. 8; 4; 2.04   6. 42; 23; 12

Lesson 7.12, page 73

1.
a

Stem	Leaves
1	3 4
2	1 8
3	1 3 4

b

Stem	Leaves
3	8 9
4	9
5	0 4 7
6	3 4
7	2 9

2.
Stem	Leaves
2	5 7
3	4 7 8
4	8 9

Stem	Leaves
7	3 5
8	1 4 7 8
9	1 3 6 9

3.
Stem	Leaves
1	3 7 9
2	4 5
3	3 8

Stem	Leaves
2	3 5 6 7
3	3 5 7
4	1 5 6

Lesson 7.13, page 74
1. 75   3. 50   5. 15
2. 9   4. 20   6. 30
7.

Lesson 7.14, page 75
1. Lopez   5. 55   9. 105
2. 30   6. Wed.   10. 195
3. Wed.   7. Thurs.
4. Martin   8. Tues.

Lesson 7.15, page 76
1. 1,800   7. 35
2. 25–30   8. Answers will vary but may include
3. 0–5   300 to 400 trees.
4. 34.7%   9. Answers will vary.
5. 65.3%   10. Students should draw a star above
6. 50   the 20–25 feet bar.

Lesson 7.16, page 77
1. mode-85; median-84; mean-82.44; range-66; IQR-15; MAD-9.79

Stem	Leaves
3	4
6	3
7	2 8 9
8	1 2 3 3 5 5 5 8
9	4 6 7 9
10	0

85 is the value that appears most frequently in the data set. 34 is the lowest value in the set and makes the mean lower. Therefore, the best measure of center to describe the data set is the median, 84.

2. mode-3; median-3; mean-3.2; range-4; IQR-2; MAD-1.04

Stem	Leaves
0	1 2 3 3 3 4 4 5 5

All of the values in this data set are single digits. The range is only 5, so the mean, 3.2, is the best measure of center to describe this data set.

Lesson 7.16, page 78
1. mode-64; median-57; mean-57.83; range-20; IQR-11; MAD-5.17

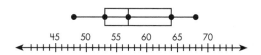

This data set has a range of 20 and is evenly distributed. The mean, 57.83, is the best measure of center to describe the set.

2. mode-45; median-45; mean-40; range-60; IQR-15; MAD-14

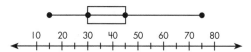

The median and mode of this data set, 45, greatly affects the way the distribution looks. Most of the data points fall either below or along the median.

Lesson 7.16, page 79

mode-15 & 20; median-20; mean-19.17;
range-35; IQR-12.5; MAD-7.64

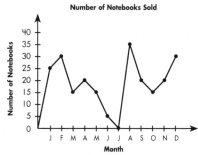

This data set has is evenly distributed in the middle, but has outliers on the low end. Therefore, the median, 20, is the best measure of center to use to describe the data set.

Language Arts Grade 6 Answers

Chapter 1

Lesson 1.1 Common and Proper Nouns

Common nouns name people, places, and things. They are general nouns (not specific). In a sentence, the noun is the person, place, or thing that can act or be acted upon.

teacher – a person
I like my *teacher*.

country – a place
I will visit another *country*.

book – a thing
What is your favorite *book*?

Proper nouns name specific people, places, and things.
Mrs. Crane – a specific person
Mrs. Crane is my favorite teacher.

United States of America – a specific place
I was born in the *United States of America*.

Animal Farm – a specific thing
Animal Farm is one of my favorite books.

Complete It
Use the word box below to complete the following sentences. Remember, common nouns are general and proper nouns are more specific. Proper nouns are also capitalized.

doctor	poem	song
Saturn	Dr. Green	planet
"Twinkle, Twinkle Little Star"		Where the Sidewalk Ends

1. I am writing a _____song_____ for music class.
2. I took my cat to see _____Dr. Green_____ when he had a cold.
3. The planet with the rings is called _____Saturn_____.
4. My mom takes me to the _____doctor_____ when I'm sick.
5. My _____poem_____ came in third place in the poetry contest.
6. Mars is the closest _____planet_____ to the earth.
7. _Where the Sidewalk Ends_ is one of my favorite books.
8. My little sister likes to sing "Twinkle, Twinkle Little Star" before she goes to bed.

82

Lesson 1.1 Common and Proper Nouns

Proof It
Correct the mistakes in the use of common and proper nouns using proofreading marks.

/ – lowercase letter
≡ – capitalize letter
^ – insert words or letters

John Muir

John Muir was born in 1838 in Dunbar, Scotland. From a very young age, he had a love of Nature. He traveled all over the world. He came to the United States to observe nature and take notes on what he saw. He wrote many nature Books. John Muir was concerned for the welfare of the land. He wanted to protect it. He asked President Theodore Roosevelt for help. The National Parks System was founded by John Muir. This System sets aside land for Parks. The first national park was Yellowstone National Park. John Muir is also the founder of the Sierra Club. The people in this Club teach others about nature and how to protect it. John Muir is known as one of the world's greatest conservation leaders.

Try It
Write a biography about someone you think is a hero. Use at least six common and six proper nouns correctly in your biography.

_____

Answers will vary.

83

Lesson 1.2 Regular and Irregular Plural Nouns

Try It
Use the lines to explain how the nouns were made into their plural forms. The first one is done for you.

Column A	Column B	
match	matches	If the noun ends in ch, add an es.
eyebrow	eyebrows	Most nouns add an s.
volcano	volcanoes	If the noun ends in o with a consonant before the o, add es.
wolf	wolves	If the noun ends in an f or fe and has the v sound, change the f to v and add es.
trophy	trophies	If the noun ends in y, change the y to i and add es.
toothbrush	toothbrushes	If the noun ends in sh, add an es.
sheriff	sheriffs	If the noun ends in an f or fe and has the f sound, add an s.

Find It
Write the irregular plural noun form of the following singular nouns on the lines provided. Use a dictionary if you need help.

1. ox _____oxen_____
2. trout _____trout_____
3. man _____men_____
4. series _____series_____
5. axis _____axes_____
6. mouse _____mice_____
7. sheep _____sheep_____
8. salmon _____salmon_____
9. woman _____women_____
10. crisis _____crises_____
11. oasis _____oases_____
12. radius _____radii_____

85

Lesson 1.3 Personal and Intensive Pronouns

A **pronoun** is a word used in place of a noun.

A **subject pronoun** can be the subject of a sentence. *I, you, he, she,* and *it* are subject pronouns.
I found the ball.   *It* is my favorite sport.

An **object pronoun** can be the object of a sentence. *Me, you, him, her,* and *it* are object pronouns.
Matt gave the ball to *me*.   Matt threw *it*.

Possessive pronouns show possession. *My, mine, your, yours, his, her, hers,* and *its* are possessive pronouns.
Anna gave *my* ball to Matt.

The plural forms of personal pronouns include:
Subject: *we, you, they*   Object: *us, you, them*
Possessive: *our, ours, your, yours, their, theirs*

Intensive pronouns end in *–self* or *–selves* and usually appear right after the subject of a sentence. They emphasize the subject.
I *myself* am too tired to go to the movies.
You *yourselves* are responsible for the outcome of the game.

Complete It
Complete each of the following sentences with an intensive pronoun. Remember, intensive pronouns end with *–self* or *–selves*.

1. Jessa _____herself_____ baked all these muffins.
2. The Boy Scouts _____themselves_____ set up all these tents.
3. The smoke _____itself_____ did all this damage to the house.
4. We _____ourselves_____ created the website in just a couple of days.
5. Oliver _____himself_____ wrote that poem.
6. You _____yourself_____ must clean up all these dominoes.
7. The doctor _herself/himself_ checked on each of the patients.
8. The kids in Pilar's class _____themselves_____ raised over $100 for the charity.

86

Language Arts Grade 6 Answers

Lesson 1.3 Personal and Intensive Pronouns

Identify It
The following skit contains subject, object, and possessive plural pronouns. Identify what each boldfaced plural pronoun is replacing on the line. Then, write whether the pronoun is a subject, object, or possessive on the line. The first one has been done for you.

Matt and Anna are on **their** _____Matt and Anna, possessive_____ way to the park to play. On the way, **they** ___Matt and Anna, subject___ meet Andrew and Stephanie.

"**We** ___Matt and Anna, subject___ are on **our** ___Matt and Anna, possessive___ way to the park," said Matt. "Can **you** _Andrew and Stephanie, subject_ join **us** ___Matt and Anna, object___?"

"Can **we** _Andrew and Stephanie, subject_ play with **your** _Matt and Anna, possessive_ ball?" asked Stephanie. "**Ours** _Andrew and Stephanie, possessive_ is missing."

"**Yours** _Andrew and Stephanie, possessive_ is missing? That's too bad," said Anna. "Sure, **you** _Andrew and Stephanie, subject_ can play with **our** _Matt and Anna, possessive_ ball."

Matt, Anna, Andrew, and Stephanie all walked to the park. They would all play together.

"I'll throw the ball to you," said Matt to Andrew. "Then you can throw the ball to **them** _Anna and Stephanie, object_," Matt said pointing to Anna and Stephanie.

"Hey," yelled Anna. "I see a ball ahead. Could it be Andrew and Stephanie's ball?"

"Yes, it could be **their** _Andrew and Stephanie, possessive_ ball," answered Matt. Matt showed Andrew and Stephanie the ball. Sure enough, it was **theirs** _Andrew and Stephanie, possessive_

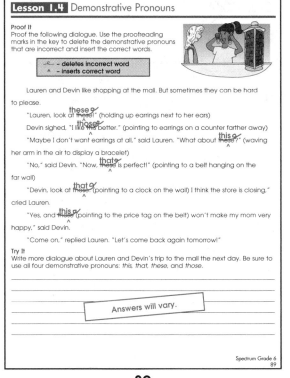

Spectrum Grade 6
87

87

Lesson 1.4 Demonstrative Pronouns

A pronoun is a word used in place of a noun. Pronouns can be a subject, object, or possessive of the sentence. Pronouns can also be demonstrative.

Demonstrative pronouns replace nouns without naming the noun.
this   that   these   those

> *This* is fun. (refers to an event or experience, for example, a roller coaster)
> *That* was wonderful. (refers to an event or experience, for example, a movie)
> *These* are good. (refers to a basket of apples)
> *Those* are better. (refers to a barrel of pears)

This and *these* are usually used when the person or object is closer to the writer and speaker. *That* and *those* are usually used when the person or object is farther away from the writer or speaker.

> *This* is fast (the roller coaster here), but *that* is faster (the roller coaster over there).
> *These* look good (the apples in the basket that is close), but *those* look better (the pears in the barrel across the room).

Demonstrative pronouns, like other pronouns, add variety to your writing and speaking.

Match It
Draw a line to match the demonstrative pronoun in Column A with the objects of the sentence in Column B.

Column A	Column B
this	many newspapers across the room
that	one magazine at the library
these	one wallet in a pocket
those	many pencils on the desk

this	many ants on the ground
that	one book on the shelf
these	many bananas at the store
those	one experience at a baseball game

Spectrum Grade 6
88

88

Lesson 1.4 Demonstrative Pronouns

Proof It
Proof the following dialogue. Use the proofreading marks in the key to delete the demonstrative pronouns that are incorrect and insert the correct words.

> ℓ - deletes incorrect word
> ^ - inserts correct word

Lauren and Devin like shopping at the mall. But sometimes they can be hard to please.

"Lauren, look at ~~these~~ these!" (holding up earrings next to her ears)

Devin sighed, "I like ~~this~~ those better." (pointing to earrings on a counter farther away)

"Maybe I don't want earrings at all," said Lauren. "What about ~~these~~ this?" (waving her arm in the air to display a bracelet)

"No," said Devin. "Now, ~~these~~ that is perfect!" (pointing to a belt hanging on the far wall)

"Devin, look at ~~these~~ that (pointing to a clock on the wall) I think the store is closing," cried Lauren.

"Yes, and ~~these~~ this (pointing to the price tag on the belt) won't make my mom very happy," said Devin.

"Come on," replied Lauren. "Let's come back again tomorrow!"

Try It
Write more dialogue about Lauren and Devin's trip to the mall the next day. Be sure to use all four demonstrative pronouns: *this, that, these,* and *those.*

___Answers will vary.___

Spectrum Grade 6
89

89

Lesson 1.5 Relative Pronouns

A pronoun is a word used in place of a noun. Pronouns can be the subject, the object, or the possessive of a sentence.

Relative pronouns are pronouns that are related to nouns that have already been stated. They combine two sentences that share a common noun.
who   whose   that   which

> The woman, *who* is a doctor, wasn't at the party.
> *Who* refers to the noun *woman.*

> The parents, *whose* children were at the party, were ready to go.
> *Whose* refers to the noun *parents.*
> (This relative pronoun shows possession.)

> The note *that* you read is incorrect.
> *That* refers to the noun *note.*

> The newspaper articles, *which* are long, must be cut.
> *Which* refers to the noun *newspaper articles.*

Complete It
Complete the following sentences by choosing the correct relative pronoun in parentheses. Circle the correct answer.

1. Someone (who) that) likes kiwi usually likes strawberries.
2. Bicyclers (which (whose) bikes are ready can go to the starting line.
3. He likes movies (which (that) have a lot of action.
4. The man, (who) whose) lives across the street, is an actor.
5. The car (who (that) you drove is blocking the driveway.
6. The bananas, (which) that) are the ripest, are used in the recipe.

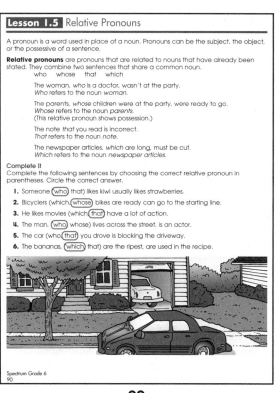

Spectrum Grade 6
90

90

Language Arts Grade 6 Answers

Lesson 1.5 Relative Pronouns

Solve It
Solve the following riddle. Use a relative pronoun to fill in the blanks.

that	who
which	whose

Who bakes apple pies?

The man ____who____ grows apples bakes pies.

Who makes the best apple pies?

The man ____whose____ apples are the sweetest bakes the best pies.

What didn't get baked into the pie?

The apple ____that____ had a bruise did not go in the pie.

What won the prize?

The pies, ____which____ were the sweetest, won the prize.

Try It
Try writing a riddle of your own. Follow the example above. Ask questions that require an answer with a relative pronoun. Use each relative pronoun at least once.

Answers will vary.

91

Lesson 1.6 Indefinite Pronouns

Indefinite pronouns are pronouns that do not specifically name the noun that comes before them (as do the relative pronouns).

all another any anybody anyone anything each everybody everyone everything few many nobody none one several some somebody someone

Many were invited to the party, but only a few came.
We donated *everything* from the attic to the charity foundation.
They looked everywhere for copies of the report, but found *none*.

Identify It
Underline the indefinite pronouns in the following paragraph.

The fair was approaching. <u>Each</u> of the cooks in town made ice cream cones for the fair. The cooks were put in pairs. <u>One</u> made the ice cream while <u>another</u> made the cones. You wouldn't think there would be any problems. However, there were <u>some</u>. <u>One</u> wanted the same flavor. <u>Another</u> wanted cherry. <u>Someone</u> wanted chocolate. <u>Several</u> even ate two scoops. That means <u>someone</u> had <u>none</u>. <u>Everyone</u> would think that is unfair. But the cooks were ready for <u>anything</u>. They made snow cones and <u>everybody</u> ate those instead. What else could happen? The sun melted the ice cream and the snow cones. Cooks quickly handed napkins to <u>everyone</u> with ice cream or snow cones. Then, they made milkshakes. <u>Everything</u> turned out fine.

92

Lesson 1.7 Pronoun Shifts

A **pronoun shift** happens when a writer changes pronouns in the middle of a sentence or paragraph. This can confuse the reader.

After *we* got our chickens, *we* discovered that *you* really need to be ready to take care of them in all kinds of weather.

In the example, the writer changes from *we* (first-person plural) to *you* (second-person singular).

Identify It
A pronoun shift occurs in each item below. Find and circle it.

1. As a photographer, he has an interesting career, because (they) get to meet so many people.
2. As new players on the team, we were nervous, but (you) just need to remember that everyone is new at some point.
3. If you want to ride this roller coaster, (they) need to be 48 inches tall.
4. Aunt Samantha said that when she was a baby (you) didn't have to ride in car seats.
5. Mr. Green said he gave (their) students all the instructions before the test.
6. They gave us (her) outgrown clothes.
7. After the choir concert, we singers gathered backstage to celebrate (their) success.
8. As a magician, she must work hard to safeguard (their) secrets.

93

Lesson 1.7 Pronoun Shifts

Complete It
Complete each sentence below by writing the correct pronoun on the line. In some cases, either *he* or *she* is an acceptable answer.

1. As a professional athlete, he must work out nearly every day if ____he____ wants to stay in shape.
2. They did not go to the Girl Scouts meeting, so ____they____ didn't hear the news.
3. Since they are under the age of 12, the children need to be accompanied by ____their____ parents.
4. Since he is leaving for college this fall, ____he____ is getting a car.
5. As the soccer coach requested, I met with her, and ____she____ said I'm welcome to join the team.
6. When they got home, ____they____ wanted to have a snack.
7. I need to get my permission slip signed if ____I____ want to go to the art museum next week.
8. Is Jorge going to join you and me at the pool, or will he call ____us____ first?
9. Mr. Crawley said he would host a class picnic, and ____he____ promised to make his taco salad.
10. As a chef, she must be willing to experiment if ____she____ wants to develop new dishes.

Try It
On the lines below, write a short paragraph about an experience you've had with your classmates. Circle each pronoun you use, and proofread your paragraph to be sure there are no pronoun shifts.

Answers will vary.

94

Language Arts Grade 6 Answers

Lesson 1.8 Verbs: Regular Present and Past Tense

A **verb** is a word that tells the action or the state of being of a sentence. In this sentence, *walk* is the verb. It tells the action of the sentence.
> The students *walk* home.

In this sentence, *shared* is the verb. It tells the action of the sentence.
> Kevin *shared* his cake with Carol at the party last night.

In the first sentence the action is taking place now. In the second sentence the action took place in the past. Add **ed** to the present tense of a **regular verb** to make it past tense. If the word already ends in the letter **e**, just add the letter **d**.

Complete It
Write each word in present tense in the first sentence and then in past tense in the second sentence.

1. act	Today, I	act	Yesterday, I	acted
2. mend	Today, I	mend	Yesterday, I	mended
3. cook	Today, I	cook	Yesterday, I	cooked
4. bake	Today, I	bake	Yesterday, I	baked
5. answer	Today, I	answer	Yesterday, I	answered
6. cycle	Today, I	cycle	Yesterday, I	cycled
7. wave	Today, I	wave	Yesterday, I	waved
8. scream	Today, I	scream	Yesterday, I	screamed
9. bike	Today, I	bike	Yesterday, I	biked
10. jump	Today, I	jump	Yesterday, I	jumped
11. mow	Today, I	mow	Yesterday, I	mowed
12. yell	Today, I	yell	Yesterday, I	yelled
13. rake	Today, I	rake	Yesterday, I	raked
14. whisper	Today, I	whisper	Yesterday, I	whispered
15. divide	Today, I	divide	Yesterday, I	divided

95

Lesson 1.8 Verbs: Regular Present and Past Tense

Proof It
Proofread the following announcement. Use the proofreading marks to correct mistakes with the present and past tense forms of verbs and insert the correctly spelled words. Not all of the verbs are from this lesson.

> ~ – deletes word
> ^ – inserts word

Hello from Northland Auditorium, home of the Riverdale Cook-Off and Bake-Off. The chefs are ready for the bake-off. The chefs cook meals last night. The judges award cooked / awarded prizes for the best meals last night. The chefs baked today. Early this morning, the judges call the chefs over. They talk with them about their recipes. The judges will now called / talked observed the baking. Judge Wilson and Judge Boggs looked over many of the cooks' look shoulders. They laughed. It must be good news. I don't think they would joked if it laugh weren't. Two cooks answered a question for the judges. They act nervous. The judges answer tasted all of the baked goods. What will win the blue ribbon? Will cookies, cakes, taste brownies, or candy captured the top prize? The judges now handed a note to the announcer. The winner is....

Try It
Write a first-hand account of a school event. Include both present and past tense regular verbs.

> **Answers will vary.**

96

Lesson 1.9 Verbs: Irregular Present and Past Tense

Identify It
Underline the irregular present and past tense verbs in this paragraph.

Aikido

They jump. They <u>fall</u>. They <u>fly</u> through the air. Who <u>are</u> they? They <u>are</u> students of Aikido. Aikido <u>is</u> a Japanese form of self-defense. Partners work together. They use wrists, joints, and elbows to block, pin, and <u>throw</u> each other. They learn the moves together and work in harmony with each other. Aikido <u>is</u> an art that tests both mind and body. It <u>is</u> a spiritual art. The founder of Aikido <u>was</u> born in 1883. He <u>wrote</u> hundreds of techniques. Aikido <u>grew</u> throughout Japan and throughout the world. Thousands of students <u>take</u> Aikido today. Aikido <u>means</u> *the way of harmony*.

Challenge:
Identify the regular present and past tense verbs and give their other form.
Challenge answers: jump/jumped, work/worked, use/used, block/blocked, pin/pinned, learn/learned, tests/tested

Try It
Write a paragraph about one of your hobbies or activities. Use at least six present tense irregular verbs and six past tense irregular verbs. Use a dictionary if you need help.

> **Answers will vary.**

98

Lesson 1.10 Subject-Verb Agreement

Subject-verb agreement means verbs must agree in number with the subject of the sentence. If the subject is singular, then use a singular verb. If the subject is plural, use a plural verb.

> The apple *tastes* good.   The apples *taste* good.
> The flower *is* beautiful.   The flowers *are* beautiful.

If the subject is a compound subject, two subjects connected by the word *and*, then a plural verb is needed.

> Tyler and Inez *bake* pies.   Tyler *bakes* pies.

If the subject is a compound subject connected by the words *or* or *nor*, then the verb will agree with the subject that is closer to the verb.

> Neither Tyler *nor* Inez *likes* blueberry pie. (Inez likes)
> Does Tyler *or* his brothers *like* banana cream pie? (brothers like)

If the subject and the verb are separated by a word or words, be sure that the verb still agrees with the subject.

> *Inez* as well as her sisters *works* at the bakery.

Complete It
Circle the correct verb for each sentence.

1. Jill (jump, **jumps**) rope after school.
2. Jill and Katie (**jump**, jumps) rope after school.
3. Jill and her friends (**jump**, jumps) rope after school.
4. Jill as well as her friends (**jump**, jumps) rope after school.
5. Ross (like, **likes**) veggie lasagna.
6. Ross and Regina (**like**, likes) veggie lasagna.
7. Ross and his brothers (**like**, likes) veggie lasagna.
8. Ross as well as his parents (like, **likes**) veggie lasagna.
9. Does Jill or her friends (**want**, wants) to ride with me?
10. Neither Jill nor Katie (want, **wants**) to go to the movies.

99

Language Arts Grade 6 Answers

Lesson 1.10 Subject-Verb Agreement

Rewrite It
Rewrite the following paragraph, correcting the subject-verb agreement mistakes as you go. Remember to be on the lookout for subjects and verbs that are separated.

Sea turtles grows in many sizes and colors. They ranges between 100 and 1300 pounds. Instead of teeth, sea turtles has beaks in their jaws. Which of their senses is most keen? That would be their sense of smell. A female sea turtle lay her eggs on land. Unfortunately, sea turtles are in danger. But in the last 100 years, the population have become almost extinct. What can we do to ensure the survival of sea turtles? We can all helps by keeping our oceans clean. We can educate ourselves about the causes of habitat destruction. We can spread the word to others. Knowledge are a powerful tool in the world of our environment. The sea turtles is counting on us.

Sea turtles grow in many sizes and colors. They range between 100 and 1300 pounds. Instead of teeth, sea turtles have beaks in their jaws. Which of their senses is most keen? That would be their sense of smell. A female sea turtle lays her eggs on land. Unfortunately, sea turtles are in danger. But in the last 100 years, the population has become almost extinct. What can we do to ensure the survival of sea turtles? We can all help by keeping our oceans clean. We can educate ourselves about the causes of habitat destruction. We can spread the word to others. Knowledge is a powerful tool in the world of our environment. The sea turtles are counting on us.

Try It
Write a nonfiction paragraph about a reptile or insect that interests you. Underline the subjects of each sentence and circle the verbs.

Answers will vary.

Lesson 1.11 Action Verbs

Action verbs tell the action of the sentence. Action verbs come in both regular and irregular forms. They have present, past, and future tense forms, too.
Sandy and Karen *visit* every spring.
Sandy and Karen *visited* last year.
Sandy and Karen *will visit* next winter.

Answers may vary. Accept all reasonable answers.

Solve It
Look at the following pictures. On the line below each picture, write the action verb that the subject in the picture is doing.

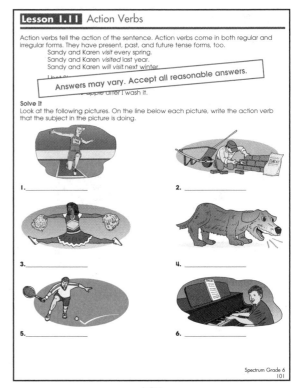

1. _____   2. _____

3. _____   4. _____

5. _____   6. _____

Lesson 1.11 Action Verbs

Match It
One verb that is used often in dialogue is *said*. Try to bring more variety to your writing by using other action verbs as a substitute for the verb *said*. Match the sentences in Column A with an action verb in Column B that could be substituted for the verb *said* in the sentence.

Column A

1. "Hey! We're over here!" said Marty __c__
2. "I like ___ ," said Kim. __e__ (Answers may vary. Possible answers:)
3. "___ ," said Alex. __i__
4. "___ I want to do more homework," said Justin. __h__
5. "We received 8 inches of snow over night," said the weather person. __d__
6. "Those are the results of my survey," said the professor. __a__
7. "Be careful riding on the wet pavement," said Mom. __g__
8. "Would you like some more lemonade?" said the server. __j__
9. "I don't like what's on my sandwich," said the customer. __f__
10. "Let's start today's lesson," said the teacher. __b__

Column B
a. concluded
b. began
c. yelled
d. reported
e. added
f. complained
g. cautioned
h. groaned
i. vowed
j. asked

Try It
Write a letter to a friend or relative. Tell him or her about a recent event in school or another activity in which you participated. Use at least 10 action verbs. Underline the verbs in your letter.

Answers will vary.

Lesson 1.12 Helping Verbs

Helping verbs are not main verbs. They help to form some of the tenses of the main verbs. Helping verbs express time and mood.

shall	may	would	has	can
will	have	should	do	did
could	had	must		

The forms of the verb *to be* are also helping verbs:
| is | are | was | were | am | been |

Verbs ending in **ing** can be a clue that there is a helping verb in the sentence. Sometimes, there is more than one helping verb in a sentence. This is called a **verb phrase**.
The Olympic star *would practice* for hours.
The Olympic star *was practicing* for hours and hours.
The Olympic star *had been practicing* for hours and hours.

Complete It
Choose a helping verb or verb phrase from the box to complete each sentence. Underline the main verb of the sentence that it helps. The main verb does not always directly follow the helping verb. Sometimes there is another word in between. Some sentences can have more than one answer.

| have | has | should | must | shall |
| had | could | would | can | had been |

1. __Shall__ we <u>dance</u> to this song?
2. That __could__ <u>be</u> the right direction, but I'm not sure.
3. Rick and Dana __had been__ <u>waiting</u> for hours when they finally got in.
4. __Would__ you <u>go</u> with me to th (Answers may vary. Possible answers:)
5. The children __can__ <u>go</u> with
6. I __have__ <u>been</u> a fan of hers for years.
7. It __has__ <u>been</u> days since we've seen each other.
8. We __should__ <u>take</u> this train; it will get us home faster.
9. It __must__ <u>be</u> this way, I see a familiar house.
10. This assignment __has__ <u>taken</u> a long time to finish.

Language Arts Grade 6 Answers

Lesson 1.13 Linking Verbs

Linking verbs connect a subject to a noun or adjective. They do not express an action.

The most common linking verbs are the forms of the verb *to be:*

is	are	was	were	been	am

Other linking verbs are those of the five senses:

smell	look	taste	feel	sound

Other linking verbs reflect a state of being:

appear	seem	become	grow	remain

A noun or adjective will follow these linking verbs in the sentence.

Identify It
Circle the linking verb and underline the noun or adjective that is linked in each sentence.

1. The crowd (appears) excited.
2. The crowd thought the play (was) good.
3. The lettuce (tastes) bitter.
4. The line (seems) long.
5. Syd, Mitzi, and Deb (were) runners.
6. Mr. Thomas (became) successful after much hard work.
7. The runners (feel) great running in the fresh air.
8. The lights (grew) dim as the play began.
9. The singer's voice (sounds) weak compared to the others.
10. Her future (remains) uncertain.
11. It (was) a long day.
12. Dinner (sounds) great.
13. They (are) late.
14. I (am) hungry.
15. The snack (is) tasty.

Spectrum Grade 6
104

Lesson 1.14 Transitive Verbs

Transitive verbs transfer their action to a direct or indirect object. If the object doesn't receive the action of the verb, the meaning of the verb is not complete.

> The hail storm *broke* the car windows.
> Transitive verb = broke
> Object = car windows (what was broken)

The meaning of the verb *broke* would not be complete without the object *car windows*.

The object and receiver of a transitive verb can be either a direct object or an indirect object.

A **direct object** receives the action directly from the subject.
> They *sent a claim.*
> Transitive verb = sent
> Direct object = claim (what was sent)

An **indirect object** is the person to whom or for whom the action is directed.
> They *sent the insurance agency a claim.*
> Transitive verb = sent
> Direct object = claim (what was sent)
> Indirect object = the insurance agency (to whom the claim was sent)

Match It
The partial sentence in Column B completes the sentence started in Column A. Column A contains the subjects of the sentences and the transitive verbs. Column B contains the direct and indirect objects. Draw a line from Column A to the sentence ending that makes the most sense in Column B.

Column A	Column B
1. Karen's father bought	his fans a story.
2. The outfielder caught	the ice cubes for later.
3. The artist drew	a picture.
4. The boys drank	the ball.
5. The teacher gave	soy beans and pumpkins.
6. The team ate	several pizzas.
7. The swimmers swam	many laps.
8. The farmer grew	them gold stars.
9. The author wrote	her a present.
10. Marie froze	the lemonade.

Spectrum Grade 6
105

Lesson 1.15 Gerunds, Participles, and Infinitives

Gerunds, **participles**, and **infinitives** are other kinds of verbs. These verbs take the role of another part of speech in some circumstances.

A **gerund** is when a verb is used as a noun. A verb can take the form of the noun when the ending **-ing** is added.
> *Cooking* is one of my favorite activities.
> (The subject *cooking* is a noun in the sentence.)

A **participle** is when a verb is used as an adjective. A verb can take the form of an adjective when the endings **-ing** or **-ed** are added.
> Those *falling* snowflakes from the sky are pretty.
> (*falling* modifies *snowflakes*)
>
> The *ordered* parts should be here on Monday.
> (*ordered* modifies *parts*)

An **infinitive** is when a verb is used as a noun, adjective, or adverb. A verb can take the form of a noun, adjective, or adverb when preceded by the word *to.*
> *To agree* with the professor can be important.
> (The verb *to agree* acts as the subject, noun, of the sentence.)
> The last student *to report* on the subject led the research team.
> (The verb *to report* acts as an adjective modifying *student.*)
> Roger observed the long movie *to report* on it for the paper.
> (The verb *to report* acts as an adverb modifying *observed.*)

Complete It
Choose a verb from the box to fill in the blanks in the sentences.

to catch	joking	sleeping
to drink	reported	to warn

1. __Sleeping__ is Jed's favorite activity on the weekends.
2. She jumped high __to catch__ the ball.
3. The __joking__ comedians performed at school.
4. Jim takes plenty of water __to drink__ on long runs.
5. The __reported__ details of the event were surprising.
6. __To warn__ the public of the oncoming storm was her job.

Spectrum Grade 6
106

Lesson 1.15 Gerunds, Participles, and Infinitives

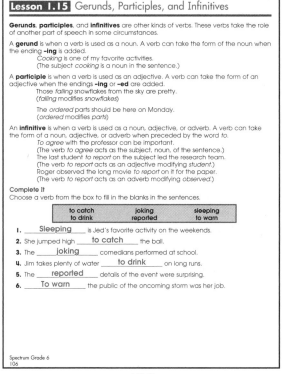

Identify It
The following sentences contain verbs that are acting as gerunds, participles, or infinitives. Identify which by placing a **G** for gerund, a **P** for participle, or an **I** for infinitive after each sentence. Then, underline the gerund, participle, or infinitive.

1. Acting is all Sally wants to do. __G__
2. The students singing on stage are from our school. __P__
3. Logs burned in this fireplace are small. __P__
4. To jump for the shot would be the best thing to do. __I__
5. Matthew brought a sandwich to eat in case the meeting ran long. __I__
6. Ann watched the special on television to learn about habitats. __I__
7. Amy studied the styles of ancient Rome to sew the appropriate costume. __I__
8. Running is an excellent exercise. __G__
9. Karen brings sweaters to wear in case it gets cold at night. __I__
10. The sound of children laughing is a wonderful sound. __P__
11. To finish your homework early is a good idea. __I__
12. The polished car sparkled in the sunlight. __P__

Try It
Make a list of six verbs. Write them on the lines below. Then, change them to gerunds, participles, and infinitives and use them in sentences. Write your new sentences on the lines provided.

_____ _____

Answers will vary.

_____
_____
_____
_____
_____
_____

Spectrum Grade 6
107

Language Arts Grade 6 Answers

Lesson 1.16 Adjectives

Adjectives are words used to describe a noun or pronoun. Most adjectives are common adjectives. Common adjectives are not proper, so they are not capitalized.

The *cold* water felt good on the *hot* day.
Water and *day* are the nouns. The adjectives *cold* and *hot* describe the nouns.

Proper adjectives are formed from proper nouns and are always capitalized.
The children wanted snow cones and *French* fries at the amusement park.
The proper adjective *French* describes the noun, *fries*.

Solve It
The words in the box are adjectives of the senses. Find and circle these words in the puzzle. They can be horizontal, vertical, diagonal, forward, and backward.

bright	loud	fresh	sour	cool
dim	sharp	sweet	spicy	rough
pretty	soothing	woodsy	tart	soft

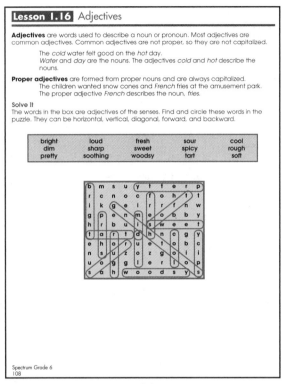

108

Lesson 1.16 Adjectives

Identify It
Circle the common adjectives and underline the proper adjectives in the paragraph.

Marblehead Lighthouse

Lighthouses are tall towers with bright lights that guide ships at night or in the fog. One famous lighthouse is located in Marblehead, Ohio, on Lake Erie. It is one of Lake Erie's most-photographed landmarks. Marblehead Lighthouse is the oldest lighthouse in continuous operation on the Great Lakes. It has been in operation since 1822. The 65-foot high tower is made of limestone. Throughout the years, the lighthouse has been operated by 15 lighthouse keepers. Two of the 15 keepers were women. Lighthouse keepers had many duties. They lighted the projection lamps, kept logs of passing ships, recorded the weather, and organized rescue efforts. As technology changed with time, the type of light used also changed. Electric light replaced lanterns in 1923. Today a 300mm lens flashes green signals every six seconds. It can be seen for up to 11 nautical miles. The lighthouse no longer has a resident keeper. The United States Coast Guard now operates the Marblehead Lighthouse. The lighthouse beacon continues to warn sailors and keep those on the lake waters safe.

Try It
Choose 10 of the 15 sensory adjectives from the puzzle on page 36. Use each of the 10 adjectives in a sentence.

Answers will vary.

109

Lesson 1.17 Adverbs

Adverbs are words used to modify a verb, an adjective, or another adverb.

An adverb tells *how, why, when, where, how often,* or *how much.*

Adverbs often end in **ly** (but not always).
how or *why*: softly, courageously, forcefully
when or *how often*: sometimes, yesterday, always
where: here, inside, below
how much: generously, barely, liberally

Match It
The categories in Column A are missing their adverbs. Select adverbs from Column B and write them in the appropriate category in Column A.

Column A	Column B
Category 1: how or why	scarcely
cleverly	today
joyfully	cleverly
luckily	outside
	joyfully
Category 2: when or how often	entirely
today	there
tomorrow	tomorrow
never	never
	luckily
Category 3: where	wholly
outside	up
there	
up	
Category 4: how much	
scarcely	
entirely	
wholly	

110

Lesson 1.17 Adverbs

Identify It
Circle the adverbs in the following paragraphs. Underline the verbs, adjectives, or adverbs they modify.

An All-American Hero

Jesse Owens lived from 1913 until 1980. He didn't have much money growing up, but he had ambition. He worked tirelessly at part-time jobs to help support his family. His high school coach noticed Jesse's talent for running. Because of work, Jesse couldn't practice with the team after school. He graciously accepted his coach's offer to train in the morning.

Jesse was anxiously recruited by many colleges and accepted an offer to the Ohio State University. However, since he was African American, he received no scholarships, despite the fact that he broke several world records while attending OSU. He continued to energetically work, study, and train. In the Berlin Olympic Games in 1936, he became the first American to win four gold medals in a single game. He also broke many track records. Remarkably, his records lasted more than 20 years.

What is even more remarkably significant is his dedication to the well-being of others that he actively exhibited later in life. He became a spokesman for living a life guided by hard work and loyalty. He eagerly sponsored and participated in youth sports programs in underprivileged neighborhoods. After his death in 1980, his wife continued to operate the Jesse Owens Foundation. Jesse Owens truly deserved the Medal of Freedom he was awarded in 1976. It is the highest honor a United States civilian can receive.

Try It
Write a sentence for each adverb in the verb box. Be sure your adverbs modify verbs, adjectives, or other adverbs.

actively	energetically
after	several
anxiously	tirelessly

Answers will vary.

111

Language Arts Grade 6 Answers

Lesson 1.18 Conjunctions

Conjunctions connect individual words or groups of words in sentences. There are three types of conjunctions.

Coordinate conjunctions connect words, phrases, or independent clauses that are equal or of the same type. Coordinate conjunctions are *and, but, or, nor, for, yet,* and *so.*

   The horse's mane is soft *and* shiny.

Correlative conjunctions are used with pairs and are used together. *Both/and, either/or,* and *neither/nor* are examples of correlative conjunctions.

   Neither pizza *nor* pasta was listed on the menu.

Subordinate conjunctions connect two clauses that are not equal. They connect dependent clauses to independent clauses in order to complete the meaning. *After, as long as, since,* and *while* are examples of subordinate conjunctions.

   We can't save for our spring vacation *until* we get part-time jobs.

Match It
Match the words in Column A with their relationship in Column B.

Column A	Column B
1. provided that the light is green	equal (coordinate)
2. cold and fluffy snow	pairs (correlative)
3. either smooth or crunchy	dependent (subordinate)
4. both mushrooms and olives	equal (coordinate)
5. before it gets dark	pairs (correlative)
6. purple or blue shirt	dependent (subordinate)
7. after the race	equal (coordinate)
8. neither pennies nor nickels	pairs (correlative)
9. music and dance	dependent (subordinate)

112

Lesson 1.18 Conjunctions

Identify It
Identify whether the following sentences use coordinate, correlative, or subordinate conjunctions by writing a **CD** for coordinate, **CR** for correlative, or **S** for subordinate before each sentence. Then, underline the conjunctions.

1. __CD__ Bobcats, members of the lynx family, are found in North America <u>and</u> Northern Eurasia.
2. __S__ <u>Although</u> they are members of the lynx family, they differ in a number of ways.
3. __CD__ Bobcats have smaller ear tufts <u>and</u> feet than lynxes.
4. __S__ <u>Because</u> of the terrain, bobcats can have different body types.
5. __CD__ Bobcats living in northern territories are smaller <u>and</u> have pale coats.
6. __CD__ Bobcats living in southern territories are larger <u>and</u> have dark coats.
7. __CD__ Bobcats can be found in swampy areas <u>but</u> also desert areas.
8. __CR__ Bobcats hunt <u>both</u> during the night <u>and</u> during the day.
9. __S__ <u>Though</u> smaller in size, bobcats are more aggressive than lynxes.
10. __CD__ Bobcats can climb <u>and</u> swim well.
11. __CR__ <u>Not only</u> bobcats <u>but</u> all big cats are exploited for their fur.
12. __C__ <u>Because</u> of this and other threats to the cat family, conservation groups are working to halt species extinction.

Try It
Write six sentences that use conjunctions. Write two sentences using coordinate conjunctions, two sentences using correlative conjunctions, and two sentences using subordinate conjunctions.

Answers will vary.

113

Lesson 1.19 Interjections

An **interjection** is a word or phrase used to express surprise or strong emotion.

Common interjections include: *ah; alas; aw; cheers; eeek; eh; hey; hi; huh; hurray; oh; oh, no; ouch; uh; uh-huh; uh-uh; voila; wow; yeah*

Exclamation marks are usually used after interjections to separate them from the rest of the sentence.

   Hurray! We are the champions!

If the feeling isn't quite as strong, a comma is used in place of the exclamation point.

   Yeah, the Oakdale Grizzlies had a great basketball season!

Sometimes question marks are used as an interjection's punctuation.

   Well? How does the team look for next year?

Solve It
What interjection from the above list would you choose to add to the following sentences? Use the pictures to help you decide. Write them on the blank in the sentences.

1. __Hi!__ It's so good to see you.

2. __Hurray!__ We've made it to the top.

3. __Ouch!__ Possible answers given.

4. __Cheers!__ Tonight we celebrate!

5. __Voila!__ Dessert is served.

6. __Oh, no!__ I hope I do better on the next test.

114

Lesson 1.19 Interjections

Rewrite It
Rewrite the following dialogue. Add interjections where you think they are appropriate to make the dialogue more exciting and interesting. Choose interjections from the previous page, or add some of your own.

"We're about ready to land. Look at that landscape," exclaimed Dana as the plane made its descent at the Kona International Airport on the big island, Hawaii. The guide book says this airport sits on miles of lava rock."

"How can that be?" asked Gabriella.

"There are five volcanoes on Hawaii. One is extinct, one is dormant, and three are still active," answered Dana.

"There are active volcanoes here?" asked Gabriella.

"The one that caused the lava flow beneath this airport is Hualalai," reported Dana. "It is still considered active. In the 1700s, it spewed lava all the way to the ocean. The airport is on top of one of the flows. The world's largest volcano, Mauna Loa, and the world's most active volcano, _____ _____ in Hawaii."

"Dana, are you sure y_____ d?" asked Gabriella.

"I plan to visit all of the _____."

"I'm hitting the beach. I've got some serious surfing to do!" exclaimed Gabriella.

Answers may vary. Possible answers :

   "Oh, boy! We're about ready to land. Look at that landscape," exclaimed Dana as the plane made its descent at the Kona International Airport on the big island, Hawaii. The guide book says this airport sits on miles of lava rock."

   "Eh? How can that be?" asked Gabriella.

   "Well, there are five volcanoes on Hawaii. One is extinct, one is dormant, and three are still active," answered Dana.

   "Oh, my! There are active volcanoes here?" asked Gabriella.

   "Yep! The one that caused the lava flow beneath this airport is Hualalai," reported Dana. "It is still considered active. In the 1700s, it spewed lava all the way to the ocean. The airport is on top of one of the flows. Eeek! The world's largest volcano, Mauna Loa, and the world's most active volcano, Kilauea, are also here on Hawaii."

   "Um, Dana, are you sure you want to vacation on this island?" asked Gabriella.

   "Oh, yes! I plan to visit all of the volcanoes," answered Dana.

   "OK, but I'm hitting the beach. I've got some serious surfing to do!" exclaimed Gabriella.

115

Language Arts Grade 6 Answers

Prepositions are words or groups of words that show the relationship between a noun or pronoun (the object of the sentence) and another word in the sentence.
They sat *upon the dock*.
In this sentence, *upon* is the preposition, and *dock* is the object of the preposition.

Common prepositions:

above	below	in	under
across	beneath	inside	until
after	beside	into	up
along	between	near	with
around	by	off	within
at	down	on	without
away	during	outside	
because	except	over	
before	for	to	
behind	from	toward	

Complete It
Complete the following sentences by circling the preposition that works best in the sentence.

1. Look (behind, down from) your car before you back out.
2. I really like the little café right (across, away from) the street.
3. The kitty likes watching the birds (outside, toward) the window.
4. Our cats only live (around, inside) the house.
5. Edna stored the photographs (through, underneath) her bed.
6. Cedric can't go on the field trip (within, without) his permission slip.
7. The commentators predicted the outcome of the game (before, until) it was over.
8. The snow piled (on top of, over to) the ice.

116

Identify It
Circle the prepositions and underline the objects of the prepositions in the paragraph.

What Is the West Wing?

The West Wing is located (in) the White House. The President (of) the United States has his office (in) the West Wing. It is called the Oval Office. The West Wing houses the executive staff's offices (in addition to) the president's office. The chief of staff's office is (across from) the Oval Office. The vice president works (beside) the chief of staff. The press secretary and the communication director's offices are (along) the main corridor. The Roosevelt Room (a conference room), the Cabinet Room (the cabinet is a group (of) advisers who are heads (of) government departments), and the President's secretary's office are a little farther (down) the corridor. (Outside) of the press secretary's window is the Rose Garden. The West Colonnade runs (alongside) the Rose Garden. The Press Room sits (inside) the West Colonnade. The Press Room sits (on top of) an old swimming pool. The swimming pool is a remnant (of) Franklin D. Roosevelt's administration. That completes the tour (of) the West Wing.

Try It
Write a paragraph describing the rooms in your home. Tell where the rooms are located and what sits outside of some of the windows. Circle the prepositions you used.

Answers will vary.

117

Prepositional phrases include the prepositions and the objects (nouns or pronouns) that follow the prepositions. A prepositional phrase includes the preposition, the object of the preposition, and the modifiers (describes other words) of the object. Prepositional phrases often tell about *when* or *where* something is happening.
They sat *upon the dock*.

If the noun in the prepositional phrase above had modifiers, they would also be included in the prepositional phrase.
They sat *upon the wooden dock*.

Match It
Match the beginnings of sentences in Column A with the prepositional phrases that match them best in Column B.

Column A
1. The clouds are
2. We can leave
3. Let's have dinner
4. The lake lies far
5. When alphabetizing the files, put the As
6. Annie can't baby sit, so Laurie is coming
7. It was raining so hard it was difficult to see
8. Swimming is permitted if you stay

Column B
within the limits.
in the sky.
after the movie.
in her place.
outside the window.
in front of the Bs.
in the morning.
beyond the forest.

118

Solve It
The following sentences describe the above ... missing. Look at the picture and complete ...

Possible answers given.

1. The kids played ___inside___ the fence.
2. A cat looked ___through___ a window.
3. A squirrel sat ___on___ the roof.
4. Chimney smoke rose ___above___ the house.
5. The basement was ___below___ the house.
6. The clouds floated ___in___ the sky.
7. The tree sat ___outside___ the fence.
8. A jogger ran ___down___ the street.

Try It
Write four sentences that include prepositional phrases. Underline the prepositional phrases in your sentences.

Answers will vary.

119

Language Arts Grade 6 Answers

Lesson 1.22 Articles

Articles are specific words that serve as adjectives before a noun. *A*, *an*, and *the* are articles.

The is a **definite article**. That means it names a specific noun.
> I go to *the* school on *the* corner.

The article *the* tells that the person goes to a specific school on a specific corner.

A and *an* are **indefinite articles**. They do not name a specific noun.
> I would like to go to *a* school on *a* corner.

The article *a* tells that the person wants to go to a school on a corner, but not a specific school or corner.

Use *a* when the noun it precedes begins with a consonant or a vowel that sounds like a consonant.
> a dog   a cat   a skunk   a one-way street

Use *an* when the noun it precedes begins with a vowel or sounds like it starts with a vowel.
> an envelope   an olive   an island   an honest person

Complete It
Complete the following sentences by circling the correct answer in parentheses.

1. Mike and Jen rented the apartment above (a, an, (the)) bookstore.
2. Henry wants to get ((a), an, the) car with four doors.
3. An amoeba is ((a), an, the) one-celled animal.
4. Coordinating the play turned out to be quite (a, (an), the) ordeal.
5. Todd wants to rent ((a), an, the) canoe for the weekend.
6. Kay brought (a, (an), the) orange to go with her lunch.
7. (A, An, (The)) orange sweater looked best on Karley.
8. Not (a, (an), the) hour went by that they didn't think about each other.
9. (A, An, (The)) Kensington Trail is beautiful.
10. Lynn wants to buy ((a), an, the) blue or red bracelet.

120

Lesson 1.22 Articles

Proof It
Proofread the following paragraph. Change any incorrect articles to the correct ones.

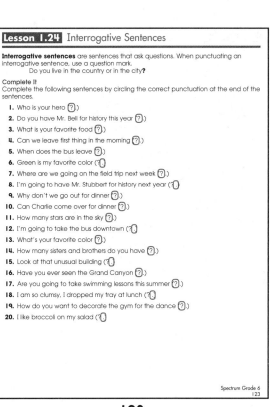

> ℯ - deletes incorrect letters, words, punctuation
> ∧ - inserts correct letters, words, punctuation

The Tonys

Almost everyone has heard of the Oscars, the an
Emmys, and a Golden Globe Awards. The Tony Awards is also a awards presentation.
A Tony Awards are given for outstanding accomplishment in theater. The Tony Awards
were named after Antoinette Perry, a actress, director, producer, and manager. She was
known for helping young people who were interested in the acting profession. An first Tony
Awards were presented in 1947 with seven categories. Today, there are 25 categories
including Best Play and Best Musical. The Tony award is the medallion that shows a image
of Antoinette Perry on one side. On an other side are a masks of comedy and tragedy.

Try It
What is your favorite play, movie, or television show? Write a paragraph describing your favorite. Underline the articles you used.

Answers will vary.

121

Lesson 1.23 Declarative Sentences

Declarative sentences are sentences that make statements. They say something about a place, person, thing, or idea. When punctuating a declarative sentence, use a period at the end.
> I have several hours of homework to do.

Identify It
Identify the following declarative sentences by placing a checkmark ✓ on the line provided. Leave the other sentences blank.

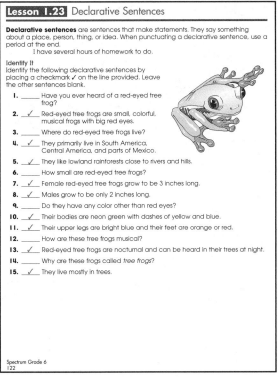

1. _____ Have you ever heard of a red-eyed tree frog?
2. __✓__ Red-eyed tree frogs are small, colorful, musical frogs with big red eyes.
3. _____ Where do red-eyed tree frogs live?
4. __✓__ They primarily live in South America, Central America, and parts of Mexico.
5. __✓__ They like lowland rainforests close to rivers and hills.
6. _____ How small are red-eyed tree frogs?
7. __✓__ Female red-eyed tree frogs grow to be 3 inches long.
8. __✓__ Males grow to be only 2 inches long.
9. _____ Do they have any color other than red eyes?
10. __✓__ Their bodies are neon green with dashes of yellow and blue.
11. __✓__ Their upper legs are bright blue and their feet are orange or red.
12. _____ How are these tree frogs musical?
13. __✓__ Red-eyed tree frogs are nocturnal and can be heard in their trees at night.
14. _____ Why are these frogs called *tree frogs*?
15. __✓__ They live mostly in trees.

122

Lesson 1.24 Interrogative Sentences

Interrogative sentences are sentences that ask questions. When punctuating an interrogative sentence, use a question mark.
> Do you live in the country or in the city**?**

Complete It
Complete the following sentences by circling the correct punctuation at the end of the sentences.

1. Who is your hero ((?).)
2. Do you have Mr. Bell for history this year ((?).)
3. What is your favorite food ((?).)
4. Can we leave first thing in the morning ((?).)
5. When does the bus leave ((?).)
6. Green is my favorite color (?(.))
7. Where are we going on the field trip next week ((?).)
8. I'm going to have Mr. Stubbert for history next year (?(.))
9. Why don't we go out for dinner ((?).)
10. Can Charlie come over for dinner ((?).)
11. How many stars are in the sky ((?).)
12. I'm going to take the bus downtown (?(.))
13. What's your favorite color ((?).)
14. How many sisters and brothers do you have ((?).)
15. Look at that unusual building (?(.))
16. Have you ever seen the Grand Canyon ((?).)
17. Are you going to take swimming lessons this summer ((?).)
18. I am so clumsy, I dropped my tray at lunch (?(.))
19. How do you want to decorate the gym for the dance ((?).)
20. I like broccoli on my salad (?(.))

123

Language Arts Grade 6 Answers

Lesson 1.25 Exclamatory Sentences

Exclamatory sentences are sentences that reveal urgency, strong surprise, or emotion. When punctuating an exclamatory sentence, use an exclamation mark.
> Watch out for the icy steps**!**

Sometimes you will find interjections in exclamatory sentences.
> *Yea!* One more test until summer break!

Exclamation marks can also be used in dialogue, when the character or speaker is making an urgent or emotional statement.
> "*Watch out!*" shouted Kelly.

Exclamation marks should be used sparingly in writing. Do not overuse them.

Match It
Match the sentences (which are missing their punctuation) in Column A with their type of sentence in Column B. Draw an arrow to make your match.

Column A	Column B
1. I will be thirteen on my next birthday	declarative
2. Hurry and open up your presents	interrogative
3. How old are you	exclamatory
4. Oh no I dropped all of my papers in a puddle	declarative
5. Is it supposed to snow all weekend	interrogative
6. Autumn is my favorite season	exclamatory
7. Where are my shoes	declarative
8. I scored 12 points in the basketball game	interrogative
9. Look out	exclamatory

Spectrum Grade 6
124

Lesson 1.26 Imperative Sentences

Imperative sentences demand that an action be performed. The subjects of imperative sentences are usually not expressed. They usually contain the understood subject *you*. Imperative sentences can be punctuated with a period or an exclamation mark.
> Get on bus #610.
> (*You* get on bus #610.)
> Answer the phone before it stops ringing!
> (*You* answer the phone before it stops ringing!)

Identify It
Identify the following sentences by writing a **D** for declarative, an **IN** for interrogative, an **E** for exclamatory, or an **IM** for imperative after each sentence.

1. Hop over that puddle! __E__
2. How many more days until spring break? __IN__
3. I won the contest! __E__
4. I don't want anchovies on my pizza. __D__
5. Let's set up a lemonade stand this summer. __IM__
6. What is the distance of a century bicycle ride? __IN__
7. Announce the winners as they come across the finish line. __IM__
8. The firefighter saved everyone in the house! __E__
9. Think about what you want to serve at the party. __IM__
10. My favorite appetizer is vegetable stuffed mushrooms. __D__
11. Whom do you admire most? __IN__
12. The fundraiser was a huge success! __E__

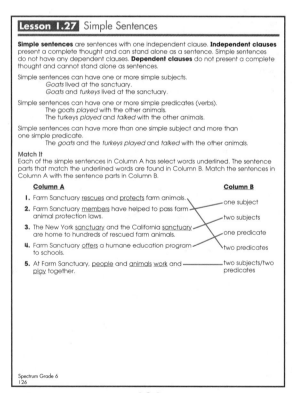

Spectrum Grade 6
125

Lesson 1.27 Simple Sentences

Simple sentences are sentences with one independent clause. **Independent clauses** present a complete thought and can stand alone as a sentence. Simple sentences do not have any dependent clauses. **Dependent clauses** do not present a complete thought and cannot stand alone as sentences.

Simple sentences can have one or more simple subjects.
> *Goats* lived at the sanctuary.
> *Goats* and *turkeys* lived at the sanctuary.

Simple sentences can have one or more simple predicates (verbs).
> The goats *played* with the other animals.
> The turkeys *played* and *talked* with the other animals.

Simple sentences can have more than one simple subject and more than one simple predicate.
> The *goats* and the *turkeys played* and *talked* with the other animals.

Match It
Each of the simple sentences in Column A has select words underlined. The sentence parts that match the underlined words are found in Column B. Match the sentences in Column A with the sentence parts in Column B.

Column A	Column B
1. Farm Sanctuary <u>rescues</u> and <u>protects</u> farm animals.	one subject
2. Farm Sanctuary <u>members</u> have helped to pass farm animal protection laws.	two subjects
3. The New York <u>sanctuary</u> and the California <u>sanctuary</u> are home to hundreds of rescued farm animals.	one predicate
4. Farm Sanctuary <u>offers</u> a humane education program to schools.	two predicates
5. At Farm Sanctuary, <u>people</u> and <u>animals work</u> and <u>play</u> together.	two subjects/two predicates

Spectrum Grade 6
126

Lesson 1.28 Compound Sentences

Compound sentences are sentences with two or more simple sentences (independent clauses) joined by a coordinate conjunction, punctuation, or both. As in simple sentences, there are no dependent clauses in compound sentences.

A compound sentence can be two sentences joined with a comma and a coordinate conjunction.
> He didn't think he was a fan of Shakespeare**,** *yet* he enjoyed the play.

A compound sentence can also be two simple sentences joined by a semicolon.
> He didn't think he was a fan of Shakespeare**;** he enjoyed the play.

Match It
Match simple sentences in Column A with simple sentences in Column B to create compound sentences. Write the compound sentences and remember to add either a coordinate conjunction or punctuation.

Column A	Column B
1. The football game was exciting.	1. They have a good record this year.
2. My favorite team is playing.	2. I'm going to get pizza after the game.
3. My school's colors are blue and white.	3. The score was close.
4. I'm going to get a	4.
5. My team won the	Answers will vary. 5. The opposing team's colors are green and gold.

1. <u>The football game was exciting; the score was close.</u>

2. <u>My favorite team is playing, and they have a good record this year.</u>

3. <u>My school's colors are blue and white; the opposing team's colors are green and gold.</u>

4. <u>I'm going to get a pretzel at halftime, or I'm going to get pizza after the game.</u>

5. <u>My team won the game, but the season isn't over yet.</u>

Spectrum Grade 6
127

Language Arts Grade 6 Answers

Lesson 1.29 Complex Sentences

Complex sentences have one independent clause and one or more dependent clauses. The independent and dependent clauses are connected with a subordinate conjunction or a relative pronoun. Dependent clauses do not present a complete thought and cannot stand alone as sentences. The dependent clause can be anywhere in the sentence.

Complex sentence (connected with subordinate conjunction):
You can go to the movies *if* you finish your homework.

Complex sentence (connected with a relative pronoun):
My mother asked me to drop off these flowers for Mrs. Hastings, *whose* house is on our way to school.

Dependent clauses follow the connecting subordinate conjunction or the relative pronoun. The dependent clause can either be the first or second part of the sentence.
Before the movie, I'll finish my homework.
I'll finish my homework *before* the movie.

Identify It
Put a checkmark on the line in front of following the complex sentences.

1. ✓ I like biking because it is good exercise.
2. ✓ Tony is going to order pasta with mushrooms, which is his favorite dish.
3. _____ History is my favorite subject.
4. ✓ Mr. Baum, who is also the baseball coach, is my favorite teacher.
5. ✓ While Kim is a good speller, Jerry is better.
6. _____ I would like a salad for lunch, yet soup sounds good, too.
7. ✓ Erin made the basketball team after two weeks of tryouts.
8. ✓ Although it's going to snow, I think we should still hike the trails.
9. ✓ Unless it rains, we'll walk, not ride.
10. ✓ We can continue hiking until it gets icy.

128

Lesson 1.30 Sentence Fragments

A **sentence fragment** is a group of words that is missing a subject, predicate, or both. A sentence fragment is also a group of words that doesn't express a complete thought, as in a dependent clause.

Doesn't have good insulation. (no subject)
Complete sentence: The window doesn't have good insulation.

The window good insulation. (no predicate)
Complete sentence: The window doesn't have good insulation.

Good insulation. (no subject or predicate)
Complete sentence: The window doesn't have good insulation.

Since the lemonade was too sour. (not a complete thought)
Complete sentence: We drank water since the lemonade was too sour.

Complete It
Complete the following sentence fragments by choosing a sentence fragment from the box that completes the sentences.

It was presented	Construction began
The statue's height	is "Liberty Enlightening the World."
stands on Liberty Island in the New York Harbor.	

1. The Statue of Liberty **stands on Liberty Island in the New York Harbor.**
_____. (look for a verb phrase)
2. **Construction began** in France in 1875.
(look for a subject and a verb)
3. **It was presented** to the United States on July 4, 1884. (look for a subject and verb)
4. The official name of the Statue of Liberty **is "Liberty Enlightening the World."**. (look for a verb phrase)
5. **The statue's height** from base to torch is 152 feet, 2 inches. (look for a subject)

129

Lesson 1.31 Combining Sentences

Combining short, choppy sentences into longer, more detailed sentences makes writing much more interesting and easier to read. Sentences can be combined in a variety of ways.

Compound Subjects and Compound Verbs:
The lightning is coming. The thunder is coming.
The *thunder and lightning* are coming.

The president of our class is honest. The president of our class is loyal.
The president of our class is *honest and loyal.*

Adjectives and Adverbs:
I went to a party. The party was a costume party.
I went to a *costume party.*

Timothy ran quickly. Timothy ran in the race.
Timothy *ran quickly* in the race.

Making Complex Sentences (using subordinate conjunctions):
Donna wanted to go to the reunion. Donna wanted to go if her best friend Diane went.
Donna wanted to go to the reunion *if* her best friend Diane went.

Match It
Under Column A are five combined sentences. Under Column B are the parts of speech that were combined. Match the sentences in Column A with the parts of speech in Column B.

Column A	Column B
1. The salesman reluctantly attended the seminar.	combined subjects
2. Dan and Rose are taking swimming lessons.	combined verbs
3. Cam's parents lived in a beautiful neighborhood.	combined adjective
4. David climbed and descended the mountain.	combined adverb
5. The phone rang while we were eating.	subordinate conjunction

130

Lesson 1.32 Writing a Paragraph

Rewrite It
The sentences in the following paragraph are out of order. Rewrite the paragraph placing the topic sentence first, the summary sentence last, and the body sentences in between.

This substance has a red pigment. Horseshoe crabs' blood has copper in it. Not all living creatures have red blood; horseshoe crabs' blood is blue! Human blood has hemoglobin that has iron in it. The color of one's blood, whether a creature big or small, depends on the makeup and chemicals in the blood. This material causes the blood to appear blue.

topic sentence: **Not all living creatures have red blood; horseshoe crabs' blood is blue!**

first body sentence: **Horseshoe crabs' blood has copper in it.**

second body sentence: **This material causes the blood to appear blue.**

third body sentence: **Human blood has hemoglobin that has iron in it.**

fourth body sentence: **This substance has a red pigment.**

end sentence: **The color of one's blood, whether a creature big or small, depends on the makeup and chemicals in the blood.**

Try It
Write a paragraph about a topic of your choosing. Select one of the types of paragraphs. Think about your topic ideas and the five steps of writing.

Answers will vary.

132

Language Arts Grade 6 Answers

133

Match It
Circle the letter of the best answer to each of the following questions.

1. Which sentence would most likely be found in a persuasive paragraph?
   a. Alexandra kicked off her sandals and raced towards the waves.
   b. According to Chinese tradition, each year is assigned an animal in the Chinese zodiac.
   c. More than half of the middle school students have said they would attend an afterschool program at the community center.

2. Which of the following sentences is mostly likely from a narrative paragraph?
   a. The man peeked through the window and saw the mass of reporters waiting on his front lawn.
   b. Throughout history, pigeons have been used to carry messages.
   c. You'll notice a difference in your energy level after cutting sugar out for only one week.

3. Which sentence would make the best topic sentence?
   a. Babe Ruth's given name was George Herman Ruth.
   b. Babe Ruth is one of the greatest athletes in the history of baseball.
   c. Babe Ruth joined the Baltimore Orioles in 1914.

4. Which sentence is most likely to be a supporting detail from the middle of a paragraph?
   a. The next time you see a bat, remember how much we rely on this small, odd creature.
   b. Bats often feed on fruit, pollen, and insects.
   c. Have you ever seen a bat on clear, starry night?

Spectrum Grade 6
133

134

Try It
On the lines below, write the rough draft of a descriptive, narrative, expository, or persuasive paragraph.

Answers will vary.

Spectrum Grade 6
134

135

Chapter 2
Lesson 2.1 Proper Nouns: Days of the Week, Months of the Year

Proper nouns are specific people, places, and things. They are capitalized.

Capitalize days of the week.
   Sunday   Monday   Tuesday   Wednesday   Thursday   Friday   Saturday

Capitalize months of the year.
   January   February   March   April   May   June   July   August   September   October   November   December

Months of the year are also capitalized when they serve as adjectives.
   They ran the marathon on a sunny *June* morning.

Solve It
Complete the following sentences by cracking the code and filling in the blanks. Remember to capitalize the days of the weeks when you write them.

1=A	4=D	7=G	10=J	13=M	16=P	19=S	22=V	25=Y
2=B	5=E	8=H	11=K	14=N	17=Q	20=T	23=W	26=Z
3=C	6=F	9=I	12=L	15=O	18=R	21=U	24=X	

1. I'm always groggy on a M o n d a y , the first day of the school week.
   13 15 14 4 1 25

2. I was born on a S u n d a y , one of the two weekend days.
   19 21 14 4 1 25

3. The day of the week with the most letters in it is W e d n e s d a y .
   23 5 4 14 5 19 4 1 25

4. F r i d a y is high school football night.
   6 18 9 4 1 25

5. T u e s d a y is one of the two days of the week that starts with the
   20 21 5 19 4 1 25   same letter.

6. T h u r s d a y is the other.
   20 8 21 18 19 4 1 25

7. I play baseball every S a t u r d a y .
   19 1 20 21 18 4 1 25

Spectrum Grade 6
135

136

Rewrite It
Rewrite the following sentences after unscrambling the names of the months. Do not forget to capitalize them.

1. The month of jeun is Adopt a Shelter Cat Month.
   The month of June is Adopt a Shelter Cat Month.

2. Earth Day, a day for environmental awareness, is celebrated in lpari.
   Earth Day, a day for environmental awareness, is celebrated in April.

3. Adopt a Shelter Dog Month is held in cbotore.
   Adopt a Shelter Dog Month is held in October.

4. St. Valentine is credited for bringing couples together on the 14th of barufrey.
   St. Valentine is credited for bringing couples together on the 14th of February.

5. The state of Colorado has its own day, and it's celebrated in stuagu.
   The state of Colorado has its own day, and it's celebrated in August.

6. Shogatsu is the name for New Year in Japan; it is celebrated in najruay.
   Shogatsu is the name for New Year in Japan; it is celebrated in January.

Try It
Write a paragraph about your favorite day of the week or month of the year.

Answers will vary.

Spectrum Grade 6
136

Language Arts Grade 6 Answers

Lesson 2.2 Proper Nouns: Historical Events, Names of Languages and Nationalities, Team Names

Historical events, nationalities, and team names are **proper nouns**.

Events, periods of time, and important documents from history are capitalized.
    Cold War   Renaissance Period   Constitution of the United States

Names of languages and nationalities are capitalized. They are also capitalized when they are used as adjectives.
    French   Hispanic   Dutch apple pie

The names of sports teams are capitalized.
    Detroit Tigers

Complete It
Complete the following sentences by circling the correct answer in parentheses. Hint: Not all choices are proper and need to be capitalized.

1. The war lasting from 1939 to 1945 was (world war II (World War II)).
2. The (italian (Italian)) language is one of the romance languages.
3. An (era) Era) is considered to be any important period of time.
4. The season begins for (baseball teams,) Baseball Teams) in April.
5. Mikhail Baryshnikov is of (russian (Russian)) descent.
6. The (boston red sox (Boston Red Sox)) won the World Series in 2004.
7. The (magna carta (Magna Carta)) was written in 1215.
8. The (english (English)) cocker spaniel was the number one dog in popularity in Britain from the 1930s through the 1950s.
9. The (victorian era (Victorian Era)) lasted from 1839 to 1901, during the reign of Queen Victoria in England.
10. The (french (French)) soufflé is a dessert served warm.
11. The first ten amendments to the Constitution of the United States is the (bill of rights (Bill of Rights)).
12. The (battle of waterloo, (Battle of Waterloo)) took place in Belgium in 1815.

137

Lesson 2.2 Proper Nouns: Historical Events, Names of Languages and Nationalities, Team Names

Solve It
Unscramble the following letters in parentheses to complete each sentence with a word from the box. Capitalize each word when necessary.

period address	patriots angels	world german	war greek

1. The Jurassic ___Period___ (rdieop) was a period in time that saw the rise of the dinosaurs.
2. ___World___ (rowdl) War II ended in Japan on V-J Day on September 2, 1945.
3. A famous speech was the Gettysburg ___Address___ (dresads) given by Abraham Lincoln.
4. The ___German___ (mgnare) chocolate cake did not really originate in Germany.
5. The New England ___Patriots___ (strapiot) football team has a patriotic mascot.
6. World ___War___ (rwa) I was also known as the Great War.
7. An angelic baseball team might be known as the Los Angeles ___Angels___ (saenlg).
8. The Greeks were the first Europeans to use an alphabet, what became known as the ___Greek___ (ekreg) alphabet.

Try It
Write a paragraph about your favorite sports team. Don't forget to use capitals when needed.

Answers will vary.

138

Lesson 2.3 Proper Nouns: Organizations, Departments of Government, Sections of the Country

Organizations, departments of government, and sections of the country are all **proper nouns** and are capitalized.

The names of organizations and associations are capitalized.
    Capital Area Humane Society   Microsoft Corporation

Capitalize the names of departments of government.
    Department of Treasury   Department of Health and Human Services

Directional words that point out particular sections of the country are capitalized. However, words that give directions are not capitalized.
    Heather grew up on the East Coast of the United States.
    Madlyn grew up on the east side of town.

Identify It
Circle the name of the organization, department of government, or section of the country in each sentence.

1. My mom and dad work for the (Department of Transportation).
2. Tina and her family are moving to the (Midwest) this summer.
3. The (National Aeronautics and Space Administration) is in charge of space exploration.
4. I volunteer for the (American Red Cross).
5. San Francisco is on the (West Coast) of the United States.
6. While walking to school, we pass the (Smithson Art Association).
7. We are traveling to the (Southwest) next year.
8. Tasha's aunt works for the (State Department).
9. Have you ever been to (New England)?
10. We must send in our tax forms by April 15 to the (Internal Revenue Service).
11. (TransUnion Carrier Services) provides cardboard boxes for moving.
12. Portland, Oregon, is in the (Northwest).

139

Lesson 2.4 Proper Nouns: Titles, Geographic Names

The titles of books, poems, songs, movies, plays, newspapers, and magazines are **proper nouns** and are capitalized. Most titles are also underlined in text. Song titles and essays, however, are in quotes.
    book: The Cat in the Hat   song: "Atomic Dog"   magazine: Time

Titles associated with names are also capitalized.
    Mayor Franklin   Senator Santos   Professor Johnson

Do not capitalize these titles if they are not directly used with the name.
    The mayor of our town is Mayor Franklin.

Geographic names, such as the names of countries, states, cities, counties, bodies of water, public areas, roads and highways, and buildings are capitalized.
    Columbia, Hawaii, Athens, Chesapeake Bay, Sierra Nevada Range, Rocky Mountain National Park, Paint Creek Trail, Globe Theatre

If the geographic name is not a specific name, do not capitalize it.
    I'm going to the lake for the weekend.

Complete It
Complete the following sentences by circling the best answer in parentheses.

1. My favorite song is ("Vertigo") "vertigo") by U2.
2. The (President, (president)) of the organization is visiting on Tuesday.
3. At 2:00 pm, (Governor,) governor) Spencer is making a speech.
4. Valerie and Gerald watched the sunset from the (Eiffel Tower,) eiffel tower).
5. Are you going to the (Mountains, (mountains)) or the beach for vacation?
6. One of my favorite books is (The Elephant Hospital) the elephant hospital).
7. Lynda walks in a park along the (Scioto River,) scioto river).
8. (Martin Luther King, Jr. Highway) Martin Luther King, Jr. highway) is located in Washington, D.C.
9. My cousin was born in (Birmingham,) birmingham), England.
10. The tiny (Village, (village)) sits next to a canal.

140

Language Arts Grade 6 Answers

Lesson 2.4 Proper Nouns: Titles, Geographic Names

Find It
Answer the following questions. If you need help, use an encyclopedia or other resource. Be sure to capitalize the answers when necessary.

1. Who is the principal of your school? _____
2. What city, state, and country do you live in? _____
3. Where were you born? _____
4. Who is the governor of your state? _____
5. What is your favorite book? _____
6. What is your favorite movie? **Answers will vary.**
7. What is your favorite poem? _____
8. What states border the state in which you live? _____
9. What is the closest national park to where you live? _____
10. What is the name of your local newspaper? _____
11. What magazine do you like to read the most? _____
12. What is the name of one of your state's senators? _____

Try It
Use the information gathered above to write a brief biography about yourself. As in your previous answers, remember to capitalize titles and geographic names when necessary. You can also include other information about yourself in addition to the facts above.

Answers will vary.

Lesson 2.5 Sentences, Direct Quotations

The first word of every **sentence** is capitalized.
The wind blew strongly through the trees.

The first word in **direct quotations** is also capitalized.
My father said, "*Finish* your homework and then we'll go for a ride."
"*I'm* almost finished now," I happily answered.

Indirect quotations are not capitalized.
My father said he had been working on his car for weeks.

If a continuous sentence in a direct quotation is split and the second half is not a new sentence, do not capitalize it. If a new sentence begins after the split, then capitalize it as you would with any sentence.
"Keep your hands and arms inside the car," said the attendant, "*and* stay seated."
"Roller coasters are my favorite rides," I said. "*I* can ride them all day."

Complete It
Complete the following sentences by circling the best answer in parentheses.

1. (The) the) girls' team beat the boys' team by three seconds.
2. T.C. said, "(Baseball) baseball) is my favorite sport."
3. "(Put) put) your donated clothing in plastic bags," said the event organizer.
4. The technician said (The) (the) car would be ready in a few hours.
5. "Don't rush through your homework," said the teacher, "(And) (and) stay focused."
6. "Be careful as you shovel the snow," mother said. "(You) you) can hurt your back."
7. (The) the) airplane was going to be delayed.
8. Renee said, "(Would) would) you like a baseball hat when we go to the park?"
9. "(Our) our) race will begin in 10 minutes," said the announcer.
10. The sales clerk said (She (she) would hold the item for one day.
11. "Lemon cream is my favorite pie," said Lisa, "(But (but) nothing beats brownies."
12. "I can't wait until my birthday," said Jack. "(My) my) parents are giving me a party."

Lesson 2.5 Sentences, Direct Quotations

Proof It
Proofread the following dialogue correcting capitalization errors.

∧	– inserts correct words or punctuation
☰	– capitalize letter

"Hi, Dad," said Jack. "We learned about tsunamis today."

"What did you learn about tsunamis?" Jack's dad asked.

Jack answered, "Well, we learned that tsunamis can move up to 500 miles per hour. We also learned about how they are formed."

"The earth's crust is made up of interlocking plates," said Jack. "The plates are floating on a hot, flexible interior that drifts. The plates sometimes collide. In a subduction, an ocean plate slides under continental plates. Over the years, the plates lock, the seafloor compresses, and the coastline warps up. Eventually, the pressure pops and the seafloor lunges landward. The coast lunges seaward. the plates push seawater all over, creating the tsunami. Geologists can study sedimentary layers near the seaside to tell when shifts have occurred in the past, maybe helping to understand when it might happen again."

Try It
Write a dialogue between you and a friend, teacher, or parent. Explain to the other person something you learned about in school. Remember the capitalization rules.

Answers will vary.

Lesson 2.6 Personal and Business Letters

A **personal letter** has five parts: heading, salutation, body, closing, and signature.

The **heading** of a personal letter is the address of the person writing the letter and the date it is written. The name of the street, the city, the state, and the month are all capitalized.
1245 Hollow Dr.
Suncrest, AZ
March 31, 2008

The **salutation** is the greeting and begins with the word *dear*. Both *dear* and the name of the person who is receiving the letter are capitalized. The salutation ends with a comma.
Dear Stanley,

The **body** is the main part of the letter and contains sentences that are capitalized as normal.

The **closing** can be written in many ways; only the first word is capitalized.
Your friend,   Sincerely,   All the best,

The **signature** is usually only your first name in a personal letter. It is also always capitalized.
Milton

Identify It
Identify the parts of the personal letter by writing the names on the lines provided. Then, circle the capital letters.

7511 Hibernia Rd.
heading Seattle, WA 40000
February 31, 2014

Dear Uncle Josh, _salutation_

How are you? My ski trip has been great. I even learned how to snowboard. I think I'll be really sore tomorrow. All of the fundraising was worth it. Thanks for helping us out. I'm glad our class got to take this trip. I hope I'll get to come back someday. _body_

Thank you, _closing_

Mike _signature_

Language Arts Grade 6 Answers

Lesson 2.6 Personal and Business Letters

A **business letter** has six parts: heading, inside address, salutation, body, closing and signature.

The **heading** of a business letter is the address of the person writing the letter and the date it is written. The name of the street, the city, the state, and the month are all capitalized.

> 4003 Fourteenth St.
> Amlin, NH 20000
> September 6, 2014

The **inside address** includes the name and complete address of the person to whom the letter is going.

> Mark Dillon, Director
> S.A.S Productions
> 100 Otterbein Ave.
> Rochester, NY 20000

The **salutation** is the greeting and begins with the word *dear*. Both *dear* and the name of the person who is receiving the letter are capitalized. The salutation ends with a colon.

> Dear Director:

The **body** is the main part of the letter and contains sentences that are capitalized as normal.

The **closing** can be written many ways. Only the first word is capitalized.

> Yours truly,   Sincerely,   Very truly,

The **signature** is your full name and is capitalized.

> Leigh D. McGregor

Try It
Write the heading, inside address, salutation, closing, and signature of a business letter. Make up the names and other information, and be sure you capitalize correctly.

heading: _____   inside address: _____

Answers will vary. Make sure capitalization is correct.

salutation: _____   closing: _____

signature: _____

145

Lesson 2.7 Periods: After Imperative Sentences, In Dialogue, In Abbreviations, In Initials

Sometimes, imperative sentences call for a **period**, as when the sentence is not urgent.
> *Pay the toll at the booth.*

Periods are used in dialogue. The period goes inside the quotation mark.
> *Jean said, "Give Mimi a drink of water."*

If the quote comes at the beginning of the sentence, use a comma at the end of the direct quotation and before the quotation mark. Place a period at the end of the sentence.
> *"If it gets cold, put on your jacket," said Robyn.*

Use a period after each part of an abbreviation. Use a period after each letter of an initial.
> *M.A. (Master of Arts)*   *Samuel L. Jackson*

Complete It
Complete the following sentences by adding periods where necessary.

1. Check out at the far counter
   Check out at the far counter.

2. Janet said, "Let's take a long walk"
   Janet said, "Let's take a long walk."

3. "Hiking is my favorite hobby," said Charlie
   "Hiking is my favorite hobby," said Charlie.

4. Kathryn received her MA from the University of Arizona.
   Kathryn received her M.A. from the University of Arizona.

5. My favorite actress is Vivica A Fox.
   My favorite actress is Vivica A. Fox.

6. "Jump over the puddle, so you will stay dry," yelled Eddie
   "Jump over the puddle, so you will stay dry," yelled Eddie.

7. Reach a little farther, and you will have touched the top
   Reach a little farther, and you will have touched the top.

8. JRR Tolkien is my favorite author.
   J.R.R. Tolkein is my favorite author.

146

Lesson 2.8 Question Marks

Question marks are used in sentences that ask questions, called interrogative sentences.
> *How was your trip?*

When used in quotations, question marks can be placed either inside or outside of the end quotation mark depending on the meaning of the sentence.

When the question mark is punctuating the quotation itself, it is placed inside the quote.
> *The coach asked, "How many push-ups can you do?"*

When the question mark is punctuating the entire sentence, it is placed outside the quote.
> *Did the coach say, "Try to do twice as many as you did last week"?*

A question mark is not used in sentences with indirect quotations.
> *Suhad asked the librarian for help finding the book.*

Match It
Draw a line to match the sentences in Column A with their descriptions in Column B.

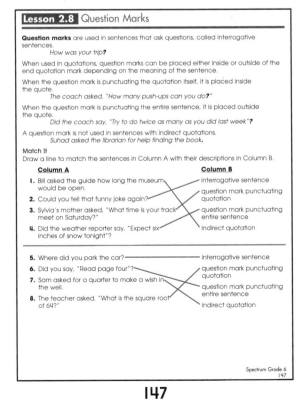

Column A	Column B
1. Bill asked the guide how long the museum would be open.	interrogative sentence
2. Could you tell that funny joke again?	question mark punctuating quotation
3. Sylvia's mother asked, "What time is your track meet on Saturday?"	question mark punctuating entire sentence
4. Did the weather reporter say, "Expect six inches of snow tonight"?	indirect quotation
5. Where did you park the car?	interrogative sentence
6. Did you say, "Read page four"?	question mark punctuating quotation
7. Sam asked for a quarter to make a wish in the well.	question mark punctuating entire sentence
8. The teacher asked, "What is the square root of 64?"	indirect quotation

147

Lesson 2.8 Question Marks

Proof It
Proofread the following dialogue, correcting the misplaced and misused question marks.

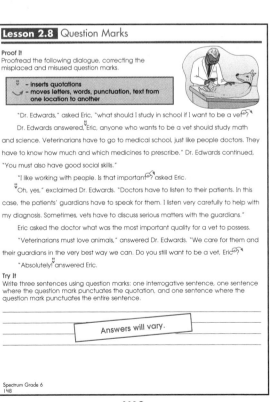

> ⋎ – inserts quotations
> ⌒ – moves letters, words, punctuation, text from one location to another

"Dr. Edwards," asked Eric, "what should I study in school if I want to be a vet?"

Dr. Edwards answered, "Eric, anyone who wants to be a vet should study math and science. Veterinarians have to go to medical school, just like people doctors. They have to know how much and which medicines to prescribe." Dr. Edwards continued, "You must also have good social skills."

"I like working with people. Is that important?" asked Eric.

"Oh, yes," exclaimed Dr. Edwards. "Doctors have to listen to their patients. In this case, the patients' guardians have to speak for them. I listen very carefully to help with my diagnosis. Sometimes, vets have to discuss serious matters with the guardians."

Eric asked the doctor what was the most important quality for a vet to possess.

"Veterinarians must love animals," answered Dr. Edwards. "We care for them and their guardians in the very best way we can. Do you still want to be a vet, Eric?"

"Absolutely!" answered Eric.

Try It
Write three sentences using question marks: one interrogative sentence, one sentence where the question mark punctuates the quotation, and one sentence where the question mark punctuates the entire sentence.

_____

Answers will vary.

_____

148

Language Arts Grade 6 Answers

Lesson 2.9 Exclamation Points

Exclamation points are used at the end of sentences that express surprise and strong emotion, called exclamatory sentences.
We have to read all three chapters for homework!

Interjections sometimes require exclamation points.
Aha! I've come up with the answer!

If you use an exclamation point, make sure the sentence expresses surprise, urgency, or strong emotion. Don't overuse exclamation points.

Complete It
Complete the following sentences by circling the best end punctuation in parentheses.

1. Can bees talk (?)
2. Scientists have discovered that bees do communicate with each other (.)
3. How do they talk (?)
4. Bees don't talk with their voices (.)
5. Bees talk through dance (?/.)
6. What do bees talk about (?)
7. Bees talk about gathering food (.)
8. One dance move tells where the food is located (./?)
9. Another dance move tells how far the food is away (.)
10. Are there more dance moves (?)
11. Yes, another move tells about how much food is in a particular location (./?)
12. Do dancing bees have a special name (?)
13. The bees who communicate about the food are called scout bees (.)
14. Scout bees dance for forager bees (.)
15. Forager bees interpret the dance and go out to get the food (.)
16. How do the forager bees understand what the moves mean (?)
17. How fast the scouts dance tells how far the food is away (.)
18. The angle the scouts dance tells where the food is and the number of times the scouts dance how much food there is (.)
19. What an amazing story (.)
20. Bees are amazing creatures (.)

Answers may vary.

Spectrum Grade 6
149

149

Lesson 2.9 Exclamation Points

Solve It
Choose a word from the box to complete the following sentences so they express strong emotion or surprise. Not all words will be used.

brave	fast	loud	show	tall
cautious	freezing	low	short	tied
close	high	luke warm	soft	warm
far	hot	mild	spicy	won

1. Don't touch the stove; it is _____ hot _____!
2. Look how _____ fast _____ that racecar driver took the curve!
3. Please turn down that _____ loud _____ music!
4. The trapeze performer is so _____ high _____ from the ground!
5. This tour through the caves is scary; the walls are too _____ close _____!
6. It's cold outside and the water is _____ freezing _____!
7. The astronauts on this mission are so _____ brave _____!
8. Be careful when you take a bite; the dip is very _____ spicy _____!
9. Yea! Our team _____ won _____ the championship!
10. The sequoia tree is so _____ tall _____!

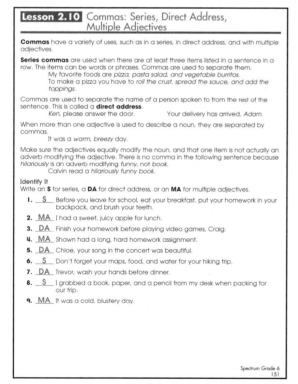

Try It
Write a paragraph describing an exciting sporting event in which you participated or watched. Use exclamation points where appropriate.

Answers will vary.

Spectrum Grade 6
150

150

Lesson 2.10 Commas: Series, Direct Address, Multiple Adjectives

Commas have a variety of uses, such as in a series, in direct address, and with multiple adjectives.

Series commas are used when there are at least three items listed in a sentence in a row. The items can be words or phrases. Commas are used to separate them.
My favorite foods are pizza, pasta salad, and vegetable burritos.
To make a pizza you have to roll the crust, spread the sauce, and add the toppings.

Commas are used to separate the name of a person spoken to from the rest of the sentence. This is called a **direct address**.
Ken, please answer the door.   *Your delivery has arrived, Adam.*

When more than one adjective is used to describe a noun, they are separated by commas.
It was a warm, breezy day.

Make sure the adjectives equally modify the noun, and that one item is not actually an adverb modifying the adjective. There is no comma in the following sentence because *hilariously* is an adverb modifying *funny*, not *book*.
Calvin read a hilariously funny book.

Identify It
Write an **S** for series, a **DA** for direct address, or an **MA** for multiple adjectives.

1. __S__ Before you leave for school, eat your breakfast, put your homework in your backpack, and brush your teeth.
2. __MA__ I had a sweet, juicy apple for lunch.
3. __DA__ Finish your homework before playing video games, Craig.
4. __MA__ Shawn had a long, hard homework assignment.
5. __DA__ Chloe, your song in the concert was beautiful.
6. __S__ Don't forget your maps, food, and water for your hiking trip.
7. __DA__ Trevor, wash your hands before dinner.
8. __S__ I grabbed a book, paper, and a pencil from my desk when packing for our trip.
9. __MA__ It was a cold, blustery day.

Spectrum Grade 6
151

151

Lesson 2.10 Commas: Series, Direct Address, Multiple Adjectives

Proof It
Rewrite the following dialogue, adding commas where they are needed.

↑ – inserts a comma

"Reese, guess what I'm doing this weekend," said Dani.

"Are you going to play basketball at the school, clean your room at home, or finish your science report?" answered Reese.

"None of the above, Reese," Dani said grinning. "I'm going to the best, brightest show on the planet. My grandparents are taking me to see Cirque du Soleil."

Reese replied, "Isn't that the circus with only human performers?"

"Yep, that's the one," answered Dani. "The brave, talented acrobats do all kinds of maneuvers high in the air on ropes. They dance, swing, and fly through the air."

"I think I even heard that they do some acts underwater!" said Reese.

"They also have hysterically funny clowns," added Dani. "I've heard that sometimes they even spray water on the audience!"

"I've got a nice, big surprise for you, Reese," beamed Dani. "My grandparents got tickets for you, your brother, and your sister."

"I hope we're sitting in the front row," shouted Reese, "even if we do get wet!"

Try It
Write six sentences of our own. Write two sentences with series, two with direct addresses, and two with multiple adjectives.

1. _____
2. _____
3. _____
4. _____
5. _____
6. _____

Answers will vary.

Spectrum Grade 6
152

152

Language Arts Grade 6 Answers

Lesson 2.11 Commas: Combining Sentences (between clauses), Set-Off Dialogue

Simple sentences may become more interesting when they are combined into compound or complex sentences. Sometimes, this means using **commas**.

Use a comma to combine two independent clauses with a coordinate conjunction. The students read three chapters, *and* they answered the questions at the end of each chapter.

When combining an independent clause with a dependent clause (a complex sentence), use a comma. The clauses are connected with a comma and subordinate conjunction.
Although the skies were sunny now, clouds were rolling in.

Commas are used when setting off dialogue from the rest of the sentence.
The salesperson said, *"Our gym has classes in aerobics, kickboxing, and cycling."*

Match It
Draw an arrow to connect the sentences in Column A with the types of sentences in Column B.

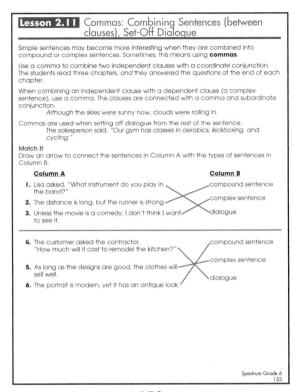

Column A
1. Lisa asked, "What instrument do you play in the band?"
2. The distance is long, but the runner is strong.
3. Unless the movie is a comedy, I don't think I want to see it.

Column B
compound sentence
complex sentence
dialogue

4. The customer asked the contractor, "How much will it cost to remodel the kitchen?"
5. As long as the designs are good, the clothes will sell well.
6. The portrait is modern, yet it has an antique look.

compound sentence
complex sentence
dialogue

Spectrum Grade 6
153

153

Lesson 2.11 Commas: Combining Sentences (between clauses), Set-Off Dialogue

Proof It
Proofread the following biography. Add or delete commas as necessary.

- deletes incorrect letters, words, punctuation
- inserts a comma

Arthur Ashe

Arthur Ashe was born in Richmond, Virginia in 1943. He started playing tennis when he was seven years old. Although the field was dominated by white athletes, Ashe won many amateur titles in his teenage years. He won a scholarship to UCLA and competed in Wimbledon for the first time during college.

Ashe continued to win many major titles. In 1968, he won the U.S. Open, becoming the top male ranked player in the United States Lawn Tennis Association. Until 1973, no African American had been permitted to compete in the South African tournament. Ashe became the first. He went on to win Wimbledon and the World Championship of Tennis. He was the top-ranked tennis player in the world in 1975.

A heart attack in 1979 forced him to retire in 1980. In 1988, Ashe suffered a devastating blow when he discovered he had contracted AIDS from a previous heart operation. Ashe was terminally ill, but he remained an active spokesperson for race relations and AIDS. Arthur Ashe died in February 1993.

Try It
Write three sentences with commas of your own: one in a compound sentence, one in a complex sentence, and one with a quotation.

Answers will vary.

Spectrum Grade 6
154

154

Lesson 2.12 Commas: Personal Letters and Business Letters

Commas are used in both personal and business letters.

Personal Letters
Commas appear in four of the five parts of the personal letter.

Heading:	2633 Lane Road Meridian, OH 30000 June 3, 2014
Salutation:	Dear Kelly,
Body:	comma usage in sentences
Closing:	Your friend,

Business Letters
Commas appear in four of the six parts of the business letter.

Heading:	2200 Meridian Drive Riverside, CA 10000 October 10, 2015
Inside address:	Ms. Corrine Fifelski, Director Lakeview Sound Design 907 Effington Boulevard Boulder, CO 20000
Body:	comma usage in sentences
Closing:	Sincerely,

Identify It
Read each line from a letter. If it is missing a comma, write an **X** on the line. If not, leave the line blank.

1. _____ 1473 Oliver Drive
2. _X_ Dear Tiffany
3. _X_ I went to the grocery store book store and shoe store.
4. _____ Your sister,
5. _X_ April 17 2004
6. _____ Portland, ME
7. _X_ I have experience in customer service and I enjoy meeting new people.
8. _X_ All my best

Spectrum Grade 6
155

155

Lesson 2.12 Commas: Personal Letters and Business Letters

Rewrite It
Rewrite the following personal letter. Add all of the required commas in your rewrite.

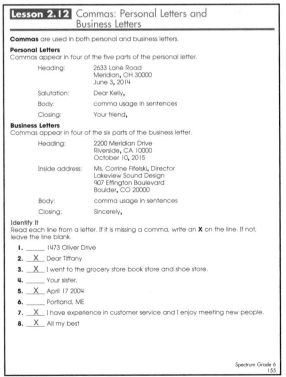

927 Cobblestone Road
Buffalo NY 50000
September 3 2014

Dear Mimi

How are you? I hope you had a great summer vacation. I saw something fantastic on my trip to visit my grandparents in Japan. Do you remember studying about World War II in history class? Well I got to see an actual living relic from World War II. In the middle of Tokyo there is a tree that was hit with a bomb. Remarkably, the tree survived! We saw lots of fascinating things on our trip through Japan, but the tree was my favorite. I can't wait to see you on your next trip to Buffalo and show you the pictures. I even brought you back a special souvenir a *maneki neko* cat. This means *beckoning cat*, and it's a lucky charm in Japan.

Your friend

Akira

927 Cobblestone Road
Buffalo, NY 50000
September 3, 2006

Dear Mimi,

How are you? I hope you had a great summer vacation. I saw something fantastic on my trip to visit my grandparents in Japan. Do you remember studying about World War II in history class? Well, I got to see an actual, living relic from World War II. In the middle of Tokyo there is a tree that was hit with a bomb. Remarkably, the tree survived! We saw lots of fascinating things on our trip through Japan, but the tree was my favorite. I can't wait to see you on your next trip to Buffalo and show you the pictures. I even brought you back a special souvenir, a maneki neko cat. This means beckoning cat, and it's a lucky charm in Japan.

Your friend,

Akira

Spectrum Grade 6
156

156

Language Arts Grade 6 Answers

Lesson 2.13 Quotation Marks

Quotation marks are used to show the exact words of a speaker. The quotation marks are placed before and after the exact words.

"Let's go to the movies tonight," said Janice. *"The new action adventure was released."*

Quotation marks are also used when a direct quotation is made within a direct quotation. In this case, single quotation marks are used to set off the inside quotation.
John said, "Miss Robinson clearly said, *'The project is due tomorrow.'"*

Single quotes express what Miss Robinson said. Double quotes express what John said.

Quotation marks are used with some titles. Quotation marks are used with the titles of short stories, poems, songs, and articles in magazines and newspapers.
"North Carolina Takes the Championship" – newspaper article

If a title is quoted within a direct quotation, then single quotation marks are used.
Melissa said, "Did you read the article *'Saving Our Oceans'* in the magazine?"

Identify It
On the lines, write a **DQ** for direct quote, a **QQ** for quote within quote, a **T** for title, and a **TQ** for title in quote.

1. __DQ__ Sandra shouted, "Our team won the game!"
2. __QQ__ Suzie responded, "I heard the coach say, 'This was my best team ever!'"
3. __T__ The magazine <u>Sports Today</u> had an article called "A Winning Season."
4. __TQ__ "What did the article 'A Winning Season' say about our team?" Sandra asked.
5. __DQ__ "The writer of the article thinks we could win the championship," Suzie said.
6. __QQ__ "He said, 'The team is strong offensively and defensively and could go all the way,'" continued Suzie.
7. __DQ__ "This is so exciting!" yelled Sandra.
8. __TQ__ Suzie said, "Let's go check out our newspaper 'Community Times' and see what they had to say!

157

Lesson 2.13 Quotation Marks

Rewrite It
Rewrite the following list of famous quotations, adding quotation marks where they are needed.

1. Arthur Ashe said, From what we get, we can make a living; what we give, however, makes a life.

   <u>Arthur Ashe said, "From what we get, we</u>
   <u>can make a living; what we give, however,</u>
   <u>makes a life."</u>

2. The most important thing is not to stop questioning, said Albert Einstein.

   <u>"The most important thing is not to stop questioning," said Albert</u>
   <u>Einstein.</u>

3. Mahatma Ghandi said, The weak can never forgive. Forgiveness is the attribute of the strong.

   <u>Mahatma Ghandi said, "The weak can never</u>
   <u>forgive. Forgiveness is the attribute of the strong."</u>

4. Although the world is full of suffering, it is full also of the overcoming of it, said Helen Keller.

   <u>"Although the world is full of suffering, it is full also of the</u>
   <u>overcoming of it," said Helen Keller.</u>

Try It
Write two sentences of dialogue that include direct quotations by characters. Write two sentences that include a title. Write two direct quotations of your own.

Answers will vary.
Make sure quotations are appropriately placed.

158

Lesson 2.14 Apostrophes

Apostrophes are used in contractions and to form possessives.

Contractions are shortened forms of words. The words are shortened by leaving out letters. Apostrophes take the place of the omitted letters.
he is = he's   can not = can't

Possessives show possession, or ownership. To form the possessive of a singular noun, add an apostrophe and an **s**.
I'll carry *Harry's* notebook.

To form the possessive of plural nouns ending in **s**, simply add the apostrophe. If the plural noun does not end in an **s**, add both the apostrophe and an **s**.
The *puppies'* guardians are very happy.
The *women's* team has won every game.

Match It
The sentences in Column A contain words with apostrophes. Match these sentences to the types of apostrophes used in Column B. Draw an arrow to make your match.

Column A	Column B
1. Felicia's jacket is in my car.	contraction
2. She's my best friend.	singular possessive
3. The men's shirts are on the second floor.	plural possessive ending in **s**
4. The girls' tickets are at the box office.	plural possessive not ending in **s**

5. The parents' cars lined the street.	contraction
6. Patty's blanket is nearly done.	singular possessive
7. The children's toys are in the toy box.	plural possessive ending in **s**
8. Teddy's got the presentation.	plural possessive not ending in **s**

159

Lesson 2.14 Apostrophes

Complete It
Complete the following sentences by circling the best answer in parentheses.

1. (I'll/Ill) make an appointment first thing in the morning.
2. (Sams/Sam's) bicycle is outside the library.
3. The (books'/book's) covers are worn.
4. Do you see the (mooses's/moose's) beautiful antlers?
5. (Don't/Do'nt) turn onto Shipman St.; it's closed.
6. You can buy your (rabbits/rabbit's) food and toys at the shelter's retail shop.
7. We'll pick up our (children's/childrens's) toys.
8. We (shouldn't/should'nt) leave without our umbrellas.
9. Did you see the (movie's/movies) review?
10. The (boys'/boy's) helmets are ready to be picked up.

Try It
Write a skit with three or more characters. Use at least three contractions and at least three singular possessives and three plural possessives.

Answers will vary.

160

Language Arts Grade 6 Answers

Lesson 2.15 Colons

Colons are used to introduce a series, to set off a clause, for emphasis, in time, and in business letter salutations.

Colons are used to introduce a series in a sentence.
My favorite vegetables include the following**:** *broccoli, red peppers, and spinach.*

Colons are sometimes used instead of a comma (in more formal cases) to set off a clause.
The radio announcer said**:** *"The game is postponed due to torrential rains."*

Colons are used to set off a word or phrase for emphasis.
The skiers got off of the mountain as they expected the worst**:** *an avalanche.*

Colons are used when writing the time.
Is your appointment at 9**:**00 or 10**:**00?

Business letters use colons in the salutation.
Dear Miss Massey**:**

Identify It
Identify why the colon is used in each sentence. Write an **S** for series, **C** for clause, **E** for emphasis, **T** for time, or **L** for letter.

1. __S__ The teacher said to do the following: read two chapters, answer the questions following each chapter, and write a paragraph about what was read.

2. __T__ My alarm goes off at 6:15 A.M.

3. __C__ The coach gave us some tips: eat right and train hard.

4. __E__ All of my hard training paid off when I saw the sign ahead: Finish.

5. __L__ Dear Dr. Brooks:

6. __C__ The host said: "Let's eat!"

7. __E__ Maya decided to see the movie when the reviewer summed it up in one word: hysterical.

8. __S__ The triathlon consisted of three events: swimming, biking, and running.

Lesson 2.16 Semicolons

A **semicolon** is a cross between a period and a comma. Semicolons can be used to join two independent clauses, to separate clauses containing commas, and to separate groups which contain commas.

Semicolons join two independent clauses when a coordinate conjunction is not used.
*The city's sounds are loud**;** I love the excitement.*

Semicolons are used to separate clauses when they already contain commas.
*After the sun sets, the lights come on**;** the city is beautiful at night.*

Semicolons are also used to separate words or phrases that already contain commas.
*Billi's new apartment has a bedroom for her, her sister, and her brother**;** a laundry room**;** an exercise room**;** and a game room.*

Rewrite It
Rewrite the following sentences adding semicolons where needed.

1. The insulation in the room wasn't very effective it was freezing.
   The insulation in the room wasn't very effective; it was freezing.

2. Although we were relieved it didn't rain, we needed it a drought was upon us.
   Although we were relieved it didn't rain, we needed it; a drought was upon us.

3. They needed equipment to start a business computer monitor printer and furniture, such as desks, chairs, and lamps.
   The needed equipment to start a business; computer; monitor; printer; and furniture, such as desks, chairs, and lamps.

4. Riana has the aptitude for science it is her favorite subject.
   Riana has the aptitude for science; it is her favorite subject.

5. Since the opening is delayed, we'll shop on Tuesday I'm looking forward to it.
   Since the opening is delayed, we'll shop on Tuesday; I'm looking forward to it.

Lesson 2.17 Hyphens

Hyphens are used to divide words, to create new words, and are used between numbers.

Use a hyphen to divide the word between syllables.
beau-ti-ful   per-form

Do not divide one-syllable words with fewer than six letters.
through   piece

Do not divide one letter from the rest of the word.
event-ful   not: e-ventful

Divide syllables after the vowel if the vowel is a syllable by itself.
come-dy   not: com-edy

Divide words with double consonants between the consonants.
swim-ming   mir-ror

Hyphens can be used to create new words when combined with *self, ex,* and *great.*
The pianist was *self-taught.*

Hyphens are used between numbers.
twenty-one

Complete It
Choose the best word in parentheses to complete each sentence.

1. Next year I'll pick an (instru-ment/ instru-ment) to play in the band.

2. Julia burned her (ton-gue,/tongue) on the hot chocolate.

3. An (o-ceanographer/ocean-ographer) studies the oceans and the plants and animals that live in them.

4. My (ex-coach,/excoach) won teacher of the year.

5. The glass holds (thirty two/ thirty-two) ounces.

6. The students are raising money for their chosen (char-ity, chari-ty).

7. Armonite would like a (ch-air/ chair) for her bedroom.

8. The clock seems to be (run-ning/ running) fast.

9. Richard's (great aunt, great-aunt) bakes the best blackberry pie.

10. Her jersey number is (sixty-four, sixty four).

Lesson 2.18 Parentheses

Parentheses are used to show supplementary material, to set off phrases in a stronger way than commas, and to enclose numbers.

Supplementary material is a word or phrase that gives additional information.
Theresa's mother *(the dentist)* will speak to our class next week.

Sometimes, words or phrases that might be set off with commas are set off with parentheses instead. It gives the information more emphasis for a stronger phrase.
Leo's apartment building, *the one with the nice window boxes,* was voted prettiest in the neighborhood.
Leo's apartment building *(the one with the nice window boxes)* was voted prettiest in the neighborhood.

Parentheses are also used to enclose numbers.
Jacklyn wants to join the track team because *(1)* it is good exercise, *(2)* she can travel to other schools and cities, and *(3)* she can meet new friends.

Match It
Match the sentences in Column A with the reason why parentheses are used in Column B. Draw an arrow to make your match.

Column A	Column B
1. When cooking rice, don't forget to (1) rinse the rice, (2) steam the rice, and (3) eat the rice!	supplementary material
2. The preliminary findings (announced yesterday) are important to the study.	set-off with emphasis
3. The dinosaur bones (a huge discovery) can be seen in the museum.	enclose numbers

4. The orientation (for freshmen) is this weekend.	supplementary material
5. Mac must (1) wash the dishes, (2) do his homework, and (3) get ready for bed.	set-off with emphasis
6. We're setting up our lemonade stand (the one that made $100 last summer) Memorial Day weekend.	enclose numbers

Language Arts Grade 6 Answers

Chapter 3
Lesson 3.1 Tricky Verb Usage

The irregular verbs *bring* and *take* are often confused with each other. When you *bring* something, it is coming in or toward you. When you *take* something, it is moving away.

The forms of *take* are *take* (present), *took* (past), and *taken* (past participle).
The forms of *bring* are *bring* (present), *brought* (past), and *brought* (past participle).

> The teacher asked her students to *bring* in newspapers.
>
> Jessica *took* magazines to her sick friend.
>
> He *had taken* the tickets to the game.

The irregular verbs *lay* and *lie* are also easily confused.

The verb *lay* means *to place*. The forms of the verb *lay* are *lay* (present), *laid* (past), and *laid* (past participle).
The verb *lie* means *to recline*. The forms of the verb *lie* are *lie* (present), *lay* (past), and *lain* (past participle).

> The teachers *lay* the papers on their desks.
>
> The kittens *lie* by the window in the sun.
>
> Yesterday, the kittens *lay* on the blankets in the laundry room.
>
> Mother *has laid* her briefcase on the same table every night for years.

Complete It
Complete the following sentences by circling the best answers in parentheses.

1. Don't (bring, (take)) the library books out of the building.
2. Brian and Matt ((take)) taken) extra water to the baseball games.
3. Last year Lilly (bring, (brought)) cupcakes on her birthday.
4. Grover (brought, (took)) six cookies out of the box.
5. Yesterday, we (take, (took)) blankets and towels to the animal shelter.
6. The children were (bring, (brought)) home when it started to thunder.
7. Marv was (took, (taken)) to the hospital when he sprained his ankle.
8. Grandma said, "Aubrey, ((bring)) take) me a glass of water, please."
9. Charlie (brought, (took)) seeds from his own garden to plant new flowers in the park.

165

Lesson 3.1 Tricky Verb Usage

Identify It
Write whether the forms of *lay* and *lie* mean *to place* or *to recline*. Write a **P** for *place* and an **R** for *recline*.

1. __R__ Don't lie in the sun without sunscreen!
2. __P__ It was unusual that the papers were missing; he had laid them in the same spot every morning.
3. __R__ Meagan and Ashley had lain in the sun too long.
4. __P__ Jean laid the covers over the plates before the rain hit.
5. __P__ Please lay the cups and plates at the end of the table.
6. __R__ The toddlers lay down for a long nap earlier today.
7. __P__ Don't lay your homework by your computer; you'll forget about it in the morning.
8. __R__ Lie on the blanket on the sand.
9. __P__ Barbara laid her blanket near the bed.
10. __R__ Maggie lay down for a quick nap yesterday.

Try It
Write six sentences of your own. Use various forms of the verbs *lie, lay, bring,* and *take*.

1. _____
2. _____
3. _____ Answers will vary.
4. _____
5. _____
6. _____

166

Lesson 3.2 Adjectives and Adverbs

Adverbs modify verbs, adjectives, and other adverbs. Some adverbs are easily confused with adjectives.

Bad is an adjective, and *badly* is an adverb.
> That was a *bad* concert; the music was too loud. (*bad* modifies the noun *concert*)
> Tyler drives *badly*; he almost ran that stop sign. (*badly* modifies the verb *drives*)

Good is an adjective, and *well* is an adverb.
> We watched a *good* game. (*good* modifies the noun *game*)
> Both teams played *well*. (*well* modifies the verb *played*)

The word *already* is an adverb. It answers the question *when*.
> It was morning and *already* time to leave.

The phrase *all ready* means *completely ready*.
> The team was *all ready* to leave.

Complete It
Circle the correct word in parentheses. Then, underline the word it modifies (except for numbers 5 and 6) and write what part of speech it is on the lines after each word.

1. We threw out the (bad, (badly)) <u>bruised</u> orange. ___ADJ___
2. Celina <u>played</u> (good, (well)) and won her match. ___V___
3. I just finished a really ((good), well) <u>book</u>; I couldn't put it down. ___N___
4. The <u>instructions</u> were ((bad), badly), and we got lost. ___N___
5. By the time the bus picked us up we were (all ready, (already)) late.
6. If everyone in the class is ((all ready), already) to go, we'll line up at the door.
7. It was a ((good), well) <u>recipe</u>; I'll make that again. ___N___
8. If our chorus <u>sings</u> (good, (well)), we'll advance to the semifinals. ___V___
9. Daryl (bad, (badly)) <u>sang</u> the last song. ___V___
10. Ally had a ((bad), badly) <u>excuse</u> for not playing in the game. ___N___

167

Lesson 3.2 Adjectives and Adverbs

Rewrite It
Rewrite the following letter, correcting the use of the words *bad, badly, good, well, all ready,* and *already* as necessary.

> Dear Grandpa,
>   I'm sorry you couldn't make it to my soccer game last Saturday. I played very good. Our team had been playing bad until a couple of weeks ago. We all got together and watched the World Cup on television. Teams from all over the world compete to determine a world champion. The United States' women's team played so good in the first Women's World Cup that they won the tournament. Our team had all ready lost several games when we watched the World Cup. We needed some well motivation. It worked. We won our next three games. Now, we're already to go to the championships.
>   Love,
>   Hannah

Dear Grandpa,
    I'm sorry you couldn't make it to my soccer game last Saturday. I played very well. Our team had been playing badly until a couple of weeks ago. We all got together and watched the World Cup on television. Teams from all over the world compete to determine a world champion. The United States' women's team played so well in the first Women's World Cup that they won the tournament. Our team had already lost several games when we watched the World Cup. We needed some good motivation. It worked. We won our next three games. Now, we're all ready to go to the championships.
                                  Love,
                                  Hannah

Try It
Write six sentences of your own. Write a sentence using each of the following words: *bad, badly, good, well, all ready, already.*

_____
_____
_____ Answers will vary.
_____
_____

168

Language Arts Grade 6 Answers

Lesson 3.3 Negatives and Double Negatives

A **negative** sentence states the opposite. Negative words include *not, no, never, nobody, nowhere, nothing, barely, hardly,* and *scarcely;* and contractions containing the word *not.*

Double negatives happen when two negative words are used in the same sentence. Don't use double negatives; it will make your sentence positive again, and it is poor grammar.

> Negative: We *won't* go anywhere without you.
> Double negative: We *won't* go *nowhere* without you.

> Negative: I *never* like to ride my bike after dark.
> Double negative: I *don't never* like to ride my bike after dark.

> Negative: I can *hardly* wait until baseball season.
> Double negative: I *can't hardly* wait until baseball season.

Rewrite It
Rewrite the following sentences. Correct the sentence if it contains a double negative.

1. I love breakfast; I can't imagine not skipping it.
   <u>I love breakfast; I can't imagine skipping it.</u>
2. I can't scarcely believe I made it all the way down the slope without falling.
   <u>I scarcely believe I made it all the way down the slope without falling.</u>
3. Samantha doesn't never like to wear her coat outside.
   <u>Samantha doesn't like to wear her coat outside.</u>
4. The class hasn't received their report cards yet.
   <u>The class hasn't received their report cards yet.</u>
5. I'm not going nowhere until it stops raining.
   <u>I'm going nowhere until it stops raining.</u>
6. Paul has barely nothing to contribute to the argument.
   <u>Paul has nothing to contribute to the argument.</u>
7. Sarah never reveals her secrets.
   <u>Sarah never reveals her secrets.</u>
8. I don't think nobody can make it to the event early.
   <u>I think nobody can make it to the event early.</u>

Lesson 3.4 Synonyms and Antonyms

Synonyms are words that have the same, or almost the same, meaning. Using synonyms can help you avoid repeating words and can make your writing more interesting.

| clever, smart | reply, answer | wreck, destroy | applaud, clap |

Antonyms are words that have opposite meanings.

| wide, narrow | accept, decline | break, repair | borrow, lend |

Find It
Think of an antonym for each word in the box. Then, find it in the word search puzzle. Words may be written horizontally or vertically, backward or forward.

| disagree | war | north | wise |
| shallow | success | remember | absent |

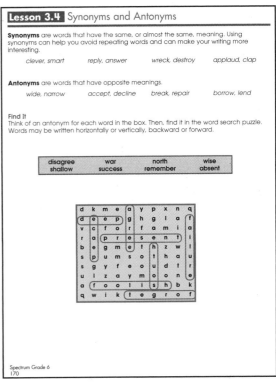

Lesson 3.4 Synonyms and Antonyms

Match It
Read each set of words below. Circle the two words in each set that are synonyms.

1. (pardon) forget (forgive) ordinary
2. damage (mend) (repair) mock
3. (likely) unlikely (probable) rarely
4. (depart) (leave) arrival mingle
5. heal insist (injure) (wound)
6. accept (decline) formula (refuse)
7. (remorse) (regret) replace joy
8. (thin) obese (slender) flexible

Rewrite It
Rewrite each sentence below. Use a synonym for **boldface** words and an antonym for <u>underlined</u> words.

1. The police officer had to **pursue** the **criminal**, who **hopped** in his car and <u>sped away.</u>
   <u>The police officer had to chase the crook, who jumped in his car and sped away.</u>
2. Harriet <u>enjoys</u> cooking with foods that have **bold** flavors.
   <u>Harriet dislikes cooking with foods that have mild flavors.</u>
3. When Enzo **finished** his book, he felt quite <u>satisfied</u> with the <u>ending.</u>
   <u>When Enzo completed his book, he felt quite unsatisfied with the beginning.</u>
4. Dr. Williams asked the **nervous** little girl to <u>exhale</u> <u>slowly.</u>
   <u>Dr. Williams asked the anxious little girl to inhale quickly.</u>

Lesson 3.5 Analogies

An **analogy** is a comparison between two pairs of words. To complete an analogy, figure out how the pairs of words are related.

> *Coop* is to *chicken* as *hive* is to *bee.*
> A coop is a home for a chicken, just as a hive is a home for a bee.

> *Petal* is to *flower* as *wing* is to *bird.*
> A petal is part of a flower, just as a wing is part of a bird.

> *Excited* is to *bored* as *silence* is to *noise.*
> Excited is the opposite of bored, just as silence is the opposite of noise.

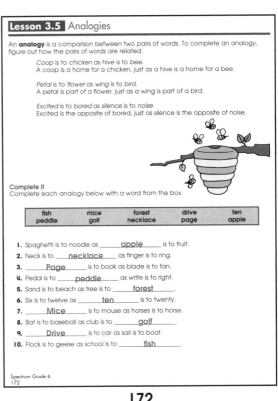

Complete It
Complete each analogy below with a word from the box.

| fish | mice | forest | drive | ten |
| peddle | golf | necklace | page | apple |

1. Spaghetti is to noodle as ___apple___ is to fruit.
2. Neck is to ___necklace___ as finger is to ring.
3. ___Page___ is to book as blade is to fan.
4. Pedal is to ___peddle___ as write is to right.
5. Sand is to beach as tree is to ___forest___.
6. Six is to twelve as ___ten___ is to twenty.
7. ___Mice___ is to mouse as horses is to horse.
8. Bat is to baseball as club is to ___golf___.
9. ___Drive___ is to car as sail is to boat.
10. Flock is to geese as school is to ___fish___.

Language Arts Grade 6 Answers

Lesson 3.5 Analogies

Identify It
Underline the word from each pair that completes the analogy.

1. Teacher is to (<u>school</u>, books) as lifeguard is to pool.
2. (<u>Bark</u>, Tall) is to dog as neigh is to horse.
3. Shy is to (bold, <u>timid</u>) as guest is to visitor.
4. Orlando is to Florida as (Wisconsin, <u>Detroit</u>) is to Michigan.
5. King is to (<u>queen</u>, kingdom) as prince is to princess.
6. Stove is to (<u>kitchen</u>, cook) as tub is to bathroom.
7. Liz is to Elizabeth as Danny is to (Tommy, <u>Daniel</u>).
8. (Spring, <u>Fall</u>) is to winter as lunch is to dinner.
9. Copper is to penny as wool is to (sheep, <u>sweater</u>).
10. Four is to quarter as (one, <u>five</u>) is to fifth.

Try It
Follow the directions to write your own analogies.

1. Write an analogy in which the words are synonyms.

2. Write an analog _Answers will vary._

3. Write an analogy that shows a numerical relationship.

Spectrum Grade 6
173

Lesson 3.6 Homophones

Homophones are words that sound the same but have different spellings and different meanings. There are hundreds of homophones in the English language.

   cereal - food made from grain
   serial - of a series

If you are unsure about which homophone to use, look up the meanings in a dictionary.

Identify It
Circle the correct homophone in each sentence.

1. My teacher will (council, (counsel)) me on what subjects to take next year.
2. This material has a smooth texture but that one is more (course, (coarse)).
3. The television program is going to be shown as a (cereal,(serial)) once a week for six weeks.
4. The ((council) counsel) meets every Wednesday evening to discuss city plans.
5. I like to ride my bike on the scenic ((course) coarse) along the river.
6. My favorite breakfast is a big bowl of ((cereal) serial).

Match It
Fill in the blanks in the sentences in Column A with a homophone from Column B.

Column A	Column B
1. I bid one _____ more and won the item.	overseas
2. Deb has a beautiful _____ on her finger.	oversees
3. The sailor was stationed _____.	ring
4. The flowers have a beautiful _____.	wring
5. _____ out the dish cloth over the sink.	cent
6. Mr. Morgan _____ metal production.	scent
7. David _____ the envelope yesterday.	sent
8. My oldest dog _____ feeding time for all of my pets.	overseas
9. I would like to travel _____ for a semester.	oversees
10. It was raining so hard I had to _____ out my shirt.	ring
11. Did I hear someone _____ the doorbell?	wring
12. The letter was _____ to the wrong address.	cent
13. The item costs three dollars and one _____.	scent
14. The perfume has a strong _____.	sent

Spectrum Grade 6
174

Lesson 3.7 Multiple-Meaning Words

Multiple-meaning words, or **homographs**, are words that are spelled the same but have different meanings. They may also sometimes have different pronunciations.

The word *bow* can mean "a looped piece of ribbon or cloth," or it can mean "to bend at the waist."

   Lexi put a *bow* on top of her gift for Chandler.
   "Be sure you *bow* to the audience at the end of the performance."

Find It
Read each sentence. Then, circle the definition that describes the meaning of the underlined word as it is used in the sentence.

1. Before leaving the house, my mother always makes sure her <u>compact</u> is in her purse.
   a. dense and tightly packed
   (b.) a small case with a mirror

2. Juan added vanilla <u>extract</u> to the cookie dough.
   a. take out
   (b.) concentrated form

3. The <u>proceeds</u> from the auction will be used to provide art scholarships.
   (a.) money from a sale
   b. moves forward

4. Officer Wilkins talked calmly with the man who was <u>upset</u> about the accident.
   a. spilled or overturned
   (b.) distressed or anxious

5. The school board was <u>inclined</u> to agree with Mr. Radkey's ideas about a sales tax.
   (a.) tended to feel a certain way
   b. sloping

6. The nurse held a <u>compress</u> against the bruise on Nina's leg.
   (a.) a cloth pad
   b. push together

Spectrum Grade 6
175

Lesson 3.7 Multiple-Meaning Words

Identify It
Read each pair of sentences. Circle **N** for noun or **V** for verb to identify the part of speech for the word in **boldface**. Each pair of sentences will have two different answers.

1. Horace dusted the **display** of books in the store's front window. (N) V
   The schools in our district **display** student artwork throughout their halls. N (V)

2. Please **number** your answer 1 through 10. N (V)
   Dr. Patel analyzed the **number** of tadpoles living in the pond. (N) V

3. After the movie, Preston and Kelly debated whether the **remake** was better than the original. (N) V
   Sonja had to **remake** the pie after she discovered one of the kittens eating it.
   N (V)

4. Louisa made the basket, **evening** the score and making the crowd go wild. N (V)
   Later this **evening**, we will go to my grandparents' house for a party. (N) V

5. The reporter explained that the **recall** only affected certain brands of baby food.
   (N) V
   Do you **recall** that time when we got a flat tire on our way to zoo? N (V)

Rewrite It
Read each sentence be___ _Answers may vary._ ___ using a different meaning for
the underlined word. Use _Possible answers :_ ___ help.

1. The book's <u>content</u> is too difficult for children under five years old to understand.
   <u>I was content to stay at home and watch a movie last night.</u>

2. The water contains <u>minute</u> amounts of chlorine and fluoride.
   <u>I'll be ready in just a minute!</u>

3. King Alfred ordered his <u>subjects</u> to work through the night to finish the bridge.
   <u>Math and science are my two favorite subjects.</u>

4. Brynna rides her <u>moped</u> near the curb so cars can safely pass her if they need to.
   <u>George moped because it was rainy and he couldn't go to the park.</u>

5. A <u>combine</u> moved slowly back and forth across the acres of wheat.
   <u>If you combine yeast, flour, and water, you can make bread.</u>

6. Several <u>inserts</u> fell to the floor as Mikki took a magazine from the rack.
   <u>Grandma inserts cream cheese into the middle of each muffin.</u>

Spectrum Grade 6
176

Spectrum Grade 6
306

Language Arts Grade 6 Answers

Lesson 3.8 Connotations and Denotations

A word's **denotation** is its actual, literal meaning. It is the meaning you would find if you looked the word up in a dictionary.

A word's **connotation** is the meaning associated with the word. The connotation may be more emotional, or tied to an idea or feeling about the word. Connotations can be positive, negative, or neutral.

For example, the words *house, home, shack,* and *residence* all mean approximately the same thing. Their denotation is "a place where people live." The connotation of these words, however, is different. *House* and *residence* both have a neutral connotation. *Home* has a positive connotation—it sounds cozy and reassuring. *Shack,* on the other hand, has a negative connotation—it sounds rundown and shabby.

Identify It
For each set of words b[...] _on (or literal definition) on the top line. On the line bes[...] e connotation, **N** for neutral connotation, and **NG** fo[...] connotation.

Answers may vary. Possible answers:

1. denotation: **to pose a question**
   ask **N**   demand **NG**   request **P**
2. denotation: **secure in oneself**
   confident **P**   pushy **NG**
3. denotation: **not fat; slim**
   slender **P**   skinny **N**
4. denotation: **different**
   odd **NG**   special **P**   unique **P**
5. denotation: **searching; inquiring**
   curious **P**   nosy **NG**   interested **P**
6. denotation: **take or use something that is not yours**
   borrow **N**   steal **NG**
7. denotation: **not spending a lot of money**
   cheap **NG**   thrifty **P**   stingy **NG**

Lesson 3.8 Connotations and Denotations

Match It
Match each word with another word that has a similar denotation but different connotation. Write the letter of the matching word on the line.

1. **d** mimic
2. **h** childish
3. **a** odor
4. **f** limit
5. **g** dog
6. **c** escape
7. **e** starving
8. **b** collect

a. scent
b. accumulate
c. depart
d. mock
e. hungry
f. restrict
g. mutt
h. childlike

Try It
Write a senten[...] below. The words in each pair have similar denotations but different connotations.

Answers may vary. Possible answers:

1. inexpensive <u>Going to the museum is a great, inexpensive way to spend the day.</u>
   cheap <u>I know these shoes were cheap, but they are already falling apart.</u>
2. puny <u>That poor, puny piglet is having a hard time getting enough milk from his mama.</u>
   small <u>The small girl patiently waited her turn in line.</u>
3. proud <u>Eli felt so proud of his winning time.</u>
   boastful <u>Georgia was boastful about her extensive fossil collection.</u>
4. smile <u>Mom gave me a huge smile as she waved good-bye.</u>
   smirk <u>It hurts my feelings when you smirk at me like that.</u>
5. soggy <u>The bread got soggy from the mustard and mayonnaise.</u>
   moist <u>The banana bread was moist and warm from the oven.</u>
6. carefree <u>Nico felt relaxed and carefree as the plane took off the ground.</u>
   irresponsible <u>It is irresponsible to leave those library books outside.</u>

Lesson 3.9 Figures of Speech: Similes, Metaphors, and Personification

Complete It
Complete each sentence below with a simile.

Answers may vary. Possible answers:

1. The jet soared through the air like **an eagle**.
2. The kitten's fur felt soft as **cotton candy**.
3. Mr. Robinson's laugh rang out like **tinkling bells**.
4. The rooster stood on the fence and crowed like **an early morning** alarm.
5. After the spring storm, the forest smelled as fresh as **a newly-cut lawn**.
6. Maya tripped as she stepped onto the stage, and her face turned as red as **a ripe tomato**.
7. With each step, Rowan's boots crunched the snow, sounding like **popcorn beneath** his feet.
8. Hannah's new scissors cut through fabric like **butter**.

Try It
Imagine you have been shipwrecked on a deserted island. Write a short paragraph describing the sights, sounds, smells, and feelings you might experience. Include at least two similes in your paragraph.

Answers will vary.

Reading Grade 6 Answers

---

1. Why were the Godfreys in Japan?

to visit Mrs. Godfrey's college roommate

2. What do you think Emily meant when she said, "American baseball may never be quite as interesting again"?

In comparison to American baseball, Japanese baseball seems more interesting and exciting to her.

3. What is one way American and Japanese baseball are similar? What is one way they are different?

Possible Answers: Some of the snacks served are the same. Japanese baseball has male cheerleaders.

4. Do you think that Alex and Emily will go to another JBall game if they have a chance? Why or why not?

Answers will vary.

Circle the word that best completes each sentence.

5. Alex and Emily decide to try food that they would not be _____ to find at an American game.
allowed (likely) impressed

6. The Godfreys are _____ to learn how American and Japanese baseball are different.
(curious) refusing apprehensive

7. Noisemakers are a popular _____ at Japanese baseball games.
explanation resource (custom)

An **idiom** is a group of words that has a special meaning. For example, the idiom *hit the hay* means *to go to bed*. Write the idiom from paragraph 8 on the line next to its meaning.

8. something of interest; something a person enjoys ___ cup of tea

9. Would you enjoy attending a sporting event in another country? Explain why or why not.

Answers will vary.

Spectrum Grade 6
193

193

---

1. Check the sentence that best states the main idea of the passage.

✓ Although baseball is thought of as an American sport, there are many fans and talented players of Japanese baseball, or yakyu.

___ American teams toured Japan in the early 1900s and played exhibition games against the local amateurs.

___ Horace Wilson brought baseball to Japan in the 1870s.

2. Number the events below to show the order in which they happened.

1 Horace Wilson introduced baseball to his students.

3 World War II interrupted Japanese baseball.

4 The Giants won nine consecutive national championships.

2 Babe Ruth and Lou Gehrig played baseball in Japan.

3. Check the phrase that best describes the author's purpose.

✓ to inform

___ to entertain

___ to persuade

4. Why is Sadahara Oh's last name so appropriate?

It means king, and he is the king of baseball in Japan.

5. Why did Japan's leaders like baseball?

It contained elements that were already part of Japanese culture.

6. What is the literal meaning of *yakyu* in Japanese?

field ball

7. During World War II, many of the players became ___ soldiers

Spectrum Grade 6
195

195

A fact is something that is known to be true. An opinion is what a person believes. It may or may not be true. Write **F** before the sentences that are facts. Write **O** before the sentences that are opinions.

1. O Sushi is delicious.

2. F The chef spreads a layer of sticky rice over the sheet of seaweed.

3. O Wasabi ruins the flavor of sushi.

4. F Mrs. Ito makes some suggestions about what to order.

5. Check the line beside the word or words that best describe what type of passage this is.

___ informational text

✓ fiction

___ tall tale

6. How are Alex and Emily different?

Alex is more adventurous than Emily is about trying new foods.

7. Why isn't everyone surprised that Alex likes sushi?

He was looking forward to trying authentic Japanese food.

8. What holds everything together in a roll of sushi?

a thin sheet of seaweed

9. What is *wasabi*?

a very spicy condiment

10. Why does Mr. Godfrey say, "Our kids are turning into some very well-seasoned eaters"?

Alex and Emily both enjoy the sushi and want to find a restaurant at home that serves it.

Spectrum Grade 6
197

197

Write the words from the passage that have the meanings below.

1. the process of growing and caring for something

cultivation

2. to trim away the unwanted parts of a tree or bush

prune

3. copied; made again

reproduces

Write **T** before the sentences that are true. Write **F** before the sentences that are false.

4. F The tradition of raising bonsais was begun in Europe.

5. T Japanese bonsais are usually grown in containers outdoors.

6. T The owner of a bonsai must spend some time caring for the plant.

7. F There are three basic styles of bonsai.

8. What do you think the phrase *time-honored tradition* means?

something that is respected because it has existed for a long period of time

9. What are the three elements needed to create a successful bonsai?

truth, goodness, and beauty

10. How are the cascade and semi-cascade styles of bonsai similar?

The leaves and the branches cascade down toward the base of the plant.

11. What purpose would a reader have for reading this selection?

___ for pleasure or entertainment

✓ for information

___ to form an opinion about bonsai

Spectrum Grade 6
199

199

Reading Grade 6 Answers

---

1. What is *composting*?

a process in which leftover scraps of fruits and vegetables are used as fertilizer

2. Name four fruits or vegetables that are grown in the Edible Schoolyard.

Answers will vary.

3. Do you think that other schools will create gardens based on Alice Waters's ideas? Why?

Answers will vary.

4. Check the sentence that best states the **main idea** of the selection, or tells what the passage is mostly about.

____ Alice Waters owns Chez Panisse Restaurant in California.

____ Students look forward to the time they spend gardening each week.

✓ Alice Waters founded the Edible Schoolyard, a program in which students learn to grow and prepare their own foods.

5. Check the words that describe Alice Waters.

✓ generous

____ unfriendly

✓ talented

✓ ambitious

____ stingy

Write the idiom from paragraph 2 on the line next to its meaning.

6. goes together hand in hand

7. Why does Alice Waters believe that students should know how to cook and garden?

Possible Answer: She wants to teach students that a healthy body and a healthy environment go together.

8. Do you have a school garden at your school? If so, what do you grow there? If not, what could you do to help start one?

Answers will vary.

Spectrum Grade 6
201

201

The **point of view** tells the reader whose view of the story he or she is reading. In **first-person point of view**, the reader knows the thoughts and feelings of the person telling the story. In **third-person point of view**, the reader only knows what an outsider knows about a character. Mark each phrase below **F** for first-person and **T** for third-person.

1. F My cousin P.J. lives in Washington.

2. T Emilio's aunt is the co-owner of a nursery.

3. T Mr. Hasselbach has a vegetable garden.

4. F I hope Ms. Milano likes our idea.

5. What problem do Drew, Emilio, and Michi have at the beginning of the story?

They have to figure out how to convince Ms. Milano that the garden is a good idea.

6. Where did Drew get the idea to start a school garden at his middle school?

from his cousin

7. How do Drew, Emilio, and Michi know that Mr. Hasselbach has a garden at home?

He brings in vegetables to school that he grew in his garden at home.

8. Name two ideas that the students have that they think will make Ms. Milano more likely to approve their plan.

Answers will vary.

Write the idiom from paragraph 6 on the line next to its meaning.

9. to start something up and running

10. What is the setting for this story?

a picnic table at a park

11. Would you like to have a garden at your school or at home? Why or why not?

Answers will vary.

Spectrum Grade 6
203

203

Circle the word that best completes each sentence below.

1. The students put a great deal of _____ into the preparation of the meal.

(effort) guidance transformation

2. Ms. Milano _____ Drew, Emilio, and Michi's contributions.

regrets (appreciates) plans

3. The stepping stones are _____ with their names and the date.

requested remembered (engraved)

4. Name two things the students did to transform the lunchroom.

Answers will vary.

5. Why did Ms. Milano give Drew, Michi, and Emilio stepping stones?

to thank them for their hard work and to help future students remember their contributions

6. Why do you think Ms. Milano was skeptical when the students first presented her with the idea of starting a school garden?

She knew it would be a lot of work and was not sure if it would be successful.

7. About how much of the food the students served did they grow themselves?

about three-quarters of the food

8. In paragraph 8, what does perseverance mean?

continuing to do something even when it gets difficult

9. List three adjectives that describe how you think Drew, Emilio, and Michi feel at the end of the story.

Possible answers: proud, excited, happy

Spectrum Grade 6
205

205

Write the words from the story that have the meanings below.

1. causing fear

bloodcurdling

2. held tightly together

clenched

3. needing immediate attention

urgently

4. well known for something unpleasant or unfavorable

notorious

5. stretching the neck to see better

craning

6. Number the events below to show the order in which they happened.

1 Savannah switched off her flashlight.

4 Savannah and her mom saw the owl's eyes gleaming in the moonlight.

5 Savannah's dad poured himself a glass of orange juice.

2 Savannah ran into her parents' bedroom.

3 Savannah's mom looked for her slippers.

7. Find one sentence that shows Savannah was frightened by the screaming she heard.

Possible answer: Savannah lay stiffly and silently in her bed waiting to see what would happen.

8. If Savannah hears a barn owl again someday, do you think she will be frightened? Why or why not?

Answers will vary.

9. What problem did Savannah have in the story?

She didn't know what was making the screaming noises.

10. Why weren't Savannah and her mom surprised when the owl's cries didn't wake up Savannah's dad?

He is notorious for sleeping through anything and has to set multiple alarms just to wake up in the morning.

11. How were Savannah and her mom able to identify the owl's call?

They listened to sound bites from a Web site that Ms. Petrovic had recommended.

Spectrum Grade 6
207

207

Spectrum Grade 6
309

Reading Grade 6 Answers

Page 209:

1. How are barn owls different from common owls?
Barn owls have a light colored heart-shaped face.

2. Why is the owl's sense of hearing important to its survival?
because they hunt at night

3. How do archaeologists know that ancient Egyptians respected owls?
They found mummified owls in Egyptian tombs.

4. What is unusual about the owl's neck and eyes?
The owl's eyes do not move, but its neck can turn about 270 degrees.

5. In what part of the world does the smallest owl live?
Mexico and the southwestern United States

6. What is one reason that owls have been feared in some cultures?
They are nocturnal creatures.

7. A **summary** is a short sentence that tells the most important facts about a topic. Check the sentence below that is the best summary for paragraph 3.
____ Owls hunt at night.
✓ Owls have a sharp sense of hearing, which helps them to be strong hunters.
____ Some owls' ear openings are positioned asymmetrically.

8. What was the author's purpose in writing this selection?
to inform the reader about the varieties, habits, and characteristics of owls.

9. In paragraph 4, enhances means
____ makes weaker
✓ makes better or stronger
____ changes

Spectrum Grade 6
209

209

Page 211:

1. How do we know that lighthouses have existed for at least 3,000 years?
In Homer's *Iliad*, which was written about 1200 B.C. he refers to lighthouses.

2. How far can the Fresnel lens project light?
28 miles

3. Why aren't lighthouse keepers necessary for today's lighthouses?
Almost all the lighthouses are automated.

4. What are two ways in which lighthouses may be different from one another?
Answers will vary.

5. Why do you think that historians think it is important to preserve lighthouses?
Answers will vary.

6. What did early versions of lighthouses look like?
They were made of iron baskets that were suspended from long poles.

7. Check the phrase that best describes the author's purpose.
✓ to share the history of lighthouses
____ to persuade the reader to visit a lighthouse
____ to explain how lighthouses were built

8. In paragraph 3, what does the word automated mean?
works by itself

9. What is the main idea of this selection?
Possible answer: Lighthouses are an interesting and important part of coastal American history.

Spectrum Grade 6
211

211

Page 213:

1. What kind of animal is Sadie? How can you tell?
Sadie is a cat. She curls up on Paloma's lap and meows.

2. What problem does Paloma have at the beginning of the story?
She is having a hard time thinking of a short story to write, and she is running out of time.

3. Find an example of a sentence or phrase Paloma uses to create tension in her story.
Answers will vary.

4. The next time she has to write a story for school, do you think Paloma will put it off again? Why or why not?
Answers will vary.

5. Where does Paloma get her story idea?
from a trip her family took to the Outer Banks

Mark each sentence below **F** if it is in first-person point of view and **T** if it is in third-person point of view.

6. F I was relying on Sadie's calmness to get me through the hurricane.

7. T Paloma reread Mr. Molina's assignment.

8. F I looked up at the staircase and shuddered.

Find the simile in paragraph 4 and write it on the line below.

9. The heavy rain beat against my lighthouse like a thousand footsteps racing up and down the walls.

10. If you were given the same assignment as Paloma, what would you write about?
Answers will vary.

Spectrum Grade 6
213

213

Page 215:

1. Number the events below to show the order in which they happened.
2 People were worried that the lighthouse would collapse.
5 The relocation was a success.
1 The Cape Hatteras Lighthouse was completed in 1870.
3 The lighthouse was removed from its existing foundation.
4 Onlookers watched the slow progress of the lighthouse's move.

2. Check the line beside the word or words that best describe what type of passage this is.
____ biography   ____ fiction
✓ historical nonfiction

3. Check the sentence that best states the main idea of the passage.
____ The Cape Hatteras Lighthouse in Buxton, North Carolina, is the tallest lighthouse in the United States.
____ The process used to move the Cape Hatteras Lighthouse was very slow.
✓ In 1999, the Cape Hatteras Lighthouse was moved further inland to prevent its destruction due to erosion.

4. What are the Diamond Shoals?
a dangerous, shallow area about 14 miles off the coast of Cape Hatteras

5. What is one reason that some people protested moving the lighthouse?
Answers will vary.

6. What is the Graveyard of the Atlantic?
an area around the Outer Banks, where thousands of ships have sunk

7. Do you agree with the decision to move to the lighthouse? Explain.
Answers will vary.

Spectrum Grade 6
215

215

Reading Grade 6 Answers

217

1. Check the words that best describe Ida Lewis.

   ✓ hardworking   ✓ strong-willed

   ✓ determined   ___ unpredictable

   ___ nosy

Write **T** before the sentences that are true. Write **F** before the sentences that are false.

2. **F** It was more common for women than for men to be lighthouse keepers.
3. **F** After his stroke, Captain Lewis was able to resume his job as lighthouse keeper.
4. **T** Ida kept the light at Lime Rock for 39 years.
5. **T** President Ulysses S. Grant visited Ida in Rhode Island.
6. **T** Today, Lime Rock Lighthouse is called Ida Lewis Lighthouse.
7. Why did all the attention make Ida uncomfortable?

   Ida was used to solitude and quiet of a lighthouse keeper's life.

8. Why do you think that we don't know for sure how many people Ida rescued?

   Answers will vary.

9. How old was Ida when she began tending the lighthouse? 15

10. What were two jobs of lighthouse keepers before lighthouses became automated?

    cleaning and polishing the lamps and lenses, keeping the lamps filled with fuel

11. Do you think you would have enjoyed being a lighthouse keeper? Why or why not?

    Answers will vary.

Spectrum Grade 6
217

219

Write **F** before the sentences that are facts. Write **O** before the sentences that are opinions.

1. **O** Keeping a photo diary is a difficult assignment.
2. **F** Dante's brother's name is Wesley.
3. **O** Dante's classmates will find it easy to create a narrative from his photos.
4. **F** Mrs. Carter spilled some orange juice.
5. **O** Mr. Carter has a good sense of humor.
6. The **protagonist** is the main character in a story, or the person the story is mostly about. Who is the protagonist in this story?

   Dante

7. Why doesn't Dante want to leave out any details of his day?

   He wants it to be a realistic narrative.

8. Why does Wesley joke that photos of him will be valuable one day?

   because he wants to be a famous basketball player

9. During what time of day does the story take place? How can you tell?

   Morning. The Carters are having breakfast and Mrs. Carter says that it is 7 o'clock in the morning.

10. What is the setting for this story?

    the kitchen in Dante's house

11. If you were to make a photo diary of an average day in your life, describe four photos you would want to be sure to include.

    Answers will vary.

Spectrum Grade 6
219

221

Write the words from the passage that have the meanings below.

1. make a copy of

   reproduce
   Par. 1

2. a piece of equipment used for a specific purpose

   device
   Par. 2

3. allowed to be reached by light

   exposed
   Par. 3

4. to make up for something

   compensate
   Par. 7

5. How is a camera's aperture similar to the iris in a human eye?

   They are both circular openings that can be adjusted to let in more or less light.

6. What is one example of a time you might want to use a slow shutter speed?

   Possible answer: taking a picture in low light

7. What does the Latin term camera obscura mean?

   dark chamber

8. How are digital cameras different from traditional cameras?

   Digital cameras use a light-sensitive electrical device.

9. What are the two main devices that control light in a camera?

   the shutter and the aperture

10. Why do you think it is easier to use an automatic camera than a manual camera?

    Answers will vary.

11. Check the phrase that best describes the author's purpose.

    ___ to persuade

    ___ to entertain

    ✓ to inform

Spectrum Grade 6
221

223

1. Why does Dante want to record his interview with Mr. Salinas?

   He does not want to be distracted by having to take notes.

2. What job did Mr. Salinas have before he became a photographer?

   high school English teacher

3. Name two people who have influenced Mr. Salinas's work.

   Possible answers: Elizabeth Chu, Walker Evans, Alfred Stieglitz

4. What does Mr. Salinas like about his job?

   Possible answer: It does not feel like a job.

Circle the word that best completes each sentence below.

5. Mr. Salinas was _____ with the work of Alfred Stieglitz and Walker Evans.

   uninterested (impressed) disappointed

6. Dante's questions for Mr. Salinas were _____.

   irritating   encouraging   (thoughtful)

7. Mr. Salinas _____ that his work can be frustrating at times.

   (mentioned)   aspired   demanded

8. After his interview with Mr. Salinas, do you think that Dante will still want to become a photographer? Explain your answer.

   Answers will vary.

9. List three adjectives you could use to describe Dante in this story.

   Possible answers: Curious, interested, polite

Spectrum Grade 6
223

Reading Grade 6 Answers

---

1. Check the line beside the word or words that best describe what type of passage this is.

    _____ historical fiction

    __✓__ biography

    _____ persuasive

2. Check the sentence below that is the best summary for paragraph 7.

    __✓__ Adams was an environmentalist who was able to help the cause he believed in through his photographs of natural places.

    _____ Adams visited Sequoia, Mount Rainier, and Glacier National Parks.

    _____ The Sierra Club is a conservation group.

3. Check the words that best describe Ansel Adams.

    __✓__ talented

    _____ anxious

    __✓__ enthusiastic

    __✓__ creative

    _____ suspicious

Write **T** before the sentences that are true. Write **F** before the sentences that are false.

4. __F__ Adams was born on the East Coast.

5. __F__ Adams received his first camera from a teacher.

6. __T__ Adams was also a talented musician.

7. __T__ The majority of Adams's photographs are black and white.

8. __F__ Adams is still alive and lives California today.

Write the idiom from paragraph 1 on the line next to its meaning.

9. to sound familiar __ring a bell__

10. In paragraph 7, it says that Adams was an "avid environmentalist." What does this mean?

    Possible answers: Someone who very strongly believes in and works for environmental causes

Spectrum Grade 6
225

225

---

1. Check the sentence that best states the main idea of the selection.

    _____ Margaret Bourke-White photographed Cleveland's steel mills in the 1920s.

    __✓__ Margaret Bourke-White was a talented photojournalist who traveled the world and broke new ground for women.

    _____ Margaret Bourke-White was one of *LIFE* magazine's first four photogrphers.

2. Is this selection a fantasy, or does it take place in reality? How can you tell?

    reality; Answers will vary.

3. Why was Bourke-White's job unusual for a woman?

    At that time it was still customary for women to work mostly in the home.

4. What did Bourke-White plan to be before she discovered photography?

    a herpetologist

5. What was unusual about Bourke-White's industrial pictures?

    made photos of machinery and factories artistic

6. Number the events below to show the order in which they happened.

    __4__ Bourke-White photographed the liberation of the concentration camps.

    __3__ Bourke-White began working for *LIFE* magazine.

    __2__ Henry Luce hired Bourke-White to work at *Fortune*.

    __1__ Bourke-White graduated from college.

7. What do you find most interesting about Margaret Bourke-White's life?

    Answers will vary.

Spectrum Grade 6
227

227

---

1. What kinds of exotic animals did Ari and his mom see when they were online?

    Answers will vary.

2. Why did Ari decide to write a letter to the television show he watched?

    Ari thought the show was irresponsible for not explaining both sides of the story.

3. Why did Mrs. Stein say that Ari was mature and responsible?

    because he made a mature decision about owning an exotic pet

4. Do you think that Ari will be a good pet owner? Why or why not?

    Answers will vary.

Mark each sentence below **F** if it is in first-person point of view and **T** if it is in third-person point of view.

5. __F__ I can't believe we're going to get a dog or cat!

6. __T__ Mrs. Stein put down her knitting.

7. __T__ Ari turned on the computer.

8. __F__ I think that writing a letter is an excellent idea.

9. Tell about a time when you read something or watched something that presented only one point of view. How did you feel about it? Did you want to learn more about the other point of view?

    Answers will vary.

Spectrum Grade 6
229

229

---

1. Check the phrase that best describes the author's purpose.

    _____ to entertain   _____ to instruct

    __✓__ to inform

2. An **analogy** is a comparison between two things that may seem to be unalike but that have at least one similarity. An analogy is used to compare two things in paragraph 7. What are they?

    dominoes and the environment

3. Name two animals that are nonnative species in southern Florida.

    Answers will vary.

4. Why is it hard to care for a full-grown Burmese python?

    because it is so large

5. Why are exotic pets more likely to survive in the wild in a state like Florida than they are in a state like Ohio or Montana?

    because Florida's climate is warmer, wetter and more tropical

6. Do you think that abandoned exotic animals will continue to be a problem in Florida? Explain your answer.

    Answers will vary.

7. How would you define the term *invasive species*?

    Possible answer: nonnative species that have a negative effect on the local environment

8. In paragraph 2, *exotic* means

    unusual; from another part of the world

9. Would you ever purchase an exotic pet? Why or why not?

    Answers will vary.

Spectrum Grade 6
231

231

Page 233

Write **F** before the sentences that are facts. Write **O** before the sentences that are opinions.

1. __F__ The Everglades National Park covers about 1.5 million acres.
2. __F__ Melaleuca trees consume a great deal of water.
3. __O__ Everyone should visit the Everglades at least once.
4. __O__ The Everglades are most beautiful in the summer.
5. __F__ The Everglades are the only place in the world where crocodiles and alligators coexist.

6. What is the author trying to persuade the reader of in this passage?
   that the Everglades are worth protecting

7. Think about what you know about rain forests. Name two ways in which rain forests and the Everglades are similar.
   Answers will vary.

8. About how many species of birds are there in Everglades National Park?
   350

9. Why were melaleuca trees planted in the Everglades?
   to consume water

Circle the word that best completes each sentence.

10. Many people believe it is important to _____ our nation's wild places.
    destroy   investigate   (preserve)

11. It can be difficult to _____ the balance of an ecosystem.
    explain   (maintain)   cancel

12. What would you find most interesting about a trip to the everglades?
    Answers will vary.

Page 235

1. What is one difference between the way that scientists view volcanoes and most other people view them?
   Possible answer: People see volcanoes as erupting mountains, but scientists see them as temporary structures.

2. For what reason is the San Andreas Fault well known?
   Possible answer: because earthquakes are common there

3. The author compares the rate at which Earth's plates move with something that is more familiar. What is the other element in the comparison?
   human fingernails

4. Name two continents that border the Ring of Fire.
   Possible answers: Asia, North America, South America

5. What percentage of the world's volcanoes are located in the Ring of Fire?
   75 percent

6. Why does magma rise to the surface?
   because it is lighter, or less dense, than the rocky material that surrounds it

7. What purpose would a reader have for reading this passage?
   ____ for pleasure or entertainment
   __✓__ for information
   ____ to learn how to solve a problem

8. In paragraph 4, which word means "the rubbing together of two objects or surfaces"?
   friction

Page 237

1. Check the line beside the word that best describes what type of passage this is.
   ____ biography
   __✓__ informational
   ____ fiction

2. What does the word *tsunami* mean in Japanese?
   harbor wave

3. What are two possible causes of tsunamis?
   earthquake or underwater volcanic eruption

4. What is one way in which tsunamis are different than other waves?
   Answers will vary.

5. What is one positive effect of the 1946 tsunamis?
   creation of the Pacific Tsunami Warning System

6. Name three countries that were affected by the tsunami of 2004.
   Thailand, India, Indonesia

7. Why didn't the Pacific Tsunami Warning System alert people of the 2004 tsunami?
   There was no warning system for the Indian Ocean.

Circle the word that best completes each sentence below.

8. Tsunamis can cause great _____.
   accuracy   (destruction)   earthquakes

9. Scientists are looking for ways to be able to better _____ the arrival of tsunamis.
   explain   control   (predict)

10. Tsunamis are not _____ caused by meteorites.
    (frequently)   oddly   powerfully

Page 239

Mark each sentence below **F** if it is in first-person point of view and **T** if it is in third-person point of view.

1. __F__ I love making s'mores!
2. __T__ Charley rinsed the dishes in a tub of clean water.
3. __F__ I went to San Antonio to visit a friend from college.
4. __T__ Mr. Rosen said that vampire bats don't live in North America.

Write **F** before the sentences that are facts. Write **O** before the sentences that are opinions.

5. __F__ Mattie gathered wood for the fire.
6. __O__ Everything is more enjoyable when you are camping.
7. __F__ Mexican free-tailed bats come to Bracken Cave to give birth and raise their young.
8. __O__ The sky is most beautiful at dusk.

9. How do you think Mattie and Charley will feel the next time they see a bat? Why?
   Answers will vary.

10. What ingredients are used to make s'mores?
    graham crackers, chocolate, and marshmallows

11. Find one sentence that shows that Mattie enjoys camping. Write it on the lines below.
    Answers will vary.

12. Where is Bracken Cave located?
    Texas

Write the idiom from paragraph 10 on the line next to its meaning.

13. watched or observed   Kept an eye on

Reading Grade 6 Answers

Page 241

1. Explain how *echolocation* works.

   Possible answer: Bats make a noise and then listen for its echo, forming a mental picture of their surroundings based on the way the echo sounds.

2. What is the author trying to persuade the reader of in this selection?

   that bats are good creatures to have around

3. How can you encourage bats to live near your home?

   by building a bat house

4. Why do you think some people are afraid of bats?

   Answers will vary.

5. Write two ways in which species of bats may differ from one another.

   Possible answers: size, coloring, eating habits

Write **T** before the sentences that are true. Write **F** before the sentences that are false.

6. __T__ Some bats pollinate plants and flowers.

7. __F__ More than 3,000 species of bats exist.

8. __T__ Bats are nocturnal creatures.

9. __T__ The smallest bat in the world weighs less than a penny.

10. __F__ Bats feed only on insects.

11. Check the phrase that best describes the author's purpose.

   ___ to instruct   _✓_ to inform   ___ to entertain

12. In paragraph 6, the author mentions bats' "incredible diversity." What does this mean?

   Possible answers: There are many different bats with different types of characteristics.

13. After reading the article, has your opinion of bats changed? Explain.

   Answers will vary.

241

Page 243

1. What analogy does Uncle Jorge make when he is talking about his everyday tires as compared to his racing tires?

   The difference between wearing running shoes and loafers.

2. How is a racing wheelchair different from a regular wheelchair? How are they similar?

   Possible answer: They both have two large wheels, but the racing wheelchair has an additional small third wheel in front.

Write **F** before the sentences that are facts. Write **O** before the sentences that are opinions.

3. __F__ Uncle Jorge has completed a marathon before.

4. __O__ Uncle Jorge will probably complete the marathon in less time than his friend.

5. __F__ Tasha and Julio ate the pretzels Uncle Jorge baked.

6. __F__ The package contained Uncle Jorge's racing gloves.

7. __O__ Uncle Jorge makes the best soft pretzels.

8. Check the words that best describe Uncle Jorge.

   ___ impatient
   _✓_ competitive
   _✓_ determined
   ___ lonely
   _✓_ enthusiastic

9. How is the Boston Marathon different from most other races?

   It's one of the few races in which you need to have a qualifying time to compete.

10. What kind of relationship do Uncle Jorge and his best friend have?

   They are close but very competitive.

243

Page 245

1. What problem does Tasha have in the story?

   She is nervous about asking people to sponsor her for the race.

2. How does Julio help her resolve the problem?

   He gives her a pep talk and gives her suggestions of people to ask.

3. Name one way in which Tasha and Julio are similar.

   Answers will vary.

4. Name one way in which Tasha and Julio are different.

   Answers will vary.

5. What charitable organization will Julio and Tasha help by running the race?

   The Leukemia Society

6. Why does Julio think that it would be a good idea to ask their neighbors to pledge money during the block party?

   He thinks that everyone will be in a good mood.

7. The **theme** of a story is its subject. It tells what idea the story is mostly about. Check the word below that best describes the theme of "A Reason to Run."

   ___ fitness   _✓_ friendship   ___ loyalty

Circle the word that best completes each sentence below.

8. Tasha feels that she can _____ with Julio's support.

   win (succeed) apply

9. Julio _____ Tasha to have more confidence in herself.

   (encourages) discourages requests

Write the idiom from paragraph 7 on the line next to its meaning.

10. easy; simple to do ___ a piece of cake ___

245

Page 247

1. What are some types of fitness activities mentioned in the selection besides running?

   hiking, ice skating, jumping rope, and playing basketball

2. What do you think cross-training is?

   exercising by participating in different types of activities that work different muscles

3. What is the best way to begin training?

   Answers will vary.

4. What purpose would a reader have for reading this selection?

   ___ for pleasure or entertainment   _✓_ to learn how to become a runner
   ___ to form an opinion about running

5. Write a summary sentence for paragraph 5.

   Possible answer: It is a good idea to vary your activities and to rest at least one day a week.

6. What kind of information could you record in a runner's log?

   the weather, your route, the distance you ran, and how you felt

7. Do you think the author is trying to persuade the reader of anything in this selection? Explain.

   Answers will vary.

8. In bullet 3, what does *hydrated* mean?

   supplied with water

9. Are you a runner? If so, explain what you like about it. If not, would you like to take up running? Why or why not?

   Answers will vary.

247

Reading Grade 6 Answers

---

1. Write one sentence from the story that indicates how the Taylors felt about discovering the bioluminescence.

Possible answer: This is incredible.

2. What happened when Sophie kicked the water?

There was an explosion of a milky-green light.

3. What explanation does Mrs. Taylor have for why the water is glowing?

She says there is a high concentration of tiny organisms in the water that create light.

4. Why do you think the Taylors didn't notice the glowing water right away?

They were looking at the stars in the sky.

5. Do you think that Sophie and Miles will try to learn more about bioluminescence when they get home? Why or why not?

Answers will vary.

Read the sentences below. Write **B** next to the sentence if it tells about something that happened before Miles and Sophie noticed the water was glowing. Write **A** if it describes something that happened after.

6. _A_ Mrs. Taylor swirled her hands in the water.

7. _B_ Mr. Taylor collected the game pieces from the coffee table.

8. _B_ Miles and Sophie picked out constellations in the night sky.

9. _B_ Miles and Sophie took off their flip-flops.

10. _A_ Mrs. Taylor knelt beside Sophie.

Write the idiom from paragraph 1 on the line next to its meaning.

11. felt refreshed _caught their second wind_

A metaphor is a comparison of two things without using the word *like* or *as*. For example, *Her fingers were icicles.* Find the metaphor in paragraph 1, and write it on the line.

12. _the sun was a ball of fire_

---

1. Write a sentence that tells the main idea of the passage.

Answers will vary.

2. Explain one way in which an animal can use bioluminescence to lure prey.

Possible answer: Patterns of bioluminence on a shark's belly may resemble small fish to predators like tuna or mackerel.

3. What kind of creature produces much of the visible bioluminescence near the ocean's surface?

dinoflagellates

4. How does bioluminescence help camouflage the bobtail squid?

It spews a cloud of bioluminescent chemicals at its predator and allows the squid to escape.

5. How is bioluminescence different from the light produced by a lightbulb?

Most of its energy is used to create light instead of heat.

6. What can cause dinoflagellates to glow?

any disturbance, including the motion of waves, a boat, a porpoise, or a hand.

7. Check the line beside the word or words that best describe what type of selection this is.

____ science fiction   _✓_ informative   ____ fantasy

8. The Latin root **mar** means *sea*. Find a word in paragraph 1 with the root **mar**.

marine

9. The Latin root **fic** means *make* or *do*. Find a word in paragraph 2 with the root **fic**.

efficient

10. The Latin root **tract** means *pull* or *drag*. Find a word in paragraph 4 with the root **tract**.

attract

---

1. Number the events below to show the order in which they happened.

_5_ Mr. Taylor shook the lifeguard's hand.

_1_ The Taylors watched a seagull catch a fish.

_3_ The lifeguard cleaned the sting with alcohol.

_2_ Sophie pointed to the sand-covered jellyfish.

_4_ The lifeguard smeared meat tenderizer on Miles' foot.

2. If you don't have alcohol and meat tenderizer at home, what else can you use to treat a jellyfish sting?

vinegar, baking soda, and water

3. Under what circumstances does the lifeguard recommend that Miles see a doctor?

if the area becomes any more irritated in the next couple of hours

4. Why does meat tenderizer soothe a jellyfish sting?

It is an enzyme which breaks down the protein of jellyfish poison.

5. What were the Taylors looking at when Miles was stung?

They were watching a seagull catch a fish.

6. How did the Taylors determine what Miles had stepped on?

Sophie saw a sand-covered jellyfish on the beach.

7. The **climax** of a story is the point of highest excitement. What is the climax in "A Stinging Surprise"?

when Miles gets stung by a jellyfish

Find the simile in paragraph 1, and write it on the line below.

8. Answers will vary.

9. Have you ever been stung by something, like a bee or some fire ants? How did you react? How did you treat it?

Answers will vary.

---

1. Why does the author say that the description of a jellyfish might sound like a riddle?

The description is worded like a riddle. The question sounds as though it does not have a real answer.

2. How much of a jellyfish's body is composed of water?

95%-99%

3. What are nematocysts?

stinging cells

4. Check the phrase that best describes the author's purpose.

____ to entertain

_✓_ to inform

____ to persuade

Write **T** before the sentences that are true. Write **F** before the sentences that are false.

5. _F_ All species of jellyfish are totally harmless to humans.

6. _T_ Jellyfish do not have most of the organs that are common in other animals.

7. _F_ Jellyfish can move only where the wind and the tides take them.

8. _F_ Only about one-third of a jellyfish's body is water.

9. _T_ A few freshwater species of jellyfish do exist.

10. What three things is a jellyfish lacking that most animals have?

brains, bones, circulatory system

11. An invertebrate has no _backbone_.

12. How do jellyfish move?

The wind and ocean currents push them along, but they can also move slowly by contracting muscles.

Reading Grade 6 Answers

---

1. What was the first TV show to be regularly shown in color?
Bonanza

2. Who are the two people that are often given credit for inventing television?
Philo Taylor Farnsworth and Vladimir Zworykin

3. What Latin and Greek roots are found in the word *television*? What do they mean?
tele and **vis**; far and sight

4. About how much would a 1930s television have cost in today's dollars?
$7,000

5. Check the phrase that best describes the author's purpose.
_____ to entertain
__✓__ to inform
_____ to persuade

Circle the word that best completes each sentence below.

6. Televisions became _____ priced after World War II.
significantly (reasonably) highly

7. John Watson's _____ thinking led to the invention of cable TV.
(creative) unimaginative selfish

8. Farnsworth and Zworykin both _____ the invention of the modern television.
developed requested (contributed to)

9. In paragraph 3, which word means "an original model"?
prototype

10. When did televisions first start becoming more common?
after WWII

Write the words from the passage that have the meanings below.

1. the way in which one is viewed or perceived
perception

2. changed for the better; reformed
redeemed

3. felt comforted and less anxious
reassured

Write **T** before the sentences that are true. Write **F** before the sentences that are false.

4. _F_ Nixon stated that he did not receive any questionable gifts.

5. _F_ About 75 percent of Americans who owned televisions watched Armstrong and Aldrin walk on the moon.

6. _T_ The Beatles appeared on the *Ed Sullivan Show* in 1964.

7. _T_ Lyndon Johnson became president after Kennedy's assassination.

8. Do you think that television as a source of news will be as important in the future as it has been in the past? Explain.
Answers will vary.

9. How did the "Checker's Speech" change the way people thought of Richard Nixon?
People liked Nixon better. They saw a side of him they had not seen before.

10. Do you think it is fair for people to base their opinions on what they see as well as what they hear? Explain.
Answers will vary.

11. What kind of effect did television have on the popularity of the Beatles?
It caused a sharp rise in their popularity.

12. How did Kennedy and Nixon appear to be different from one another during their televised debate?
Nixon was scowling and uncomfortable, and Kennedy was smiling and looked confident.

---

1. The Latin root **ann** means *year*. Find a word in paragraph 2 with the root **ann**.
annual

2. The Greek root **graph** means *write*. Find a word in paragraph 9 with the root **graph**.
autographed

3. The Latin root **loc** means *place*. Find a word in paragraph 11 with the root **loc**.
local

Write **F** before the sentences that are facts. Write **O** before the sentences that are opinions.

4. _O_ Tanika worries too much.

5. _O_ This year's book fair will be better than previous fairs.

6. _F_ Rachael Weinstock's mom is the author of a picture book.

7. _F_ Caleb's class has a turtle and some fish.

Mark each sentence below **F** if it is in first-person point of view and **T** if it is in third-person point of view.

8. _F_ I think this book fair will be a success.

9. _T_ Caleb looked through the list books the librarians ordered.

10. _F_ My sister might have some sports equipment we could use.

11. What are two ideas that Tanika and Caleb have to make this year's book fair more exciting?
They want to set up areas with different themes and have authors come to sign their books.

12. Why does Caleb think that Mr. Davies might be able to help?
He used to be an editor for a children's book publisher.

Read the descriptions below. Write **C** next to the phrase if it describes Caleb. Write **T** if it describes Tanika.

13. _C_ feels calm and confident about the success of the book fair

14. _T_ suggests setting up areas with different themes

15. _T_ offers to bring in ice skates and mittens for the winter display

---

1. Why do Caleb and Tanika think that the students should be able to vote on the books that will be added to the library?
The fair was a team effort. Students from every class contributed.

2. Do you think that Caleb and Tanika work well together as a team? Why or why not?
Answers will vary.

3. Why did Mr. Rutledge and Mrs. Angley decide to ask for Caleb and Tanika's help?
The book fair was the most successful fair the school had held. Tanika and Caleb deserved a lot of the credit.

4. What is the setting for this story?
the school library

5. Do you think that Caleb and Tanika will choose to work together on future projects? Explain.
Answers will vary.

6. Check the line beside the word or words that best describe what type of selection this is.
_____ a tall tale   __✓__ realistic fiction   _____ historical fiction

7. In paragraph 6, what does *allocating* mean?
distributing; dividing up

8. If you were in Caleb or Tanika's place, how would you choose to spend the money?
Answers will vary.

Reading Grade 6 Answers

Page 265

1. Check the words that best describe Louis Sachar.
   - ✓ creative
   - ✓ intelligent
   - ✓ humorous
   - ___ nosy
   - ___ unpredictable

2. What purpose would a reader have for reading this selection?
   - ✓ for information about the life and work of Louis Sachar
   - ___ to learn how to solve a problem
   - ___ to form an opinion about the work of Louis Sachar

3. Check the line beside the word or words that best describe what type of selection this is.
   - ___ autobiography
   - ___ historical nonfiction
   - ✓ biography

4. Name two series of books that Louis Sachar has written.
   Marvin Redpost and Wayside School

5. Why didn't Sachar become a full-time writer as soon as his first book was published?
   He didn't feel confident he could make a living as a writer.

6. What happens after Sachar has completed the first draft of a book?
   He rewrites it fives or six times before he sends it to his publisher.

7. Name two sources of ideas for Sachar's stories and characters.
   Possible answers: his memories of childhood; his experience teaching; his daughter's life

8. If you were to write a short story or a novel, what sources of ideas could you use? Be specific.
   Answers will vary.

265

Page 267

1. Check the phrase that best describes the author's purpose.
   - ✓ to instruct
   - ___ to entertain
   - ___ to inform

2. Name three things you might record in a writer's notebook.
   Possible answers: dreams, song lyrics, everyday thoughts and observations

3. What does the author mean by "Do your homework"?
   Carefully research publishers and magazines, and follow their guidelines.

4. Why is perseverance an important quality for a writer to have?
   You may receive many rejections before you are published.

5. Why do you think that most writers like to read?
   Answers will vary.

6. On the lines below, write a summary of Step 3.
   It is important that you write every day so that you can get into the habit and so that you can clear your mind of things that are less important or uninteresting.

7. Why do you need to write every day?
   It's a good way to clear your mind, stay in practice, and make room for the "good stuff."

8. What do you think the author's feelings about writing as a professional are? Why?
   Answers will vary.

267

Page 269

1. Why didn't the narrator escape from the sinking ship on one of the lifeboats?
   He believed that a captain should go down with his ship.

2. Name three items the narrator found in the canvas bag.
   Possible answers: a knife, a blanket, a bottle of water, four cans of food, and a box of matches.

3. **Personification** is a literary device in which human characteristics are given to inanimate objects. In the sentence *Sam's bed beckoned to him invitingly*, Sam's bed is personified. Find an example of personification in the story, and write it on the line below.
   the sun was glaring angrily at me

4. What do you think the book Tyler was reading when he fell asleep was about?
   a shipwreck; a castaway

5. From what point of view are the first seven paragraphs of the story told?
   first-person point of view

6. From what point of view is the last paragraph told?
   third-person point of view

7. What purpose would a reader have for reading this selection?
   - ___ for information
   - ___ to answer a specific question
   - ✓ for entertainment

Find the metaphor in paragraph 3, and write it on the line.
   8. My stomach was an animal.

9. Why is most of this selection in italics?
   It is a dream.

269

Page 271

1. What nationality was Selkirk?
   Scottish

2. Why do you think Selkirk called out to the *Cinque Ports* as it sailed away from the island?
   He was having second thoughts about his decision.

3. How do we know so many details about Selkirk's experiences on the island?
   Woodes Rogers, the captain of the Duke, wrote a book that included Selkirk's experiences.

5. What is one difference between Robinson Crusoe and Alexander Selkirk?
   Possible answer: Selkirk asked to be left on his island and Crusoe was shipwrecked.

6. Is *Robinson Crusoe* fantasy, or does it take place in reality?
   fantasy

7. Is *A Cruising Voyage Round the World* fantasy, or does it take place in reality?
   It takes place in reality.

Circle the word that best completes each sentence below.

8. Selkirk's use of _____ thinking allowed him to survive on the island.
   optimistic (creative) frequent

9. It was difficult for Selkirk to _____ to life in society.
   (readjust) communicate accustom

10. Woodes Rogers's book _____ Selkirk's experiences.
    neglected ridiculed (detailed)

11. After reading this article, would you be interested in reading *Robinson Crusoe*? Why or why not?
    Answers will vary.

271

Reading Grade 6 Answers

Page 273

1. Number the events below to show the order in which they happened.

   _5_ Joseph showed Chiara and her mom several of his favorite desert plants.

   _4_ Chiara ate her breakfast in the car.

   _1_ The Giardinis moved to Arizona from Massachusetts.

   _3_ Mrs. Giardini said she missed the greenery in her old backyard.

   _2_ Chiara found her mother sitting on the deck sipping coffee.

2. What problem do Chiara and her mom have at the beginning of the story?
   They miss the garden and the greenery at their old home in Massachusetts.

3. Do you think that planting a garden will help the Giardinis feel more at home in Arizona? Why or why not?
   Answers will vary.

4. What is one way in which Massachusetts and Arizona are different?
   Possible answers: the temperature; the landscape

5. What does Mrs. Giardini mean when she says, "Arizona and Massachusetts could be different planets"?
   The two states seem very different to her.

6. Name the two different settings in this story.
   the Giardini's house; the nursery

7. Why were Chiara and her mom surprised to hear that they could plant colorful, blooming plants?
   Possible answer: They weren't expecting those kinds of plants to do well in the desert.

8. Why does Joseph recommend that Chiara and her mom plant native plants?
   They do well in that climate, and they won't need a lot of water.

Spectrum Grade 6
273

273

Page 275

Write the words from the passage that have the meanings below.

1. the process by which liquid changes into vapor or gas
   evaporation

2. water that falls to Earth in the form of rain or snow
   precipitation

3. hills of sand that are pushed into shape by the wind
   dunes

4. dry; having little rainfall
   arid

5. an area of flat land that is higher than the surrounding land
   plateau

6. How much of Earth's land surface do deserts cover?
   about one-third

7. Who was Marco Polo?
   a Venetian traveler and explorer

8. Why do some people compare sand dunes to ocean waves?
   They resemble giant, frozen waves.

9. What is an oasis? What is the plural form of oasis?
   an area of moisture and plant life in the desert; oases

Write **T** before the sentences that are true. Write **F** before the sentences that are false.

10. _F_ Most of Earth's deserts are made of sand.

11. _T_ The Sahara receives almost no rainfall.

12. _T_ The Mojave Desert is the largest American desert.

13. _F_ The Gobi is located in northern Africa.

Spectrum Grade 6
275

275

Page 277

1. How did Godfrey Daniels publicize the Mojave Desert phone booth?
   He wrote about it on the Internet and posted its number there.

2. Do you think the National Parks Service and Pacific-Bell made the right decision to remove the phone booth? Explain.
   Answers will vary.

3. What happens if someone calls the phone booth today?
   The phone will ring only on the caller's end.

4. Why was the phone booth originally installed?
   for use by miners and their families

5. On the lines below, write the main idea of paragraph 6.
   People liked making a connection with strangers because is made the world seem smaller.

Write **T** before the sentences that are true. Write **F** before the sentences that are false.

6. _T_ The phone booth was originally intended to be used by miners.

7. _F_ The phone booth is still in working order today.

8. _T_ Godfrey Daniels posted the number of the booth on the Internet.

9. _F_ The phone booth was located in Arizona.

10. _T_ People seemed to like the idea of connecting with others in faraway places.

11. If the phone booth was still in place today, would you want to call the number? Explain.
    Answers will vary.

Spectrum Grade 6
277

277
